Distributed Tracing in Practice

Instrumenting, Analyzing, and Debugging Microservices

*Austin Parker, Daniel Spoonhower, Jonathan Mace, and
Rebecca Isaacs with Ben Sigelman*

Beijing · Boston · Farnham · Sebastopol · Tokyo

Distributed Tracing in Practice

by Austin Parker, Daniel Spoonhower, Jonathan Mace, and Rebecca Isaacs, with Ben Sigelman

Published by O'Reilly Media, Inc., 1005 Gravenstein Highway North, Sebastopol, CA 95472.

O'Reilly books may be purchased for educational, business, or sales promotional use. Online editions are also available for most titles (*http://oreilly.com*). For more information, contact our corporate/institutional sales department: 800-998-9938 or *corporate@oreilly.com*.

Acquisitions Editor: John Devins
Development Editor: Sarah Grey
Production Editor: Katherine Tozer
Copyeditor: Chris Morris
Proofreader: JM Olejarz

Indexer: Sue Klefstad
Interior Designer: David Futato
Cover Designer: Karen Montgomery
Illustrator: Rebecca Demarest

April 2020:   First Edition

Revision History for the First Edition
2020-04-13   First Release

See *http://oreilly.com/catalog/errata.csp?isbn=9781492056638* for release details.

978-1-492-05663-8

[LSI]

Table of Contents

Foreword

Human beings have struggled to understand production software for exactly as long as human beings have had production software. We have these marvelously fast machines, but they don't speak our language and—despite their speed and all of the hype about artificial intelligence—they are still entirely unreflective and opaque.

For many (many) decades, our efforts to understand production software ultimately boiled down to two types of telemetry data: log data and time series statistics. The time series data—also known as metrics—helped us understand that "something terrible" was happening inside of our computers. If we were lucky, the logging data would help us understand specifically what that terrible thing was.

But then everything changed: our software needed more than just one computer. In fact, it needed thousands of them.

We broke the software into tiny, independently operated services and distributed those fragmented services across the planet, atomized among the millions of computers housed in massive datacenters. And with so many processes involved in every end-user request, the logs and statistics from individual machines told only a sliver of the story. It felt like we were flying blind.

I started working on distributed tracing in early 2005. At the time, I was a 25-year-old software engineer working—somewhat grudgingly, if I'm being candid—on a far-flung service within the Google AdWords backend infrastructure. Like the rest of the company, I was trying to write software capable of withstanding a punishing load from the outside world (by this point, Google was already a verb and we had scaled well into uncharted territory for commodity hardware). We were running *microservices* before that term had been invented, and when we needed some new abstraction layer or infrastructure, we were almost always forced to write it in-house (for one thing, GitHub hadn't even been incorporated yet).

To make a long story short, we kept the ship afloat…but it was a mess. And nobody except for the old-timer super-geniuses (read: not me) had any clue where the bodies were buried or how it all actually fit together.

That's when I met Sharon Perl, truly by accident. She had been a research scientist at DEC's Systems Research Center in the 1990s (i.e., when it was cool!) and came to Google in the very early days: 2001, if I remember correctly. In that short impromptu conversation with Sharon, I asked her what she was working on, and she rattled off a list of interesting systems software projects: a distributed blob store, a Google-scale identity service, a distributed lockservice…and then this thing called *Dapper*. Dapper was "a distributed tracing system," whatever that was.

Needless to say, I had never heard of a distributed tracing system—in 2005, hardly any nonacademic had—but it sounded fascinating. At the time, Dapper was just a prototype that Sharon codeveloped with Mike Burrows and Luiz Barroso. They had patched Google's internal RPC subsystem and control-flow packages in order to propagate a few GUIDs alongside each request as the request bounced from service to service. It wasn't fully operational, but an early proof-of-concept showed that the fundamentals were sound. For the first time, an ordinary Google engineer actually had some hope of understanding what happened to an individual web request in the 150 milliseconds it took to touch hundreds or thousands of distinct microservices.

I was hooked. Here was something truly novel, powerful, and—from a personal standpoint—wildly understaffed! So I started to dig into the Dapper codebase, clean things up, round edges, and deal with more than my share of internal bureaucracy (among other things, Dapper had a daemon running with root privileges on every piece of production hardware at Google and, wisely, they put some process around that sort of thing). Suffice it to say, after a year or two of wall time and some phenomenal work from a team of engineers, we were able to deploy Dapper across all of Google's backend software. To the best of my knowledge, this was the first time any organization had run distributed tracing continuously for a production system at scale.

…and so we deployed Dapper across all of Google, and we solved observability.

If only! The truth is that Dapper was a point solution to some painful yet isolated problems. In the early days, it was hard to get people to even use it, much less benefit from it. My team's KPI was the number of weekly logins, and I remember when the number hovered in the low double digits, month after month. We would dream up clever analytical features, deploy them, wait for the thundering herds of enthusiastic users, and then feel disappointed.

Eventually we did find a way to increase usage and thus organizational value to Google, but it wasn't with new analytical features or insightful visualizations. In fact, it was something really basic that only required a few hundred lines of code: one of my colleagues integrated links to relevant Dapper traces into a tool that Google engineers already used many times a day. It turns out that some small fraction of people would click on those links, and sometimes they found something really valuable on the other side.

That was it. Just a simple integration into an existing workflow. Beyond the data engineering and instrumentation challenges, distributed tracing is hard because it's often thought of not just as a new set of telemetry but as a distinct, segregated product experience. No matter how compelling that product experience is, developers (like all people) are creatures of habit who do not want to learn a new tool to check proactively. Tracing data and insights must fit into the context of preexisting workflows and tasks to be done. This is the best way to give tracing-oriented insights the exposure needed to justify the investment in a fundamentally new data source.

Distributed tracing is still in its infancy. Thinking back to the early days of the Dapper project, when I was just ramping up on the codebase, I asked Luiz Barroso if he could spare 30 minutes to help me understand a few things. Luiz was already quite distinguished, but was (and remains) humble, friendly, and generous with his time, so he agreed. When I met with him, I must have sounded a bit naive, but I was also unfathomably excited about what I wanted to do to Dapper. I wanted to build in a just-in-time sampling mechanism, create a declarative programming language for user-defined queries that execute across application services, integrate kernel traces, and more. I asked him what he thought. Ever the voice of wisdom, he let me down easy and explained that simply getting Dapper into production would be a major accomplishment and would take years. "Start there," he said.

Luiz was right about that. Fifteen years later, much of our industry hasn't gotten a whole lot further than that, at least in production. Distributed tracing is worth it, but it's hard! Still, it's a very young discipline, and the last section of this book provides a window on what's still to come. In another 15 years, we will look back on distributed tracing circa 2020 as both critical and primitive. By understanding where the technology is going, we'll be better able to position ourselves to adapt to the dynamic landscape surrounding tracing and observability in general.

Stepping back, it's important to remember that nobody works with "just one microservice."

Our industry moved to microservices so that our dev teams could operate with independence, and to a certain extent, we got our wish—at least where continuous integration/continuous deployment is concerned. But this "independence" was an illusion; in production, these microservices are in fact highly interdependent, and a failure or slowdown in one service propagates across the stack of microservices, leaving chaos and confusion (and many frantic Slack messages) in its wake.

Distributed traces must be part of the solution to this problem. They are the only window we have into how the hundreds of services in deep, multilayered microservice architectures actually interact as they fulfill end-to-end user requests. They may be a relative newcomer to the telemetry world compared to time series stats and vanilla logs, but they are also the most vital when it comes to understanding the larger system. Without tracing data, we are reduced to guess-and-check across seas of disorganized logging data and metrics dashboards.

Yet it's not nearly as simple as adding distributed tracing. While healthy observability in distributed systems must involve distributed traces, we still need to figure out how. How do we make distributed tracing useful? How do we adopt it? How do we integrate it into our existing workflows and processes? And how do we future-proof these efforts?

These are fascinating and challenging questions, and they are the subject of this book. We hope you enjoy it.

— Ben Sigelman
Cofounder and CEO of Lightstep
and cocreator of Dapper

Introduction: What Is Distributed Tracing?

If you're reading this book, you may already have some idea what the words *distributed tracing* mean. You may also have no idea what they mean—for all we know, you're simply a fan of bandicoots (the animal on the cover). We won't judge, promise.

Either way, you're reading this to gain some insight into what distributed tracing is, and how you can use it to understand the performance and operation of your microservices and other software. With that in mind, let's start out with a simple definition.

Distributed tracing (also called distributed request tracing) is a type of correlated logging that helps you gain visibility into the operation of a distributed software system for use cases such as performance profiling, debugging in production, and root cause analysis of failures or other incidents. It gives you the ability to understand exactly what a particular individual service is doing as part of the whole, enabling you to ask and answer questions about the performance of your services and your distributed system as a whole.

That was easy—see you next book!

What's that? Why's everyone asking for a refund? Oh…

We're being told that you need a little more than that. Well, let's take a step back and talk about software, specifically distributed software, so that we can better understand the problems that distributed tracing solves.

Distributed Architectures and You

The art and science of developing, deploying, and operating software is constantly in flux. New advances in computing hardware and software have dramatically pushed the boundaries of what an *application* looks like over the years. While there's an interesting digression here about how "everything old is new again," we'll focus on changes over the past two decades or so, for the sake of brevity.

Prior to advances in virtualization and containerization, if you needed to deploy some sort of web-based application, you would need a physical server, possibly one dedicated to your application itself. As traffic increased to your application, you would either need to increase the physical resources of that server (adding RAM, for example) or you would need multiple servers that each ran their own copy of your application.

With a monolithic server process, this horizontal scaling often led to unfavorable trade-offs in cost, performance, and organizational overhead. Running multiple instances of your server meant you were duplicating all functionality of the server, rather than scaling individual subcomponents independently. With traditional infrastructure, you were often forced to make a decision about how many minutes (or hours!) of degraded performance was acceptable while you brought additional capacity online—servers aren't cheap to run, so why would you run at peak capacity if you didn't need to? Finally, as the size and complexity of your application increased, along with the amount of developers who were working on it, testing and validating new changes became more difficult. As your organization grew, it became unreasonable for developers to understand a single codebase, not to mention the shape of the entire system. Increasingly smaller changes increased the odds of a ripple effect that led to total application failure as their impact radiated out from one component to another.

Time marched on, however, and solutions to these problems were built. Software was created that abstracted away the details of physical hardware such as virtualization, allowing for a single physical server to be split into multiple logical servers. Docker and other containerization technologies extended this concept, providing a light-weight and user-friendly abstraction over heavier-weight virtual machines, moving the question of "who deploys this software" from operators to developers. The popularization of cloud computing and its notion of on-demand computing resources solved the problem of resource scaling, as it became possible to increase the amount of RAM or CPU cores for a given server at the click of a button. Finally, the idea of microservice architectures came about to address the complexity imposed by ever-larger and more complicated software-oriented businesses by structuring large applications around loosely coupled independent services.

Today, it's arguable that most applications are *distributed* in some fashion, even if they don't use microservices. Simple client-server applications themselves are distributed —consider the classic question of "A call to my server has timed out; was the response lost, or was the work not done at all?" Additionally, they may have a variety of distributed dependencies, such as datastores that are consumed as a service offered by a cloud provider, or a whole host of third-party APIs that provide everything from analytics to push notifications and more.

Why is distributed software so popular? The arguments for distributed software are pretty clear:

Scalability

A distributed application can more easily respond to demand, and its scaling can be more efficient. If a lot of people are trying to log in to your application, you could scale out only the login services, for example.

Reliability

Failures in one component shouldn't bring down the entire application. Distributed applications are more resilient because they split up functions through a variety of service processes and hosts, ensuring that even if a dependent service goes offline, it shouldn't impact the rest of the application.

Maintainability

Distributed software is more easily maintainable for a couple of reasons. Dividing services from each other can increase how maintainable each component is by allowing it to focus on a smaller set of responsibilities. In addition, you're freer to add features and capabilities without implementing (and maintaining) them yourself—for example, adding a speech-to-text function in an application by relying on some cloud provider's speech-to-text service.

This is the tip of the iceberg, so to speak, in terms of the benefits of distributed architectures. Of course, it's not all sunshine and roses, and into every life, a little rain must fall...

Deep Systems

A distributed architecture is a prime example of what software architects often call a *deep system*.[1] These systems are notable not because of their width, but because of their complexity. If you think about certain services or classes of services in a distributed architecture, you should be able to identify the difference. A pool of cache nodes scales wide (as in, you simply add more instances to handle demand), but other services scale differently. Requests may route through three, four, fourteen, or forty different layers of services, and each of those layers may have other dependencies that you aren't aware of. Even if you have a comparatively simple service, your software probably has dozens of dependencies on code that you didn't write, or on managed services through a cloud provider, or even on the underlying orchestration software that manages its state.

The problem with deep systems is ultimately a human one. It quickly becomes unrealistic for a single human, or even a group of them, to understand enough of the

---

1 [Sig19]

services that are in the critical path of even a single request and continue maintaining it. The scope of what you as a service owner can control versus what you're implicitly responsible for is illustrated in Figure P-1. This calculus becomes a recipe for stress and burnout, as you're forced into a reactive state against other service owners, constantly fighting fires, and trying to figure out how your services interact with each other.

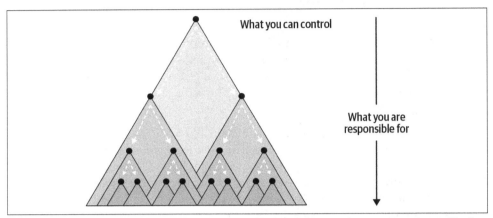

Figure P-1. The service that you can control has dependencies that you're responsible for but have no direct control over.

Distributed architectures require a reimagined approach to understanding the health and performance of software. It's not enough to simply look at a single stack trace or watch graphs of CPU and memory utilization. As software scales—in depth, but also in breadth—telemetry data like logs and metrics alone don't provide the clarity you require to quickly identify problems in production.

The Difficulties of Understanding Distributed Architectures

Distributing your software presents new and exciting challenges. Suddenly, failures and crashes become harder to pin down. The service that you're responsible for may be receiving data that's malformed or unexpected from a source that you don't control because that service is managed by a team halfway across the globe (or a remote team). Failures in services that you thought were rock-solid suddenly cause cascading failures and errors across all of your services. To borrow a phrase from Twitter, you've got a microservices murder mystery (see Figure P-2) on your hands.

Honest Status Page
@honest_update

We replaced our monolith with micro services so that every outage could be more like a murder mystery.

7:10 PM · Oct 7, 2015 · Buffer

Figure P-2. It's funny because it's true.

To extend the metaphor, monitoring helps determine where the body is, but it doesn't reveal why the murder occurred. Distributed tracing fills in those gaps by allowing you to easily comprehend your entire system by providing solutions to three major pain points:

Obfuscation

As your application becomes more distributed, the coherence of failures begins to decrease. That is to say, the *distance* between cause and effect increases. An outage at your cloud provider's blob storage could fan out to cause huge cascading latency for everyone, or a single difficult-to-diagnose failure at a particular service many hops away that prevents you from uncovering the proximate cause.

Inconsistency

Distributed applications might be reliable overall, but the state of individual components can be much less consistent than they would be in monolithic or non-distributed applications. In addition, since each component of a distributed application is designed to be highly independent, the state of those components will be inconsistent—what happens when someone does a deployment, for example? Do all of the other components understand what to do? How does that impact the overall application?

Decentralized

Critical data about the performance of your services will be, by definition, decentralized. How do you go looking for failures in a service when there may be a thousand copies of that service running, on hundreds of hosts? How do you correlate those failures? The greatest strength of distributing your application is also the greatest impediment to understanding how it actually functions!

You may be wondering, "How do we address these difficulties?" Spoiler: distributed tracing.

How Does Distributed Tracing Help?

Distributed tracing emerges as a critical tool in managing the explosion of complexity that our deep systems bring. It provides context that spans the life of a request and can be used to understand the interactions and shape of your architecture. However, these individual traces are just the beginning—in aggregate, traces can give you important insights about what's *actually going on* in your distributed system, allowing you not only to correlate interesting data about your services (for example, that most of your errors are happening on a specific host or in a specific database cluster), but also to filter and rank the importance of other types of telemetry. Effectively, distributed traces provide context that helps you filter problem-solving down to only things that are relevant to your investigation, so you don't have to guess and check multiple logs and dashboards. In this way, distributed tracing is actually at the center of a modern observability platform, and it becomes a critical component of your distributed architecture rather than an isolated tool.

So, what is a trace? The easiest way to understand is to think about your software in terms of requests. Each of your components is in the business of doing some sort of work in response to a request (aka *RPC*, from *remote procedure call*) from another service. This could be as prosaic as a web page requesting some structured data from a service endpoint to present to a user, or as complex as a highly parallelized search process. The actual nature of the work doesn't matter too much, although there are certain patterns that we'll discuss later on that lend themselves to certain styles of tracing. While distributed tracing can function in most distributed systems, as we'll discuss in Chapter 4, its strengths are best demonstrated in modeling the RPC relationships between your services.

In addition to the RPC relationships, think about the work that each of those services does. Maybe they're authenticating and authorizing user roles, performing mathematical calculations, or simply transforming data from one format to another. These services are communicating with each other through RPCs, sending requests and receiving responses. Regardless of what they're doing, one thing that all of these services have in common is that the work they're performing takes some length of time. The basic pattern of services and RPCs is illustrated in Figure P-3.

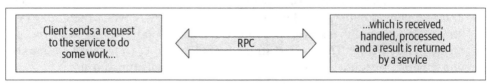

Figure P-3. A request from a client process to a service process.

We call the work that each service is doing a *span*, as in the span of time that it takes for the work to occur. These spans can be annotated with metadata (known as *attributes* or *tags*) and events (also referred to as *logs*). The RPCs between services are represented through *relationships* that model the nature of the request and the order in which the requests occur. This relationship is propagated by way of the *trace context*, some data that uniquely identifies a trace and each individual span within it. The span data that is created by each service is then forwarded to some external process, where it can be aggregated into a *trace*, analyzed for further insights, and stored for further analysis. A simple example of a trace can be seen in Figure P-4, showing a trace between two services, as well as a subtrace inside the first service.

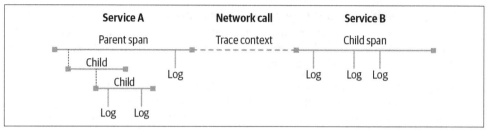

Figure P-4. A simple trace.

Distributed tracing mitigates the obfuscation present in distributed architectures by ensuring that each logical request through your services is presented as that—a single logical request. It ensures that all of the data relevant to a given execution of your business logic remain coupled at the point that they're analyzed and presented. It addresses the inconsistency issue by allowing queries to be made using relationships between services along specific APIs or other routes, letting you ask questions like "What happens to my API when this other service is down?" Finally, it addresses the decentralization issue by providing a method to ensure that processes can contribute trace data independently to a collector that can centralize it later, allowing you to visualize and understand requests that may be running across multiple datacenters, regions, or other distributions.

With all this in mind, what are some things that you can do with distributed tracing? What makes it crucial to understanding distributed systems? We've compiled several real-world examples:

- A major transactional email and messaging company implemented distributed tracing across its backend platform, including tracing calls to Redis. This trace data quickly showed that there was an unneeded loop in its calls to Redis, which was fetching data from the cache more than necessary. In removing this unneeded call, the company reduced the time it took to send an email anywhere from 100 to 1,000 milliseconds! This worked out to be a roughly 85% reduction in the time for every single email sent—and this is for a platform that was sending over one billion emails a day! Not only was the company able to discover this unneeded call, it was able to validate the impact of removing it on other services and quantify the value of the work.

- An industrial data company was able to use distributed trace data in order to easily compare requests during an incident where a primary database was overloaded to an earlier baseline. The ability to view aggregate statistical data about historical performance along with the context of individual requests during the regression dramatically reduced the time required to determine the root cause of the incident.

- A major health and fitness company implemented distributed tracing across its applications. As they analyzed the performance of their document database, engineers were able to identify repeated calls that could be consolidated, leading to reduced latency and more efficient code.

- A video-delivery platform used distributed tracing to troubleshoot latency issues from managed services that its system relied on. It was able to positively identify an issue with its cloud provider's Kafka pipeline before the vendor did, enabling a rapid response to the incident and restoration of desired performance.

These are just a handful of examples—distributed tracing has also demonstrated value in teams that are trying to better understand their continuous integration systems by providing visibility into their test pipeline, into the operation of global-scale search technologies at Google, and as a cornerstone of open source projects like OpenTelemetry. The question truly is: what is distributed tracing to you?

Distributed Tracing and You

Distributed tracing, again, is a method to understand distributed software. That's a lot like saying that water is wet, though—not terribly helpful, and reductive to a fault. Indeed, the best way to understand distributed tracing is to see it in practice, which is where this book comes in!

In the coming chapters, we'll cover the three major things you need to know to get started with implementing distributed tracing for your applications and discuss strategies that you can apply to solve the problems caused by distributed architectures. You'll learn about the different ways to instrument your software for distributed tracing and the styles of tracing and monitoring available to you. We'll discuss how to collect all of the data that your instrumentation produces and the various performance considerations and costs around the collection and storage of trace data. After that, we'll cover how to generate value from your trace data and turn it into useful, operational insights. Finally, we'll talk about the future of distributed tracing.

By the end of this book, you should understand the exciting world of distributed tracing and know where, how, and when to implement it for your software. Ultimately, the goal of *Distributed Tracing in Practice* is to allow you to build, operate, and understand your software more easily. We hope that the lessons in this text will help you in building the next generation of monitoring and observability practice at your organization.

Conventions Used in This Book

The following typographical conventions are used in this book:

Italic
: Indicates new terms, URLs, email addresses, filenames, and file extensions.

`Constant width`
: Used for program listings, as well as within paragraphs to refer to program elements such as variable or function names, databases, datatypes, environment variables, statements, and keywords.

`Constant width bold`
: Shows commands or other text that should be typed literally by the user.

`Constant width italic`
: Shows text that should be replaced with user-supplied values or by values determined by context.

 This element signifies a general note.

Using Code Examples

Supplemental material (code examples, exercises, etc.) is available for download on GitHub (*https://github.com/distributed-tracing-in-practice*).

If you have a technical question or a problem using the code examples, please send email to *bookquestions@oreilly.com*.

This book is here to help you get your job done. In general, if example code is offered with this book, you may use it in your programs and documentation. You do not need to contact us for permission unless you're reproducing a significant portion of the code. For example, writing a program that uses several chunks of code from this book does not require permission. Selling or distributing examples from O'Reilly books does require permission. Answering a question by citing this book and quoting example code does not require permission. Incorporating a significant amount of example code from this book into your product's documentation does require permission.

We appreciate, but generally do not require, attribution. An attribution usually includes the title, author, publisher, and ISBN. For example: *"Distributed Tracing in Practice* by Austin Parker, Daniel Spoonhower, Jonathan Mace, and Rebecca Isaacs with Ben Sigelman (O'Reilly). Copyright 2020 Ben Sigelman, Austin Parker, Daniel Spoonhower, Jonathan Mace, and Rebecca Isaacs, 978-1-492-05663-8."

If you feel your use of code examples falls outside fair use or the permission given above, feel free to contact us at *permissions@oreilly.com*.

O'Reilly Online Learning

 For more than 40 years, *O'Reilly Media* has provided technology and business training, knowledge, and insight to help companies succeed.

Our unique network of experts and innovators share their knowledge and expertise through books, articles, and our online learning platform. O'Reilly's online learning platform gives you on-demand access to live training courses, in-depth learning paths, interactive coding environments, and a vast collection of text and video from O'Reilly and 200+ other publishers. Visit *http://oreilly.com* for more information.

How to Contact Us

Please address comments and questions concerning this book to the publisher:

O'Reilly Media, Inc.
1005 Gravenstein Highway North
Sebastopol, CA 95472
800-998-9938 (in the United States or Canada)
707-829-0515 (international or local)
707-829-0104 (fax)

We have a web page for this book, where we list errata, examples, and any additional information. You can access this page at *https://oreil.ly/distributed-tracing*.

Email *bookquestions@oreilly.com* to comment or ask technical questions about this book.

For news and information about our books and courses, visit *http://oreilly.com*.

Find us on Facebook: *http://facebook.com/oreilly*

Follow us on Twitter: *http://twitter.com/oreillymedia*

Watch us on YouTube: *http://www.youtube.com/oreillymedia*

Acknowledgments

Austin Parker

Special thanks to everyone at O'Reilly who helped make this possible—our editors, Sarah Grey, Virginia Wilson, and Katherine Tozer; the production staff who worked tirelessly indexing, revising, redrawing, and making sure things fit on the page. Thanks to our technical reviewers for their insights and feedback; you made this a better book! I'd also like to thank Ben Sigelman and the rest of the crew at Lightstep for all their support—truly, without y'all, none of this would have happened.

I'd like to thank my parents, for having me, and to my Dad for being a daily inspiration. Love you both. To my wife: <3.

In solidarity, Austin.

Daniel Spoonhower

I'd like to thank everyone at Lightstep for supporting Austin and me through this work, and especially those that answered my many questions about their experience implementing and using tracing. I'd like to thank Bob Harper and Guy Blelloch for helping me to understand the value of clear writing (and for giving me some practice in writing under a deadline). I'd also like to thank my family for helping me find the time to work on this book.

Rebecca Isaacs

I would like to acknowledge the experience, advice and good ideas of my colleagues, many of whom have high expectations for the utility of distributed tracing in production settings. I would also like to thank Paul Barham for his insights and wisdom about tracing and analysis of distributed systems.

CHAPTER 1

The Problem with Distributed Tracing

I HAVE NO TOOLS BECAUSE I'VE DESTROYED MY TOOLS WITH MY TOOLS.
—James Mickens[1]

The concept of tracing the execution of a computer program is not a new one in any sense. Being able to understand the call stack of a program is fairly critical, you might say, to all manner of profiling, debugging, and monitoring tasks. Indeed, stack traces are likely to be the second most utilized debugging tool in the world, right behind print statements liberally scattered throughout a codebase. Our tools, processes, and technologies have improved over the past two decades and demand new methodologies and patterns of thinking, though. As we recalled in the Introduction, modern architectures such as microservices have fundamentally broken these classic methods of profiling, debugging, and monitoring. Distributed tracing stands ready to alleviate these issues to fix the holes in our tools that we have destroyed with our tools.

There's just one problem—distributed tracing can be hard. Why is this the case? Three fundamental problems generally occur when you're trying to get started with distributed tracing.

First, you need to be able to generate trace data. Support for distributed tracing as a first-class citizen in your runtime may be spotty or nonexistent. Your software might not be structured to easily accept the instrumentation code required to emit tracing data. You may use patterns that are antithetical to the request-based style of most distributed tracing platforms. Often, distributed tracing initiatives are dead on arrival due to the challenges of instrumenting an existing codebase.

---

1 [Mic13]

Another problem is how you collect and store the trace data generated by your software. Imagine hundreds or thousands of services, each emitting small chunks of trace data for each request, potentially millions of times per second. How do you capture that data and store it for analysis and retrieval? How do you decide what to keep, and how long to keep it? How do you scale the collection of your data in time with requests to your services?

Finally, once you've got all of this data, how do you actually derive value from it? How do you translate the raw trace data that you're receiving into actionable insights and actions? How do you use trace data to provide context to other service telemetry, reducing the time required to diagnose issues? Can you turn your trace data into value for other parts of the business, outside of just engineers? These questions, and more, stymie and confuse many who are trying to get started with distributed tracing.

The result of a distributed tracing deployment is a tool that grants you visibility into your deep system and the ability to easily understand how individual services in a request contribute to the overall performance of each request. The trace data you'll generate can be used not only to display the overall shape of your distributed system (see Figure 1-1), but also to view individual service performance inside a single request.

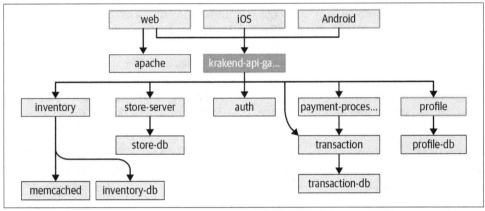

Figure 1-1. A service map generated from distributed trace data.

As Figure 1-2 shows, you'll be able to inspect requests as they move from frontend clients into backend services and understand how—and why—latency or errors are occurring, and what impact they're having on the entire request. These traces provide a wealth of information that you'll find invaluable when troubleshooting problems in production, such as metadata that indicates which host or region a particular service is running on. You'll have the ability to search, sort, filter, group, and generally slice and dice this trace data how you please in order to quickly troubleshoot problems or understand how different dimensions are impacting your service performance.

Figure 1-2. A sample trace demonstrating a request initiated by a frontend web client.

So, how do you get from here to there? What do you need to build a successful distributed tracing deployment?

The Pieces of a Distributed Tracing Deployment

To answer these questions and help you organize your thinking about the subject, we've broken down distributed tracing deployments into three main areas of focus, which is also how we've organized the book. These three pieces build off of each other, but may be generally useful to different people at different times—by no means do you need to be an expert on all three! Inside each section you'll find helpful explanations, lessons, and examples of how to build and deliver a distributed tracing deployment at your organization that should help in building confidence in your systems and software.

Instrumentation, Chapter 2

Distributed tracing requires traces. Trace data can be generated through *instrumentation* of your service processes or by transforming existing telemetry data into trace data. In this section, you'll learn about *spans*, the building blocks of request-based distributed traces, and how they may be generated by your services. We'll discuss the state of the art in *instrumentation frameworks* such as OpenTelemetry, a widely supported open source project that offers an instrumentation API (and more) that allows for easy bootstrapping of distributed tracing into your software. In addition, we'll discuss the best practices for instrumenting legacy code as well as greenfield development.

Deployment, Chapter 5

Once you're generating trace data, you need to send it somewhere. Deploying tracing for your organization requires an understanding of where your software runs—for end users and their clients, as well as on servers—and how it's operated. You'll need to understand the security, privacy, and compliance implications of collecting and storing trace data. You may encounter trade-offs in overhead relating to how much data is kept, and how much is discarded through a process known as *sampling*. We'll discuss best practices around all of these topics and help you figure out how to quickly deploy tracing infrastructure for your system.

Delivering value, Chapter 7

Once your services are generating trace data and you've deployed the necessary infrastructure to collect it, the real fun begins! How do you combine traces with your other observability tools and techniques such as metrics and logs? How do you measure what matters—and how do you define what matters to begin with? Distributed tracing provides the tools you'll need to answer these questions, and we'll help you figure it out in this section. You'll learn how to use traces to improve your baseline performance, as well as how tracing assists you in getting back to that baseline when things catch on fire.

All that said, there's still an open question here: how does distributed tracing relate to microservices, and distributed architectures more generally? We touched on this in Introduction: What Is Distributed Tracing?, but let's digress for a moment to review the relationship between these things.

Distributed Tracing, Microservices, Serverless, Oh My!

There's a certain line of thinking about microservices, now that we're several years past them being the "hot thing" in every analyst's portfolio of "Top Trends for 20XX" —namely, that the battle has been won. The exploding popularity of cloud computing, Kubernetes, containerization, and other development tools which enable rapid provisioning and deployment of hardware (or hardware-like abstractions) has

---

transformed the industry, undoubtedly. These factors can make it feel like asking the question "Should I use microservices?" would be to out oneself as a fool or charlatan.

Take a step back here and we'll look at some real-world data. First and foremost, there's some evidence that containers aren't exactly as popular in production as the hype may make them seem: only 25% of developers use them in production.[2] Quite a few engineering organizations are still using traditional monoliths for a lot of their work. Why? One reason may be, ironically enough, the *lack* of accessible distributed tracing tools.

Developer and author Martin Fowler identifies three primary considerations for those adopting microservices: the ability to rapidly provision hardware, the ability to rapidly deploy software, and a monitoring regime that can detect serious problems quickly.[3] The things we love about microservices (independence, idempotence, etc.) are also the things that make them difficult to understand, especially when things go wrong. Serverless technologies add further confusion to this equation by giving you less visibility into the runtime environment of a particular function and often being stubbornly resistant to monitoring through your favorite tools.

How, then, should we consider distributed tracing arrayed against these questions? First, distributed tracing solves the monitoring question raised by Fowler by providing visibility into the operation of your microservice architecture. It allows you to gain critical insights into the performance and status of individual services as part of a chain of requests in a way that would be difficult or time-consuming to do otherwise. Distributed tracing gives you the ability to understand exactly what a *particular, individual service* is doing as part of the whole, enabling you to ask and answer questions about the performance of your services and your distributed system.

Traditional metrics and logging alone simply can't compare to the additional context provided by distributed tracing. Metrics, for example, will allow you to get an aggregate understanding of what's happening to all instances of a given service, and even allow you to narrow your query to specific groups of services, but fail to account for infinite cardinality.[4]

Logs, on the other hand, provide extremely fine-grained detail on a given service, but have no built-in way to provide that detail in the context of a request. While you can use metrics and logs to discover and address problems in your distributed system, distributed tracing provides context that helps you narrow down the search space

---

2 [Sta19]

3 [Fow14]

4 *Cardinality* is a mathematical term that refers to the number of elements in a set or group. In the context of metrics, it's the number of unique combinations of metric names and key/value attributes attached to those names. We'll discuss this more in later chapters.

required to discover the root cause of an incident while it's occurring (when every moment counts).

As we mentioned in the Introduction, trying to manage and understand a complex, microservice-based distributed architecture can lead to stress and burnout. If you're thinking about migrating to microservices, are in the middle of a transition from a monolith to microservices, or are already tasked with wrangling an immense microservice architecture, then you might be experiencing this stress too, when considering how to understand the health and performance of your software. Distributed tracing might not be a panacea, but as part of a larger observability strategy, it can become a critical component of how you operate reliable distributed systems.

The Benefits of Tracing

What are the specific benefits you can achieve with distributed tracing? We'll talk about this throughout the rest of the book, but let's review the high-level quick wins first:

- Distributed tracing can transform the way that you develop and deliver software, no doubt about it. It has benefits not only for software quality, but for your organization's health.

- Distributed tracing can improve developer productivity and your development output. It is the best and easiest way for developers to understand the behavior of distributed systems in production. You will spend less time troubleshooting and debugging a distributed system by using distributed tracing than you would without it, and you'll discover problems you wouldn't otherwise realize you had.

- Distributed tracing supports modern polyglot development. Since distributed tracing is agnostic to your programming language, monitoring vendor, and runtime environment, you can propagate a single trace from an iOS-native client through a C++ high-performance proxy through a Java or C# backend to a webscale database and back, all visualized in a single place, using a single tool. No other set of tools allows you this freedom and flexibility.

- Distributed tracing reduces the overhead required for deployments and rollbacks by quickly giving you visibility into changes. This not only reduces the mean time to resolution of incidents, but decreases the time to market for new features and the mean time to detection of performance regressions. This also improves communication and collaboration across teams because your developers aren't siloed into a particular monitoring stack for their slice of the pie—everyone, from frontend developers to database nerds, can look at the same data to understand how changes impact the overall system.

Setting the Table

After all that, we hope that we have your attention! Let's recap:

- Distributed tracing is a tool that allows for profiling and monitoring distributed systems by way of *traces*, data that represents requests as they flow through a system.
- Distributed tracing is agnostic to your programming language, runtime, or deployment environment and can be used with almost every type of application or service.
- Distributed tracing improves teamwork and coordination, and reduces time to detect and resolve performance issues with your application.

To realize these benefits, first you'll need some trace data. Then you'll need to collect it, and finally you'll have to analyze it. Let's start at the beginning, then, and talk about instrumenting your code for distributed tracing.

CHAPTER 2

An Ontology of Instrumentation

When you sketch a system diagram, what do you start with? We often start with a simple box representing a single service, as in Figure 2-1.

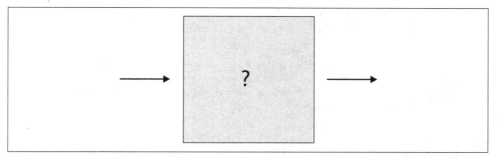

Figure 2-1. A visual representation of a service, component, function, or what have you.

This box is extended, added to, and connected to a variety of other boxes through dashed and solid lines, arrows, and other logically connected fabric. At the end of the day, we can't really escape the idea of our software being this series of connected boxes on some sort of plane. Often, we aren't able to conceptualize of our boxes as much other than a simple function that accepts inputs, does something to them, and sends the output to another box off in the distance (see Figure 2-2).

We already instrument our boxes in various ways during development to understand what's happening inside each one—after all, practically no software is bug-free, and any system accepting input from users is likely to receive something the developer did not expect. You can think of *instrumentation* as anything that assists you in monitoring or measuring the performance and state of an application—so you'll write some logs that indicate when a user inputs invalid parameters to your function, or perhaps when an operation is disallowed.

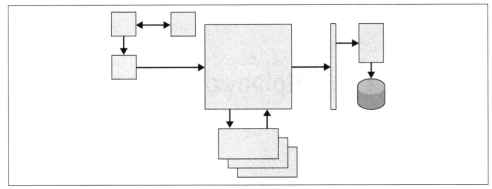

Figure 2-2. Multiple services, components, functions, etc. linked together visually.

Now, if you're reading this, we'll assume you're interested in instrumenting your code for *tracing*, which has its own set of concerns and edge cases that you'll need to address. In this chapter, we'll cover the two critical things you need to understand in order to begin instrumenting an application and talk about the trade-offs between them. Finally, we'll demonstrate how to apply the instrumentation techniques we present in order to trace a simple service that communicates over HTTP.

 As mentioned in the Introduction, a span is a unit of work performed by a service. We'll discuss more concrete representations of them in Chapter 3, but in the upcoming sections we represent them as JSON blobs.

White Box Versus Black Box

The first major topic we'll cover is the distinction between *white box* and *black box* instrumentation. Remember the little square from Figure 2-1 that contained the service we were interested in monitoring? Turn it on its side and imagine that it's a box —like in Figure 2-3.

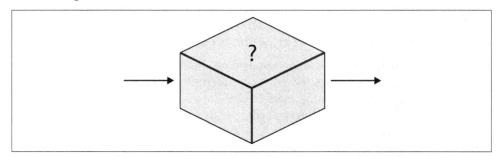

Figure 2-3. A visual representation of a service from Figure 2-1, but in three dimensions.

To an outside observer, such as a user or consumer of our service, this box is completely opaque. You may have some guarantees, such as, "If I put something in this box, I'll get something else out of it," but the actual mechanism of this operation is unknown and unknowable to you, the user. Consider a scenario where, as an external end user, you wanted to know the performance of the mechanism inside the box—all you're able to do is measure the length of time it takes from when you put something into when you're given your result. You don't have any real ability to model what's happening inside the box—other than pure conjecture, which isn't really useful in this circumstance—and thus the amount of data you can reasonably make inferences about is fairly small. We consider this sort of instrumentation to be operating against a *black box*.

Let's apply this metaphor to a daemon process running on a system and the various dimensions we can measure it in. As an operator of this process, I can view interesting and potentially valuable data about the process by inspecting /proc/<pid>/status]—for example, the amount of memory mapped to the process (as VmSize).[1] I can view open file handles, calculate the percentage of CPU utilization by the process over a fixed time range with some fancy math, and do all sorts of things. However, little of this helps me trace the application. For that, I'll need to observe the set of *observable inputs* to my process:

- I/O devices
- System calls
- Network activity
- External libraries
- Process operations

We can discard several of these in the context of distributed systems; as a matter of fact, we can generally focus on just one—network activity. By and large, distributed applications running across multiple physical or virtual servers will have the majority of their inputs defined by an RPC (remote procedure call) that is delivered across a LAN or WAN link. This does not diminish the utility or importance of these other forms of input (they can be critical for debugging or deep, kernel-level tracing), but it does help to focus our discussion.

Thus, one example of a black box trace would be to observe, through some sort of proxy, the incoming and outgoing network traffic of a process. If we know that our black box accepts requests in the format /api/:operation/:resourceId, and

---

1 Or through Get-Process in PowerShell, for our Windows friends!

responds with some message, we could use the proxy to create a span that looks something like Example 2-1.

Example 2-1. Black box trace

```
{
    'operationName': '/api/<operation>',
    'duration': <endTime—startTime>
    'tags': [
        {'resource': '<id>'},
        {'service': '<processName>'},
        {'wasSuccess': true}
        // And so forth—pid, other metrics
    ]
}
```

By analyzing the traffic as it enters and exits the process, we can collect the data required to build a useful span.

Up to this point, we've been talking about *black box* instrumentation, presupposing that we don't know what's going on inside the box. What if we opened it up to look inside, as in Figure 2-4? We can easily create and validate a hypothesis due to our knowledge of the inner workings of a service we write—after all, we wrote it! It is this knowledge of the service and the ability to modify it that comprises white box instrumentation.

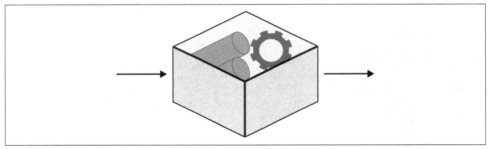

Figure 2-4. When you open the box, you can view all of the inputs, outputs, and how they're transformed.

With the ability to look inside the service and modify its code, we can instrument our software in much more powerful ways. The ability to fully comprehend the internal workings of the service, the data model that it operates on, and the exact call graph that comprises its execution flow allows for writing trace instrumentation that is more comprehensive and more useful than we might otherwise. Recall our earlier example—when limited to merely observing the inputs and outputs, we could lack critical pieces of information for our span, such as the relationships between external RPC calls created by our service or requests to other components of our distributed application, such as a database. With white box instrumentation, we do not have to think of the entire internal transaction as a single logical whole, but can consider it as almost a subtrace of our greater transaction.

Given this, you might be wondering, "Why wouldn't I always use white box instrumentation?" Quite simply: sometimes, you cannot. This is common in larger engineering teams with more legacy software to maintain—consider a modern API frontend that is backed by a legacy mainframe application. Even if you could modify the source code to your legacy services (which is not always possible), would you *want* to? In these circumstances, you might be able to represent only the work performed in your legacy component via black box instrumentation. Keep in mind, you do not necessarily need to create your black box spans from the system that operates a service; a typical pattern is to use the calling service with its white box instrumentation to create a separate span for the black box process.

Application Versus System

Our second topic is the distinction between application and system instrumentation. Much has been written about the difference between application and system *monitoring*, and instrumentation for distributed tracing follows similar lines. We'll briefly review the distinction and discuss how it applies to instrumentation for distributed tracing.

Traditionally, the people who operated applications and the people who operated the servers that ran those applications had different concerns. A system operator might be concerned with the health of disk drives, the amount of memory available on a server, or other *system* metrics. Meanwhile, an application operator would have more prosaic questions—is the application responding to requests, and is it performing acceptably? The application operator, thus, might monitor their application by using a script to access the application over the network every few seconds and report any failures. The system operator, however, would use similar scripts to query the server's operating system to understand when a disk was running out of space.

In the context of distributed tracing, we're usually less concerned with these sort of metrics (or, to be more accurate, we gather them through other sources), but they shouldn't be ignored. Indeed, we can think of this as more of a question about what component *generates* our traces. In short, do we generate spans in our application code, or does some service or subsystem that is running our application code do it for us?

Consider our simple service from the last section—we know it has some inputs and produces some outputs. Let's add some more boxes to our service diagram in Figure 2-5.

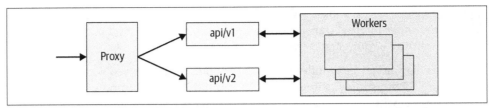

Figure 2-5. A simple system diagram of an API server, service proxy, and worker process.

All of these services could be independently instrumented for traces, emitting spans as a single request passes through them—in fact, this is a very common pattern and the easiest way to get started with tracing distributed systems. However, applications are often ignorant of what's going on outside of their immediate context—indeed, a stateless service would be ignorant of anything happening outside of the context of a specific request! In this case, we need to pull back a bit, looking not only at the services that are running, but the substrate they exist in. This is where system instrumentation comes into play.

Systems can be many exciting things—consider container orchestration systems such as Kubernetes or managed platforms such as DC/OS. We can use these systems to generate trace data in the form of spans or context baggage that provides turn-key instrumentation to applications or to enhance the quality of spans emitted by application code. Since these orchestrators and platforms act, practically, as the operating system for services running on them (see Figure 2-6), you're able to extract useful *system* data such as memory usage, CPU share utilization, and other data external to the process or its container and share that with the application or emit it as a separate span for analysis.

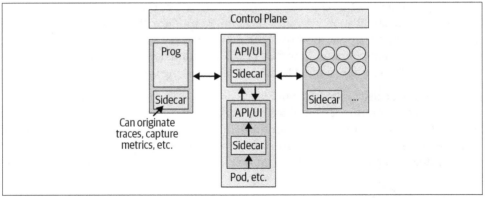

Figure 2-6. The services from Figure 2-5, but running inside a platform that exposes system data.

So, when should you use application instrumentation and when should you use system instrumentation? Ideally, you'd use both. At the time of this writing, it's generally easier to get started with pure application instrumentation, but new technology such as service meshes dramatically reduces the difficulty of implementing system instrumentation. In the future, we expect that managed orchestration platforms such as Google Kubernetes Engine or AWS Fargate will provide seamless span context propagation to services running on them.

Agents Versus Libraries

The third topic we'll cover is the distinction between agent-based and library-based instrumentation. What do we mean by *agents* and *libraries*? Remember, a white box presupposes that the person writing instrumentation has access to the source code of the application being instrumented and can use that knowledge to generate more logically accurate instrumentation. This closely maps to the concept of instrumenting with a library. Conversely, the black box assumes you don't have that interior knowledge of the application source—agents are more analogous to this case, since they operate outside of the process itself.

The terms *agent* and *library* are used quite a bit in the modern tracing space, sometimes interchangeably, with confusing results. There are libraries that brand themselves as agents, agents that call themselves libraries, and a lot of things in between. We suggest that the biggest distinction between the two comes down to intent. The intent of a library is to make it easier to write instrumentation that can be shared across multiple services, easing the pain of adoption for creating distributed traces across a polyglot distributed system. Agents, conversely, intend to make it very easy to trace and observe *existing* systems without rewriting code.

A library-based instrumentation approach can be characterized by its reliance on an application-level dependency on some shared, standardized library that is used throughout its services. These libraries provide a sane and standardized API for handling the key components of creating instrumentation and propagating context. Libraries can support a polyglot heterogeneous application by defining a relatively small API that supports the least-common set of features shared by all of the target languages. Indeed, it's generally possible with a library-based strategy to write your instrumentation against a thin interface wrapper and only depend on a concrete implementation of your library at runtime via dependency injection. That said, library-based instrumentation generally relies on developers to write instrumentation code.

Agent-based instrumentation relies on some sort of external process or processes to instrument processes at runtime. There are a wide variety of agents and strategies for instrumenting with agents, but there are really two major methods agents use to instrument a service directly. The first is some external process or monitoring service that injects code into your service and uses this to create a trace of the service as various functions are called. The second method is through some sort of in-process agent that is imported to the runtime environment of a process and uses a system of user-defined rules to trace specific actions. Of special note is indirect usage of agents to capture data that can be transformed into trace data—one such interesting application is to extend the black box approach and use some sort of existing data source for service state, like structured or unstructured log files, which the agent then transforms into trace data.

Really, as with everything else in this chapter, you're going to need to blend these approaches. Even with modern code, if you haven't been considering how to instrument your services from the jump, there's going to be an implementation cost to add tracing libraries to your existing services and applications. Some of your older services may not be able to have tracing added at all, and will require agents in order to be instrumented. That said, even if you have fairly modern software and services, you can jump-start tracing with agents to more quickly prove value or to prop up overall system visibility for teams that don't have high-quality library-based instrumentation.

Propagating Context

So far, we've discussed various strategies for instrumenting our services to emit spans that describe the work our services are doing. These spans, as standalone pieces of data, aren't very exciting. In order to create *traces*, we will need some way to communicate certain details about our spans to other services or other parts of our process. The mechanism by which we communicate these details to other services is generally known as *context propagation*.

Let's start by talking about what we're propagating, then we'll move into how it's propagated. Let's assume we have a simple service proxy that provides functions around user management. What would a span look like? (These span representations are covered in more detail in Chapter 3 when we discuss OpenTelemetry.)

Our span in Example 2-2 has some pretty basic information—the operation we're concerned with, a tag—but there's something new as well. We've added a spanId field that provides an identifier for this particular span. Conceptually, each of our services is going to emit a span for the work that it's doing, represented in Figure 2-7.

Example 2-2. Basic span

```
{
    operationName: "api/getUser",
    spanId: "09f42f7e-e606-4923-831b-7dd612683720",
    tags: [
        {
            key: "userName",
```

```
            value: "testUser"
        },
    ],
    // Start time, duration, etc.
}
```

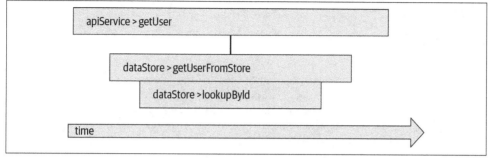

Figure 2-7. Relationship between the API proxy and the datastore services.

What's going on in our datastore service? Let's look at Example 2-3.

Example 2-3. Datastore service

```
{
    operationName: "getUserFromStore",
    spanId: "dac303fb-6c1c-4816-ac86-ce717cee1714",
    tags: [
        {
            key: "userId",
            value: 105832
        }
    ],
    // Start time, duration, etc.
}
```

One of the benefits of distributed tracing is that your spans exist largely independently of each other. As we'll talk about in later chapters, you can collect and centralize data from multiple sources, so we want a way for each of these spans to know the relationship between them that doesn't require us to send too much data around. For distributed RPCs like this, it's popular to send the *trace context* between services in an HTTP header, and have the child service create a span with a defined parent-child relationship. Our second span's data structure would look something like Example 2-4, in contrast.

Example 2-4. Span with a defined parent-child relationship

```
{
    operationName: "getUserFromStore",
```

```
    spanId: "dac303fb-6c1c-4816-ac86-ce717cee1714",
    parentSpanId: "09f42f7e-e606-4923-831b-7dd612683720",
    tags: [
        {
            key: "userId",
            value: 105832
        }
    ],
    // Start time, duration, etc.
}
```

 The trace context (sometimes simplified to just *context*) is covered more in Chapter 3 and later in this chapter. For now, think of it as a set of globally unique identifiers for a trace and each of its spans. Typically, these identifiers are a bunch of random bits or a large random number.

Those are the basics—let's dive in for a more detailed look at the two different types of propagation: *interprocess* and *intraprocess*.

Interprocess Propagation

One key notion of microservice architectures is that we can think of each service as fairly independent of its peers. A service should do one logical thing reliably and robustly. This allows our services to scale horizontally in response to demand or other signals. This notion maps very well to span-based distributed tracing—each service, logically, would have a single span that corresponds to the work being performed by that service. It's often helpful to conceive of this by considering the RPCs that make up your microservices as a sort of call stack. Imagine an application with a few components, building off what we've been discussing earlier, as in Figure 2-8.

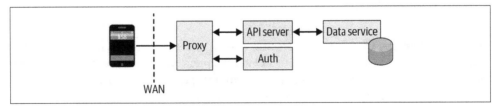

Figure 2-8. A service diagram from client to datastore.

Now let's manually trace a request through the system, starting at the client:

```
client
api-proxy
auth
api-server
datastore
```

Any transaction you make, logically, needs to follow this series of RPC calls: the client talks to the api-proxy, the api-proxy authenticates the request and passes it along to the api-server, which talks to the datastore, which returns the result all the way back to the client. The work each of those services performs would be a single, logical span. We can intuit that we'll need some mechanism to propagate the *trace context* through this chain of requests so that each subsequent call can use that information to form a parent-child relationship with its predecessor.

For the purposes of this section, let's presume that our services communicate with each other using HTTP. However, the principles that we're discussing aren't limited to interprocess communication over HTTP—they can be performed over a variety of transport methods such as gRPC, Apache Thrift, SOAP, etc.

Why HTTP?

Here and throughout the book, we tend to use HTTP and RESTful API idioms when discussing RPCs. This is mostly an affordance to the relative simplicity of HTTP, the familiarity that most of our readers have with it, and the fact that conceptually the model of a RESTful API with HTTP as the message-passing system is easily modeled by distributed traces.

Ultimately, when you're making an RPC between any two of these services, you need two things to happen. The caller needs a way to take the current span context and serialize the required information to propagate the trace context to the next hop. The callee needs a way to discover the span context (if it exists) and create a child span using this data. The first action, serializing the current span context, is also known as an *inject* operation, whereas the latter is an *extract*. We're "injecting" the span context into the transport, and "extracting" it back out. These inject and extract operations happen at the edge of our service in code—you'd generally want to use some sort of middleware in your HTTP service that would automatically perform these operations when a new request is created or received.

The terms *trace context* and *span context* are used interchangeably throughout the text. In general, they denote the same context—unique identifiers about a trace and span.

Broadly speaking, inject and extract semantics are fairly universal—you either pass in a span context, or get one back as the result. The span context is simple enough—it's an object that contains the identifier for a span. The exact implementation of a span context varies somewhat across implementations, but open source projects such as OpenTracing have defined a span context as an object containing a SpanID, a

TraceID, and an array of baggage (which contains arbitrary key-value pairs). In general, we want these identifiers to be fairly unique—a span ID should be unique within a TraceID, and a TraceID should be unique within a very large space. How large? That depends entirely on the amount of traces your system is generating, but a random 64-bit value is usually sufficient. The W3C's forthcoming general specification for trace context is standardizing around 128-bit identifiers, such as UUIDv4, which allows for very low probabilities of collisions (to reach a 50% probability of a single collision with UUIDv4, you'd need to generate 2.71 quintillion identifiers—that's one billion IDs a second for 85 years!) and should be sufficient for any single system.

Aside from IDs, there's *baggage*, as mentioned earlier—this is a convenient way to propagate information from earlier services to later ones. Imagine that you would like to propagate some piece of information from the client through every span such as a user ID, a version, etc. You *could* use baggage to do this, but use it with care! Everything you put into baggage will exist on every hop after you add it, and the overhead of pushing that additional data across the network may incur noticeable performance penalties.

How should we use these methods? It's best that they happen in a fairly touch-free way. A good practice is to include middleware in your HTTP request pipeline that attempts to extract the span context from each incoming request and adds it to the request object. In your route handler, you can then look for the incoming span context and create a new child span. Similarly, wrapping your outgoing HTTP requests with a function that looks for an existing span and injects it into the outgoing request ensures that the next service down the line can pick it up if properly instrumented. A productive way to begin instrumenting an existing application is through this strategy, as a matter of fact—we'll talk more about that later.

It is very important that your team or organization develops standards for the format of propagated contexts. Eventually, the W3C's standardization efforts will reduce this burden, but as of this writing, you'll need to ensure that upstream and downstream service owners all agree on the format for your span context. Standardizing around some shared code for performing inject/extract works well and is easy to do in more homogenous environments. In a more polyglot world, such as one where you've got microservices written and running in a variety of languages, make sure that documentation is clear and widely shared about the specific headers that will carry your trace context, and the format of that data. Open source telemetry frameworks also ease the burden of dealing with this problem, which we'll cover in Chapter 3.

Intraprocess Propagation

Where interprocess propagation is concerned with passing a trace context between different services, intraprocess propagation is concerned with passing the trace context around inside a single process. Why would we want to do this? If our microservice applications are being designed like we all hope they are, we would have a single span per service, right?

Not all applications are pretty arrangements of microservices. We would hazard a guess that *most* applications aren't. We're seeing a greater and greater number of what we call "gentrified" applications—new, greenfield development tacked on to large brownfield monoliths. These hybrid applications often do involve a great deal of microservices surrounding the core monolith—and wouldn't you know it, we'd like to trace both those microservices *and* the calls they make inside the monolith. Even in microservices, it's extremely likely that we'll want to trace individual functions, or requests into our database.

In addition, not all microservices are equally micro—think about a worker service that parallelizes work across multiple threads or across multiple remote services. In all of these cases, it would be highly beneficial to be able to propagate a trace inside a service in order to create spans that more accurately represent the work being performed.

The basic concepts here are very similar to the ones discussed in the section on inter-process propagation, with one critical difference. Since we aren't making RPCs, we don't need to concern ourselves with injecting or extracting our span context and serializing or deserializing it across a process boundary. In general, we're more concerned with the *scope* of a span. The details of this are fairly language-specific, but we'll give an overview of the concept. In a multithreaded or asynchronous processing scenario, we can define an *active* span as the span that is in scope of the work that our process is doing at any given point. Consider the pseudocode in Example 2-5.

Example 2-5. Active span

```
async function bigSearch(*context, key, dataset...) {
    for dataset d {
        let result = await d.findInSet(*context, key)
    }
    return result
}

async function (dataset) findInSet(*context, key) {
    while *context.isNotCancelled {
        let found = d.find(key)
        if found {
            *context = *context.Cancel
            return found
        }
    }
}
```

Our `bigSearch` function can take some arbitrary amount of datasets, a context, and a key to look up in those sets. For each set, it starts a thread and begins to search for the key. When the key is found, it cancels the context and returns the result, causing all other searches to short-circuit as well. We can visualize this in the timing graph shown in Figure 2-9, which would be generated by the pseudocode in Example 2-6.

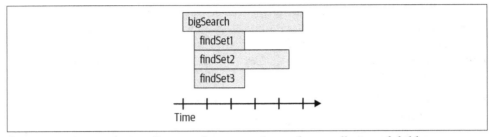

Figure 2-9. A span timing diagram demonstrating early cancellation of child spans.

How do you create these relationships in spans? As mentioned, we can create parent-child relations between spans using a span context, and the same principle applies here. Since we don't have to cross an RPC boundary, the simplest way is to pass the span context as a parameter to child functions, like in Example 2-6.

Example 2-6. Span context as a parameter to child functions

```
async function bigSearch(*context, key, dataset...) {
    let span = startSpan("bigSearch")
    span.setTag("searchKey", key)
    for dataset d {
        let result = await d.findInSet(*context, key, span.context)
    }
    span.finish()
    return result
}

async function (dataset) findInSet(*context, key, spanContext) {
    let childSpan = startSpanFromContext("findInSet", spanContext)
    while *context.isNotCancelled {
        let found = d.find(key)
        if found {
            *context = *context.Cancel
            span.log("found span in dataset", d)
            span.finish()
            return found
        }
    }
    span.setTag("cancelled", true)
    span.finish()
}
```

The preceding pseudocode is written in the style of Go or other languages where a user-managed process context object is available. In languages such as Java or C#, thread-local storage would offer similar functions. The key thing to note is that you need to pass the *span context* into child functions that you wish to create spans for and use whatever language facility exists to do so. It can be as simple as passing a single span object around via function parameters.

Each of the child spans in this case would have a single parent, but it's kind of ugly to have to modify our method signatures to accept span contexts everywhere. Worry not, there's an easier way to do it through a mechanism known as a *scope manager*, but that's dependent on the specific technology and language you're using. In general, a scope manager removes the manual part of this process by using thread-local storage to automatically preserve a reference to the active span for a function and can use that reference to create new child spans from the active one. We'll discuss explicit implementations of scope managers in Chapter 3. For now, just know that you don't have to limit your traces simply to RPCs!

The Shape of Distributed Tracing

Now that we've introduced some of the basic concepts around instrumenting services, let's dive in to make it a bit more real. You might have an understanding of differing forms of instrumentation and how they can interact with each other, but how do we tie these concepts back to the sort of software and services you might be familiar with? In general, there's a certain pattern—or shape—of how distributed traces act, and interact, with common software architectural styles. Let's review them and give some pointers on which sort of instrumentation approaches would work best.

Tracing-Friendly Microservices and Serverless

Distributed tracing and microservices/serverless were, quite literally, made for each other. Historically, distributed tracing technology has been built by large engineering organizations with thousands or tens of thousands of microservices that are operated and maintained by hundreds or thousands of people. It may surprise you, then, that not all microservices are created equal when it comes to being traced. As a matter of fact, span-based distributed request tracing has several characteristics that you can hew to in order to create more useful traces from your microservices or serverless architectures. We'll cover some quick dos and don'ts here.

Generally with microservices or serverless, consider white box instrumentation first
Your microservices should be small enough that you can make the necessary changes to allow for library-based instrumentation practices, where your tracing code is integrated into the service itself. This allows for trace data that's not only

more accurately scoped to the actual function of the service, but also offers you the opportunity to build out tracing over time as services are updated to take advantage of it. Capture semantic information about each service in your trace data. A well-traced microservice should attach relevant semantic attributes (such as the OpenTelemetry `span.kind` attribute) to the spans that it generates. This gives you a more complete and accurate view of what your services are doing and is especially beneficial in a microservice architecture as you have fewer guarantees about trace data consumers being aware of what your service *does*.

Create attributes for the important things!
Think about what you'd want to know if you were trying to debug a production fire at 3 a.m., then add that. Some recommended attributes/tags are `hostname`, `region` or `datacenter`, and `service.version`. One great idea that we're starting to see more of is a `README` attribute, or some other pointer to an internal system that indicates where people can ask questions or find out more information about the service. Ensure that ingress and egress are traced.[2] As we've mentioned, it's best practice to have the process of creating spans for incoming and outgoing requests to be handled automatically by your RPC library.

Finally, start with what you know
If you have particular trouble spots, latency-sensitive services, or other areas of interest, then the quickest way to make useful traces is to start building them from there. It can often be easier to add a little bit of instrumentation to understand the problems you're having *now* rather than waiting for a large-scale instrumentation plan to be developed and executed, and we'll go into more detail on this later.

There are also some things to avoid:

Don't neglect to set "rules of the road"
The most critical aspect of successful instrumentation is that each service is able to create spans that are part of a larger distributed trace. This means that one of your first steps should be to ensure that standard context propagation headers and formats are being used. Chapter 4 will dive in deeper to a variety of open source frameworks for distributed tracing; we'd suggest using one of those.

In general, don't try to trace extremely long operations
Distributed request tracing works best when the entire traced operation takes place in a fairly short (minutes) time span. There are several reasons for this, such as data retention periods for trace analyzers and sampling considerations (which we'll get into later), but for now let's just say that it's not a great fit. If you

---

2 Ingress and egress refer to traffic that enters, or exits, a network boundary, respectively. Broadly, these are used to refer to any or all incoming or outgoing requests from a service.

are trying to trace operations with an extremely long execution time, don't fret, there are options to address those use cases.

If you own a service that isn't in the critical path, don't assume you don't need to do anything

You might think that your service isn't important, or that it doesn't have a role to play in a trace. At the very least, you'll want to ensure that all of your services pass tracing headers through that may be coming from their callers to their callees. We would suggest, though, that if you're going to go ahead and do that, it doesn't take a lot more work to wrap your microservice in a span and send it on its way, giving everyone a more complete view of the work of the application.

Finally, don't hold trace data locally for very long

This is more of a concern with a serverless service, but it's good advice in general —preferably, you're regularly exfiltrating your trace data from your service to some external collector. Some of this is to ensure that your analysis system is able to capture and analyze each request in its entirety while that trace is still relevant. More importantly, this practice reduces the potential for lost data if an instance of your service becomes unavailable due to a crash or some other disaster.

Tracing in a Monolith

We've stated that distributed tracing is primarily the domain of microservices, so some of you might be looking forlornly at your monoliths of yore, silently mouthing "Is tracing not for me, then?" Humble reader, hope is not lost—but you will need different tactics to instrument a monolith.

When instrumenting monoliths, you should first take stock of what you already have and consider why you're adding tracing. We see a few rationales for this. One is that you're decomposing your monolith and have decided to adopt tracing, but need to extend traces into the monolith from the new microservice components. Another is that you're adopting tracing at a different layer of the system (for example, at your client/frontend) and would like to capture end-to-end performance data to identify hotspots. Whatever your reasons are, instrumenting a monolith looks both similar and dissimilar to instrumenting a microservice.

As mentioned earlier, you should take stock of how you're observing the monolith already to determine the best path forward. Are your existing metrics and logs valuable? Studying how your on-call teams and engineers are using existing observability data to inform their on-call practice can be useful in understanding where tracing would be beneficial to your monolith. For example, one common pattern we've seen with engineers who retrofit tracing into their monolithic applications is to use agents or other out-of-process services to capture log data and marshal it into trace data. This is a fairly low-touch method of adding tracing to a monolith, yes, but if the logs you're using aren't valuable to begin with, then the trace data you generate is also going to be of limited value.

That said, what distinguishes tracing in a monolith from tracing in a microservice? First, and most critical, is your instrumentation methodology. Attempting to trace a monolith as a black box can be challenging to the point of futility. Many monolithic applications are characterized by a high level of concurrency and parallel processing on different threads or thread-shaped objects, requiring some level of white box introspection of what's happening inside the process itself. Ingress and egress operations may be extremely difficult to quantify due to the complexity of the monolith, especially if the monolith exposes multiple versions of an API that each support different RPC styles—consider a monolithic service that exposes a v1...vn API where each version adds and/or deprecates a particular RPC transport (SOAP, JSON over HTTP, Apache Thrift, etc.).

The Right Abstraction to Instrument

In general, divorced from whatever framework you're using, it's best to instrument at the layer of abstraction *below* the one you're trying to understand and inspect. Instrumenting below the layer of inspection gives you more visibility into your system with less effort. In addition, if you've instrumented below the layer you're inspecting, then it is generally easier to pull a context "up" in order to get more details in a particular service or part of your code than it is to push an existing context "down" into the underlying framework.

One strategy that can serve you well when instrumenting a monolithic service for tracing is to rely on agent-based approaches to inject instrumentation into the service framework layer. Consider the Spring Framework for Java—if your application is built on Spring, you'll get more bang for the buck by instrumenting the Spring classes themselves as opposed to your own code. Conveniently enough, these popular frameworks often have open source instrumentation available, saving you the trouble of implementing it yourself. Framework instrumentation can get you started, and in some cases might be enough to understand the broad performance shape of requests, but will often need to be paired with some level of manual instrumentation to capture the nuances of your business logic. There aren't many silver bullets here, to be blunt— you'll need to carefully consider the structure of your application code, and how calls propagate through your service. You need to pay special attention to the intraprocess propagation of spans and traces inside your service, as there aren't necessarily clean lines of separation like you'd get in a microservice architecture.

Along those same lines, spend some time thinking about exactly what functions or intraprocess calls need to be their own spans, and which can be combined with a common parent span. It may not be necessary, or desirable, to add a trace for every single function call in your monolith. It usually isn't!

Finally, it can be helpful to create a model of your monolith's various internal components and use those to orient your thinking around what "should be traced." Consider a simple ecommerce monolith that provides some sort of UI, an inventory component, an account management component, and an order management component (see Figure 2-10). In a monolith, each of these components may share code with others, and they may have very fuzzy boundaries in some cases, but they're the logical divisions available to you that can provide context to trace data. For example, it might be that some piece of shared functionality fails more often when called from the account management component versus the order management component—having trace data that corresponds to the component instead of the function will make it easier to identify the reason.

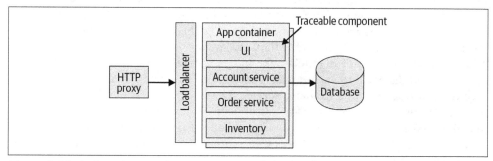

Figure 2-10. A shopping cart/ecommerce monolithic application.

There are a lot of things you'll want to do the same way as you would if you were tracing a microservice, though. You'll still want to capture semantic information about your service (or internal component) in each span, and you'll want to create attributes for hostname, IP address, etc. If you're using agents or framework-based instrumentation for your monolith, much of this work may be done for you. Ultimately, there's nothing that stops you from tracing monoliths or having trace data from monoliths be a part of a larger trace. In the worst case, where you don't have any ability to modify or introspect your existing process, you can always fall back on wrapping the monolith in some sort of request proxy and generating trace data through that—it's always better to have a span than no span.

Tracing in Web and Mobile Clients

Most of this book has been written from the implied perspective of a backend service, running in your datacenter or on a cloud provider. What about when your code doesn't run on something you control quite so neatly? As mentioned earlier, one of the benefits of distributed tracing is that it allows for visibility into the complete, end-to-end life cycle of a request—not just a narrow slice of it.

So, what does a distributed trace look like when it begins at the beginning? Mobile computing through cell phones, tablets, and other small-scale devices has become the gateway to software for millions of people, and so we've seen a rise in client-side single-page applications and native mobile applications. You should consider how you're tracing these parts of your application, and be aware of some of their special requirements. For the sake of brevity, we'll refer to these client applications as *frontend* services for the rest of this section.

Instrumenting a frontend service looks an awful lot like instrumenting any other service, with the same sort of stipulations and watchwords—be sure to trace egress (so, any communication between your client and your server), add semantic tags, and so forth. The biggest question is one of verbosity. How much detail in your frontend trace data is too much? There's a wealth of information available in Web APIs through the Performance interface (*https://oreil.ly/Hngwz*) on the amount of time it takes to load resources (such as HTML, CSS, JavaScript, and image assets), how long redirects and other HTTP methods take to execute, and how long it takes to create the DOM and display it to an end user. This can be extremely valuable information to include in a trace of your frontend service. However, it's possible that it can be an overwhelming amount of data for consumers of your traces—both humans and machines. We'll discuss the trade-offs around collecting and storing trace data in later chapters, but suffice to say that there's some amount of overhead for creating, collecting, and storing trace data.

One option is, of course, to collect everything you can and leverage your analysis tools to cut through the chaff. This is becoming more popular as the sophistication of analysis tools increases. Another option is to create two separate traces—a trace that represents the work being done by the frontend client, such as performance and timing information around rendering the DOM or drawing UI elements, and a separate trace that represents the work being done by the frontend communicating with back-end components, such as loading data from an API. These traces can be linked by a single, shared attribute. Consider the humans who are consuming your trace data in order to make a decision here—how much data do they need in order to understand the performance profile of a request, and what are they responsible for?

Other challenges than verbosity are involved in instrumenting frontend services, of course. Many of them are challenges endemic to the nature of mobile or web services in general—inconsistent network availability, a significantly wider variance in the performance of end-user hardware, etc. Here are some common scenarios to watch out for when instrumenting frontend services:

Loss of WAN connectivity

Your instrumentation and reporting should check to make sure they can report spans before they start recording, and potentially *NoOp* (short for no operation) to avoid unneeded allocations and work if there's no chance that the trace data can be sent to your backend.

Unexpected loss of focus for your service

In general, background processes on mobile devices are constrained in what they can do or how long they can do it. Make sure that your tracer is listening for events that indicate a loss of focus, and hurry up to flush whatever trace data is available to your trace analyzer.

Debounce your spans

If your application has a button, someone is probably going to click it in frustration. You should be debouncing any sort of long-running request, so make sure that span creation is *also* debounced to avoid creating a lot of unnecessary spans (although it might be fun to count how many rage taps you get and monitor that!).

Be careful with PII

As privacy laws and regulations continue to develop, you should be extremely careful about what you're logging or recording from a device. We are not lawyers (and we're especially not *your* lawyers), so you should check the specifics with your legal counsel, but the European Union's General Data Protection Regulation (GDPR) asserts that users have a right to understand how you're using their personal data, to request access to that personal data, and to request that their data be deleted. In the interest of not having to delete swaths of telemetry data at the request of your end users, it would behoove you to simply not track personal data to begin with. Again, talk to a lawyer for details.

If you feel a bit lost, don't worry—we just dumped a lot on you. It might be useful to keep these pointers in mind and reference them after you've finished the book and have a better understanding of not only instrumentation, but also collection and analysis of trace data. In Chapter 3, we'll discuss various open source telemetry and tracing frameworks that you can use to address many of the challenges raised when tracing microservices, serverless, monolithic, or frontend services.

Open Source Instrumentation: Interfaces, Libraries, and Frameworks

As a technology, tracing—even distributed tracing—isn't brand-new. Developers have been building distributed systems in some form or another for decades and have turned to tracing solutions to understand these systems. One thing many of these solutions have in common, however, is that they tend to be very focused. Sometimes this focus is for a particular technology stack or language; sometimes it relies on the usage of a particular middleware provider; sometimes it's just a home-rolled solution that's been maintained for years by engineers who aren't with your company anymore. More recently, we've seen this sort of behavior continue to proliferate aided by cloud vendors and other platform providers.

Some might say, "Well, what's the problem here?" After all, for a great many people, these proprietary or otherwise closed solutions work fine, or at least are providing value to their users. While that certainly can be the case, these solutions are often more brittle than they appear at first glance. The foremost argument against proprietary instrumentation is that it often leaves you at the mercy of the authors of the instrumentation solution when it comes to adapting your software for new languages, methodologies, and challenges caused by increasing scale or business requirements.

Remember—one of the few constants in life, and especially in computing, is change. At the time of this writing, Microsoft is one of the largest contributors to open source software. If you went back in time 20 years and told someone that, they'd likely be shocked! Relying on the current state of vendors and cloud providers and popular languages or runtimes will invariably lock you into decisions that you might not want to be locked into.

There is a solution to this dilemma, one that's been widely adopted by users, vendors, and software authors—the open source model of instrumentation. What we mean, in practice, is that rather than relying on languages and runtimes to provide the tools for instrumenting software, the community in general provides them. In this chapter, we'll discuss the current state of the art when it comes to these open source solutions, as well as some of the historical context and forerunner projects that you're likely to encounter in the wild. We'll also cover the API and methodology behind instrumenting software with these packages, such as OpenTelemetry.

The Importance of Abstract Instrumentation

Why is it important to embrace abstract instrumentation in the first place? It's a good question, especially if you're already using a platform or tech stack that provides some sort of tracing functionality, and are thinking about adopting it to monitor your services. Historically, this information has been available at several locations that tend to "make sense" (for example, at the boundaries of your services, or via some ingress layer such as a load balancer, web proxy, or other routing service). These trace identifiers, such as the `X-Amzn-TraceID` of Amazon's Elastic Load Balancer (ELB) or the fairly opaque tracing headers supplied by Microsoft's IIS (Internet Information Services), are able to provide a fairly thorough view into a single request as it moves through your services. That said, there are a few critical areas where these legacy tracing methods fall short.

The first test that these tracing methods fail is portability. Take, for example, IIS Request Tracing. It might not surprise you to learn that using this requires you to also use IIS as your web server/proxy, which also implies that your software runs on Windows Server. While we won't suggest that there's no software that runs (and generates perhaps a massive amount of business value) on Windows Server, we would also suggest that it's not quite as popular these days as it once was. The associated costs of this lock-in can be deleterious, however. You may delay or defer maintenance and upgrades to your monitoring, opening you up to security vulnerabilities. Advancements in monitoring platforms may provide you with improved insights and lower costs, but you may be unable to take advantage of them because you'll be locked into your existing instrumentation. Finally, even if you're generally happy with the level of control and insight that your proprietary instrumentation grants you, you may find it difficult to convince new team members of its greatness if they've learned to appreciate newer tools.

The second test that proprietary tracing methods fail is being *adaptable* to distributed applications. This is obvious when attempting to instrument a client-server relationship over some external link, such as the internet. Without some abstract instrumentation on both sides (the mobile application or client web application, and the backend server), you'll often have to resort to manual hacks to fit and transform data being generated by two potentially separate systems. Often, these proprietary systems will begin their traces at the ingress point rather than at the client, which can segregate your data rather than provide a single, end-to-end view into a request. These systems often lack internal extensibility, which is to say that you may find it challenging or impossible to create subtraces of service functionality outside of the top-level HTTP request. Additionally, you'll find that these systems may struggle at instrumenting transport methods that *aren't* carried across HTTP, leaving you with a tangled mess of incompatible trace data being generated by your HTTP, gRPC, SOAP, or other carriers. This can stymie refactoring for performance or integration with new services and technologies.

The third and final test that these methods fail is they promote *vendor lock-in* by necessity or by design. Don't like the analysis tools available? Too bad! Don't care for a particular instrumentation API? You're stuck with it unless you wrap the provided API in your own. Even this can only do so much, depending on the underlying design of the system. One surprisingly common situation we've seen is that this lock-in can paralyze teams that are spinning up new services because there may be business reasons that prevent the allocation of additional analytic capacity. A popular pricing model for monitoring, for example, relies on the amount of hosts or containers that are being monitored at any given time—if you're locked into a vendor with this pricing strategy, it can actually act as a damper on the amount of new instrumentation added to your application due to cost concerns. While this may seem like a savvy way to save a few bucks while developing a new and unproven idea, you don't know if this new service will take off (or, worse, become a sneaky failure-prone piece of code causing difficulties, headaches, and many late-night alerts for other teams).

Abstract, open source instrumentation solves these problems neatly. Your instrumentation is portable to any underlying operating system (OS) that supports the language you're writing it in—Linux, Windows, macOS, iOS, whatever! Since it's open source, even if it doesn't work right now, you have the ability to fork it and add support if required. Thankfully, the major open source instrumentation interfaces and frameworks have wide support for the majority of general purpose programming languages in use today...although if you wanted to port it to Perl, we're sure someone would be grateful. As you might expect from a widely supported framework, open source and abstract instrumentation are very adaptable to your changing requirements and needs.

As your services decompose into smaller services, you'll find that abstract instrumentation fits in very neatly with your new service boundaries, regardless of how they're being written, deployed, or run. Abstract instrumentation makes it easier to integrate your instrumentation with other technologies as well, such as service meshes or container orchestration platforms. Not to mention, as you integrate new services into your distributed application, abstract instrumentation grants you the flexibility to share a common *language* of instrumentation across disparate teams. Finally, and most importantly, abstract instrumentation prevents vendor lock-in of analysis or instrumentation. Since the instrumentation APIs, trace data format, propagation headers, wire format, and more are defined openly and publicly, you'll be able to use them (either directly or through a shim) with any sort of analysis system you can imagine. At the time of this writing, almost every major monitoring vendor supports at least one—and usually more—open source tracing formats, thus allowing you the flexibility of *write once, run anywhere* with your instrumentation code.

Now that we've gone over the benefits of these instrumentation frameworks, let's take a look at the most popular ones available, starting with the newest: OpenTelemetry.

OpenTelemetry

Writing an instrumentation library is, in a word, difficult. While the actual process of collecting and generating telemetry from a service is conceptually fairly straightforward, implementing that process in a highly performant way that also can get buy-in from a diverse group of users is extremely challenging. The foremost reason is that however much any two pieces of software have in common, they're likely to be very different. While this might be somewhat reductionist, it's a useful thing to keep in mind when discussing the challenges of writing instrumentation libraries for a general audience. However, there are several good reasons that you might prefer a general-purpose instrumentation library over a bespoke one:

- A general-purpose library will be more likely to be more performant in the general use case.
- The authors of the general-purpose library are more likely to have considered edge cases and other situations.
- Using a general-purpose library can save you months of maintenance headaches in adapting, extending, and using a bespoke one.

As your software becomes more complex, and development cycles become more strained, the rationale for the general-purpose library grows. You probably don't have the time or desire to implement your own telemetry collector or API. You might not have the expertise to create or maintain bespoke telemetry libraries in every language used by your application, or you may find the organizational dynamics of creating an internal standard insurmountable. Finally, you probably don't want to have to reinvent the wheel in terms of generating telemetry data from your dependencies—RPC frameworks, HTTP libraries, etc.

OpenTelemetry solves these problems and a host of others for you. The primary goal of OpenTelemetry is to provide a single set of APIs, libraries, agents, and collectors that you can use to capture distributed tracing and metric telemetry from your application. In doing so, OpenTelemetry imagines a world where portable, high-quality telemetry data is a built-in feature of cloud native software.

OpenTelemetry was formally announced in May 2019 as the next major release of both OpenTracing and OpenCensus. These two projects had similar goals but different ways of achieving them. The seeds for OpenTelemetry were planted in the fall of 2018 in several wide-ranging Twitter threads that crystallized the major stumbling block facing both projects—the appearance of a "standards war" between the two. Open source project authors, seeing that there were two incompatible standards for instrumentation, would defer adding tracing to their libraries and frameworks in the absence of consensus about which they should focus on. (For more information, see "OpenTracing" on page 43 and "OpenCensus" on page 48.)

These and other disagreements led to back-channel negotiations and discussions between the founders of each project along with a neutral mediator. A small technical team was formed to prototype a merged API, which became the initial prototype of OpenTelemetry. Spring 2019 saw work continue on the prototype, along with efforts to codify the new governance structure—taking lessons from other successful open source projects, like Kubernetes. After the announcement in May, contributors from a wide variety of companies, including Microsoft, Google, Lightstep, and Datadog, worked in concert to formalize the specification, application programming interface (API), software development kit (SDK), and other components.

Which brings us to now. OpenTelemetry, at the time of this writing, is still in an alpha phase. The project anticipates a beta by the time you're reading this, but as is the nature of open source, the timeline may change. With that in mind, we'll focus this section mostly on the distributed tracing components in OpenTelemetry, along with critical parts of its design.

OpenTelemetry comprises three major components. These are the API, the SDK, and the Collector. These components implement the OpenTelemetry specification and data model, and are designed to be interoperable and composable with each other. What does this mean? In short, parts of these components can be "swapped out" with differing implementations, as long as those reimplementations conform to the specification and the data model.

As Figure 3-1 shows, there are two main parts of any given OpenTelemetry library. The API contains the interfaces required for writing instrumentation code along with a minimal (or NoOp) implementation of the SDK. Generally, the API will be packaged with the SDK, which implements the core functionality of the API such as managing span state and context, serializing and deserializing span context from the wire, and other features. External to the SDK are *exporters*, plug-ins that translate and transmit the OpenTelemetry trace data to a suitable backend service for analysis. Each of these components is decoupled from the others; you can use the API with no SDK (see Figure 3-2), for example, or selectively reimplement parts of the SDK.

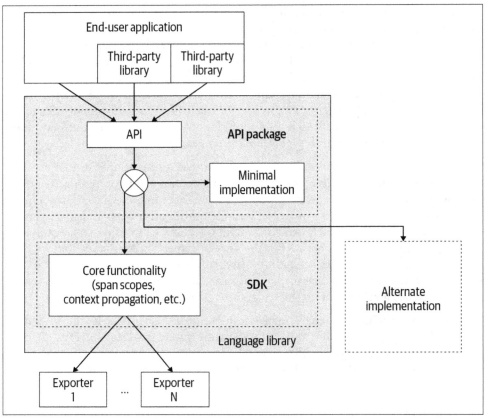

Figure 3-1. A generic OpenTelemetry library.

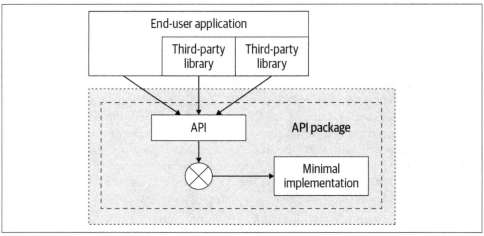

Figure 3-2. Minimal implementation of OpenTelemetry.

If you're writing code that will primarily be used as a library, then you would use the API by itself. If you're writing a service that will run—either alone or in concert with other services—you'd use the API and SDK.

The rationale is fairly simple. Let's say you're writing a library that performs some convenient function, like an optimized search on some set of data. Your users want to be able to trace your code—giving them insight into the number of iterations it requires to find the desired search term, for example. You can accomplish this very easily by adding tracing instrumentation and creating either a single span that represents the work being done by your library, or multiple spans representing each iteration (if you parallelized the algorithm in some way, this latter approach might be more useful). However, you want your library to be fairly performant and to have few external dependencies; after all, it's an optimized piece of code. In this case, you'd only take a dependency on the OpenTelemetry API package. When someone imports and uses your library, which is also using the OpenTelemetry SDK, your library would automatically swap over to using the full implementation rather than the minimal one, allowing your end users to trace the activity of your code.

The OpenTelemetry API provides three major things: distributed context propagation, management, application tracing, and application metrics. We'll focus on the first two in this book.

First, tracing. The primary building block of spans in OpenTelemetry is the `Tracer`. The `Tracer` provides methods for creating and activating new `Span` objects along with the ability to track and manage the active `Span` in the process context. Each `Tracer` is configured with Propagator objects, which allow for transferring the span context across process boundaries. The API provides a `TracerProvider` which allows for the creation of new `Tracer` objects, which each have a required name and an optional version. OpenTelemetry refers to this concept as *named tracers*, which act as a namespacing mechanism for multiple logical components inside a single process. For example, if you were to instrument a service that used an HTTP framework to communicate with other services, you would name the tracer for our service's business logic something like `myService`, while instrumentation for the HTTP framework would be named `opentelemetry.net.http`. This helps in preventing collisions in span name, attribute key, or other factors. Optionally, we can assign a version string to our tracer that should correspond to the version of the instrumentation library itself (i.e., `semver:1.0.0`).

Each tracer has to provide three methods—getting the current span, creating a new span, and activating a given span as the current one. In addition, it should provide methods to configure other important tracing components, like propagator objects. When creating a new span, the tracer will first check whether there's an active span, and create the new one as its child. A span or span context can also be provided when creating a new span as its parent. Each span is required to contain a span context, which is an immutable data structure that contains identifiers for the trace, span, and other flags and state values:

TraceID
:   16-byte array with at least one nonzero byte.

SpanId
:   8-byte array with at least one nonzero byte.

TraceFlags
:   Details about the trace. Present in all traces, unlike Tracestate.

Tracestate
:   System-specific configuration data, which allows for multiple tracing systems to participate in the same trace.[1]

IsValid
:   A Boolean flag, which returns true if the TraceID and SpanId are valid (or non-zero).

IsRemote
:   A Boolean flag, which returns true if the span context was propagated from a remote parent.

The span is a data structure that represents a single operation in a trace. Each trace contains a root span that represents the end-to-end latency of a request and, optionally, subspans that correspond to suboperations. The span encapsulates information like the name of the operation, its span context, a parent span, the start and end timestamp of the operation, a map of attributes, links to other spans, a list of events with timestamps, and a status. Some of these are more self-explanatory than others. The start time of a span should be set to the time that it was created, but you can override this with an arbitrary timestamp as well. Once a span has been created, you can change its name, set attribute keys and values, and add links to other spans and events—but only before the span has finished. Once an end time has been set, these values become immutable. Since the span is not intended to propagate information inside a process, you should not provide access to span fields *other* than span context.

There are a few new concepts here, so we'll break them down.

The name of the span is a requirement when creating a new span, but it's one of the only absolutely required parameters. Depending on the implementation, a span may be automatically created as the child of the current active span, but you also have the option to indicate that it should be a new root span. The span kind field is used to

---

1 For more details, see the W3C documentation (*https://oreil.ly/6sPwi*).

describe the relationship between a given span and its parents and children in the trace. The two properties that it describes are if the span is the parent or child of a remote operation and if the span represents a synchronous call. A single span should only have a single span kind in order for the field to be meaningful to analysis systems. See Table 3-2 for a complete description of span kind values.

Attributes are a collection of key-value pairs that can be created either at span creation time or during the lifetime of the span. In general, you want to set known attributes at span creation. Links are between arbitrary amounts of spans that have some causal relationship. They can exist between spans in a single trace or across multiple traces. When would you use link objects? First, you may want to use them to represent *batch* operations, where a single span was initiated from multiple incoming spans, each representing a single item in the batch. Additionally, a link can declare the relationship between an originating trace and a following trace. Consider a trace entering a trusted boundary of a service such as remote client code, like a web browser, and being forced to generate a new trace rather than relying on the incoming context. The root span in the new trace would be linked to the old trace.

Finally, as mentioned earlier, the start and stop timestamps are required but are generally automatically generated. You *can* tell the API to create a span with an arbitrary start and stop timestamp, which is useful if you're creating some sort of proxy that transforms existing telemetry data (such as a log file) into a trace.

Once you've created a tracer and a span, what can you do with them? The API provides several required methods:

- Get the SpanContext.
- Check whether the span IsRecording information.
- SetAttributes on the span.
- AddEvents to the span.
- SetStatus of the span.
- UpdateName of the span.
- End the span.

While some of these are fairly self-explanatory, such as ending the span, others are more nuanced. IsRecording is one of these—this method returns a Boolean value indicating whether the span is recording events, attributes, etc. The intended design of this flag is to avoid potentially expensive computation of attributes or events when a span is not being recorded. An interesting wrinkle to this is that the flag is independent of the sampling decision of the trace. An individual span may record events even if the trace that it is a member of has been sampled out (based on flags in the span context). The rationale is that you may want to record and process the latency of all requests with instrumentation while sending only a subset of the instrumented requests to the backend. SetStatus lets you modify the status of a span operation. By default, a span will have a status of Ok, indicating that the operation that the span represents completed successfully. You can see a full list and description of valid statuses (which will look familiar if you've used gRPC) in Table 3-1 and Table 3-2. Keep in mind that you can also create your own status codes through the API, which would be useful for creating statuses that map to your own RPC system.

Table 3-1. OpenTelemetry span status canonical codes

Code	Description
Ok	The operation completed successfully.
Cancelled	The operation was cancelled (typically, by the caller).
Unknown	An unknown error occurred.
InvalidArgument	The client specified an invalid argument. Differs from FailedPrecondition, as this indicates that the arguments were invalid regardless of the system state.
DeadlineExceeded	Deadline (timeout) expired before operation could complete.
NotFound	The entity requested could not be found.
AlreadyExists	The entity already exists (if we were trying to create it).
PermissionDenied	The caller was authenticated, but did not have permission to execute the desired operation.
ResourceExhausted	Some resource was exhausted, such as an API rate limit, per-user quota, or physical resource like disk space.
FailedPrecondition	The operation was rejected because the system is not in the appropriate state for the execution of the requested operation.
Aborted	The operation was aborted.
OutOfRange	The operation was attempted outside a valid range. Unlike InvalidArgument, this error indicates the problem may be fixed if the system state changes.
Unimplemented	The requested operation is not implemented or supported in this service.
Internal	An internal error occurred.
Unavailable	The requested service is unavailable.
DataLoss	Unrecoverable data loss or corruption occurred.
Unauthenticated	The request is not valid due to invalid or missing authentication credentials.

Table 3-2. OpenTelemetry SpanKind reference

Kind	Description	Asynchronous
CLIENT	This span represents a synchronous request to a remote service; it is the parent of its associated SERVER span.	False
SERVER	This span represents a synchronous request from a client on the remote service; it is the child of its associated CLIENT span.	False
PRODUCER	This span represents the parent of an asynchronous request. It is expected to end before its associated CONSUMER span.	True
CONSUMER	This span represents the child of an asynchronous request. It is the child of an associated PRODUCER span.	True
INTERNAL	This span does not represent any RPC; instead, it is an internal operation within a service and has no interaction with remote parents or children.	n/a

SetAttributes allows you to add key-value pairs to a span. These attributes, which are also commonly referred to as tags, are the primary method of aggregating and indexing spans in a backend analysis system. Attribute keys must be strings, and attribute values may be strings, Boolean, or numeric values. If you try to set an attribute that already exists, the new value will overwrite the existing one. AddEvents allows you to add timestamped events to a span. An event is roughly analogous to a log statement. These events can also have attributes, allowing you to make structured event data.

That was a lot of ground to cover, so let's illustrate with Example 3-1.

Example 3-1. Attributes

```
import io.grpc.ManagedChannel;
import io.grpc.ManagedChannelBuilder;
import io.opentelemetry.OpenTelemetry;
import io.opentelemetry.exporters.jaeger.JaegerGrpcSpanExporter;
import io.opentelemetry.sdk.OpenTelemetrySdk;
import io.opentelemetry.sdk.trace.export.SimpleSpansProcessor;
import io.opentelemetry.trace.Span;
import io.opentelemetry.trace.Tracer;

public class OpenTelemetryExample {
  // Get a tracer from the tracer factory
  private Tracer tracer = OpenTelemetry.getTracerFactory()
                              .get("OpenTelemetryExample"); ❶
  // Export traces to Jaeger
  private JaegerGrpcSpanExporter jaegerExporter;

  public JaegerExample(String ip, int port) {
    this.ip = ip;
    this.port = port;
  }
```

```
private void setupJaegerExporter() {
  // Set up a gRPC channel to export span data to Jaeger
  ManagedChannel jaegerChannel = ManagedChannelBuilder.forAddress(ip, port)
                                                      .build();
  // Build the Jaeger exporter
  this.jaegerExporter =
      JaegerGrpcSpanExporter.newBuilder()
          .setServiceName("OpenTelemetryExample")
          .setChannel(jaegerChannel)
          .setDeadline(30)
          .build();
  // Register the Jaeger exporter with the span processor on our tracer
  OpenTelemetrySdk.getTracerFactory()
      .addSpanProcessor(SimpleSpansProcessor.newBuilder(this.jaegerExporter)
      .build()); ❷
}

private void makeSpan() {
  // Generate a span
  Span span = this.tracer.spanBuilder("test span").startSpan(); ❸
  span.addEvent("about to do work");
  // Simulate some work happening
  doWork();
  span.addEvent("finished doing work");
  span.end();
}

private void doWork() {
  try {
    Thread.sleep(1000);
  } catch (InterruptedException e) {
  }
}

public static void main(String[] args) {
  JaegerExample example = new JaegerExample("localhost", 14250);
  example.setupJaegerExporter();
  example.makeSpan();

  // Wait for things to complete
  try {
    Thread.sleep(1000);
  } catch (InterruptedException e) {
  }
}
}
```

❶   All spans created by this tracer will be prefixed with the name you enter here.

---

❷   There are other span processors available in OpenTelemetry—this one sends each span as it finishes. Alternatively, you can use a batching processor that sends groups of spans on some time interval.

❸   You could also add attributes or other metadata here.

As you can see, the basics are pretty straightforward. Create a tracer, register an exporter, then create spans. You'll need to do a bit more to instrument your actual services, however (more about instrumenting a *real* service in Chapter 4). What haven't we discussed about OpenTelemetry? First, we didn't touch on the metrics component, since this text is focused on distributed tracing. Second, we didn't discuss the distributed context components of OpenTelemetry in detail—you can read more about those in Appendix B.

OpenTelemetry is the new standard for instrumenting your code for distributed tracing. Its broad base of support from major cloud and observability vendors ensures that it will have the necessary resources for maintenance and improvements over time, and it's expected to gain adoption rapidly in existing and new open source frameworks and libraries. We'll take you through its predecessors now and help you understand not only the differences between them and OpenTelemetry, but also the similarities.

OpenTracing and OpenCensus

OpenTracing and OpenCensus are both highly successful open source projects and have been broadly adopted by developers for instrumenting their distributed systems. In this section, we'll discuss the specifications and APIs of these frameworks and some of the drawbacks that led to the creation of OpenTelemetry.

OpenTracing

OpenTracing was launched in 2016 with the goal of fixing the broken state of tracing instrumentation.[2] While large tech companies like Google had used distributed tracing for over a decade, overall adoption was slow. The OpenTracing authors saw this as a failure at the point of instrumentation—the wide variety of processes that a request would pass through all required instrumentation to interoperate, and the existing instrumentation options would necessarily bind you to a specific tracing vendor.

As we've mentioned, the trace context must remain unbroken through the entire request in order to provide end-to-end visibility. This was the primary rationale behind OpenTracing: to provide a standard mechanism for instrumentation that

---

2 [Sig16]

wouldn't bind any particular package, library, or service author to a particular tracing vendor. Prior efforts in this space focused on standardization of data formats and context encoding rather than APIs to manage spans and propagation of the trace context between services. While this could be useful, the authors determined that it wasn't required for the widespread adoption of distributed tracing.

Indeed, the problem was (and, in large part, still is) that the point of instrumentation matters a great deal. Instrumenting your application code and business logic can be useful, yes—but instrumenting the middleware and the frameworks your application relies on can be much more valuable: you benefit from the instrumentation without additional effort during development *and* can extend the instrumentation into your business logic easily. How did the authors seek to accomplish this? To achieve the goal of vendor neutrality, OpenTracing could not be overly opinionated about data formats, context propagation encoding, or other factors. Instead, they built a semantic specification that was portable across programming languages and provided an interface package that others could implement. The overall design can be seen in Figure 3-3.

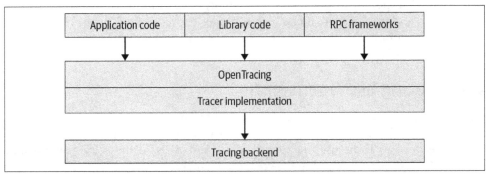

Figure 3-3. The OpenTracing ecosystem design.[3]

What does the OpenTracing API look like? It's primarily focused on span and context management; it has a fairly constrained API surface. There are three main objects defined in the OpenTracing API: tracer, span, and span context. We'll discuss each of them in turn.

A tracer is capable of creating spans and responsible for serialization and deserialization of them across process boundaries. Tracers must satisfy all of the following requirements:

---

3 Figure based off of an image at OpenTracing (*https://oreil.ly/JhXBy*).

- Start a new span.
- Inject a span context into a carrier.
- Extract a span context from a carrier.

A span started by a tracer must have a name—a human-readable string that represents the work being done by the span. The specification prescribes that the "operation name should be the most general string that identifies a (statistically) interesting class of Span instances." As we've mentioned, this is because the name is the primary aggregation key for your traces. A span may also be created with references to other span context objects, an explicit starting time, and key-value pairs of tag data. Span contexts are also operated on by the tracer for context propagation purposes through the `inject` and `extract` methods.

First, we should define what a *carrier* is: a data structure that "carries" the encoded span context, such as a text map or blob of binary data. OpenTracing requires three formats for injection and extraction: text map, HTTP headers, and binary. Text map and HTTP headers are very similar in that they're both string-to-string maps, but HTTP headers require that both the keys and values satisfy RFC 7230 (*https://oreil.ly/ GgfXg*). Binary is a single arbitrary blob of bytes that represent the span context.

In practice, it is this last part—injecting and extracting a span context—that has caused much consternation in the distributed tracing community. As OpenTracing did not specify a data format for the context headers (in part due to significant existing work in the space from projects such as Zipkin, which we'll discuss in "Other Notable Formats and Projects" on page 53), several different keys are commonly seen in the wild. These include `x-ot-span-context` (a binary blob used by Envoy), the B3 headers (`x-b3-TraceID`, `x-b3-spanid`, etc.) and Jaeger's `uber-TraceID`, which are both HTTP headers, and more (Jaeger is an OpenTracing tracer and trace analyzer). In addition, many organizations that had an existing tracing implementation would use or reuse their tracing headers and adapt them to the OpenTracing API. As described earlier, many of these issues are made moot by the adoption of W3C Trace-Context, which provides a universal standard for propagating trace state over the wire, but it's likely that we'll see these legacy headers in use for years to come.

OpenTracing's second primary object type is the span. A span implementation must satisfy the following requirements:

- Retrieve the span context of the span.
- Overwrite the name.
- Finish (or complete) the span.
- Set a tag on the span.
- Create a log message on the span.

- Set an item in the span baggage.
- Get an item in the span baggage.

Some of these methods are fairly self-explanatory, such as overwriting the name of the span. One important note is that after a span is finished, *no methods other than retrieving the span context may be called on it.* As with starting a span, finishing a span accepts an optional explicit timestamp—if unsupplied, the current time will be used. Logs are an interesting field on spans because they can accept an arbitrary value, as opposed to tags, which can only accept string, numeric, or Boolean value types. This means, for example, that complex objects can be logged and, subject to the capabilities of the trace analyzer or OpenTracing implementation, interpreted.

Finally, we come to baggage. *Baggage items* are key-value pairs where both the key and value must be a string. Unlike tags or logs, baggage items are applied to the given span, its span context, and *all span objects that directly or transitively reference that span.* When you add baggage items, they're attached to the span context rather than to the span itself, so when you inject that context and extract it on the other side of an RPC, the baggage has gone along for the ride and can be retrieved. Baggage is a powerful tool because it allows developers to easily pass values throughout their system, so it should be used with care. Some interesting applications of baggage are to pass values from a client system (such as client OS or application version) to a backend system where they can be used to apply more metadata to spans, or even for conditional logic statements in the backend such as selecting which method handles a given request.

Finally, the span context. We've discussed it in this chapter and others, and its history in OpenTracing is complex. Originally, it only exposed a single method—an iterator for all baggage items. The authors left the actual implementation largely up to authors of tracers that implemented OpenTracing in a bid for compatibility. Over time, the specification was extended to offer accessors for the TraceID and SpanID (`ToTraceID` and `ToSpanID`, respectively), which would return a string representation of the trace and span ID values. This was not extended to every language prior to the development of OpenTelemetry, however, so it's unlikely to be seen in the wild. For the most part, as far as the specification is concerned, a `SpanContext` is an opaque identifier.

What does it look like in practice? Let's go through a small example in Java (see Example 3-2).

Example 3-2. SpanContext

```
import io.jaegertracing.Configuration;
import io.jaegertracing.Configuration.ReporterConfiguration;
import io.jaegertracing.Configuration.SamplerConfiguration;
import io.jaegertracing.internal.JaegerTracer;
import io.jaegertracing.internal.samplers.ConstSampler; ❶
```

```
import io.opentracing.Span;
import io.opentracing.util.GlobalTracer; ❷

...

SamplerConfiguration samplerConfig = SamplerConfiguration.fromEnv()
    .withType(ConstSampler.TYPE)
    .withParam(1); ❸

ReporterConfiguration reporterConfig = ReporterConfiguration.fromEnv()
    .withLogSpans(true);

Configuration config = new Configuration("helloWorld")
    .withSampler(samplerConfig)
    .withReporter(reporterConfig);

GlobalTracer.register(config.getTracer()); ❹

...

try (Span parent = GlobalTracer.get().buildSpan("hello").start()) { ❺
    parent.setTag("parentSpan", true);
    parent.log("event", "hello world!");
    try (Span child = GlobalTracer.get().buildSpan("child").asChildOf(parent)
                                    .start()) { ❻
        child.setTag("childSpan", true);
    }
}
```

❶ Since OpenTracing doesn't provide an implementation of the tracer, you'll need to import the Jaeger packages.

❷ The OpenTracing packages here are for the span and global tracer API.

❸ Since OpenTracing doesn't have a first-class sampling API, Jaeger provides it.

❹ OpenTracing's GlobalTracer provides a single instance of the tracer class (singleton) to the process.

❺ buildSpan takes a single argument, the name of the span.

❻ OpenTracing in Java supports a try-with-resources pattern that can finish a span automatically when it goes out of scope. Automatic context management in the Java tracer implicitly forms a parent-child relationship between these two spans.

As you can see, the API for OpenTracing is fairly small—too small, ironically enough. What drove adoption of OpenTracing was also what made it hard to use, in many ways. A common scenario for a new developer who had heard about distributed tracing was to discover the OpenTracing website and try to install an OpenTracing package for their language, only to find that it didn't actually *do* anything.

OpenTracing provided mock and NoOp tracers in each language for the benefit of testing and validation, but there was no simple or easy way to "get started" without first understanding the design of the library. In addition, some of the trade-offs made for the sake of simplicity turned out to be difficult for end users to cope with. Implementers of the OpenTracing API would often add nonstandard features that patched holes or added convenience for users, breaking some of the fundamental promises of vendor neutrality.

OpenTracing also presented users with a tracing-only framework. There was no associated metrics API, for example, to allow for the recording of counters, gauges, or other common metric primitives. Users wanted more.

OpenCensus

In early 2018, Google released an open source version of its internal Census project, naming it OpenCensus (*https://oreil.ly/C-1Vx*). Census was designed under different circumstances and with different constraints than OpenTracing. The goal of the Census project was to provide a uniform method for instrumenting and capturing trace and metric data from Google services automatically. The Census team built deep integrations into technologies such as gRPC, affording any developer who used these technologies basic tracing and metrics for no additional work.

The design of Census, thus, was extremely different from the thin API offered by OpenTracing. Census was an entire SDK for tracing and metrics, providing a full implementation in addition to the API, tightly coupled and deeply entwined with gRPC for activities such as context propagation. Open-sourcing Census was in many ways an effort to extend the existing Google tracing infrastructure to external users of Google services—since Google services such as Spanner were traced using Census, external requests that were *also* traced using Census could be connected seamlessly. In addition, maintaining a tracing and metrics framework and integrating it with a variety of tools and vendors can be extremely costly, making the economics of open-sourcing the project a win for Google.

The fundamental design of OpenCensus differed significantly from OpenTracing, as Figure 3-4 shows. In addition to a tracing API, as mentioned, a metrics API was included. Context propagation could be handled automatically thanks to all implementations using the same format for propagating trace context. It supported the automatic collection of traces and metrics from integrated frameworks along with a local viewer for this data (called "zPages"), making it more immediately useful out of the box. Finally, rather than relying on runtime-swappable implementations of its API to capture and export data to a trace analyzer, it provided a pluggable exporter model that allowed it to upload data to almost any backend. Like the design, the specification is different—rather than focus on a few primitive types, it defines several different components that build upon each other, as shown in Figure 3-5.

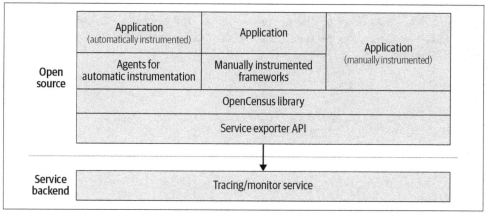

Figure 3-4. OpenCensus ecosystem design.[4]

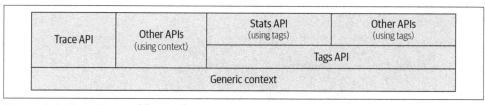

Figure 3-5. OpenCensus library design.[5]

The OpenCensus libraries are built on a base of in-process context propagation. Where OpenTracing left this mechanism as an exercise to the implementer, Open-Census required explicit or implicit propagation of subcontexts inside a process. Where a language-supported generic context exists (such as Golang's `context.Con text`), that implementation must be used.

All other APIs are built on this generic context. The Tracing API is extremely similar, however, to the OpenTracing API in terms of the creation and construction of span objects. The SDK provides a tracer that spans can be started from (with a required name, as in OpenTracing), but the way you do this is different than in OpenTracing. OpenCensus allows for the creation of *root spans* and *child spans*—spans that do not, or do, have a parent. When creating a span, the span may be attached or detached from the underlying context. Unlike OpenTracing, there is no mechanism to modify

4 Figure based off of an image on GitHub (*https://oreil.ly/wWqdW*).

5 Figure based off of an image on GitHub (*https://oreil.ly/wWqdW*).

the start or stop time of a span at creation or completion. There is also no explicit span context object; instead, SpanID and TraceID are fields set on the span itself. OpenCensus additionally defines several unique fields such as `Status` and `SpanKind`, semantic fields that describe the operation status (for example, OK, CANCELLED, and PERMISSION_DENIED) and its type (SERVER, CLIENT, or UNSPECIFIED). A full list of fields follows:

- `SpanID`
- `TraceID`
- `ParentSpanID`
- `StartTime`
- `EndTime`
- `Status`
- `Link`
- `SpanKind`
- `TraceOptions`
- `Tracestate`
- `Time Events` (Annotations and `Message Events`)

Of note is the Time Events field, which represents a collection of events that occurred during the lifetime of the span. Annotations contain both attributes (key-value pairs) as well as a log message.

In addition to the Span API, OpenCensus provides an API to control sampling. In-process sampling allows you to record only a certain number of spans based on various conditions. Samplers can be configured on the global tracer, or set per span. There are four provided samplers:

- `Always` (always return `true` for a sampling decision)
- `Never` (always return `false` for a sampling decision)
- `Probabilistic` (random chance of returning `true` or `false` based on a rate, by default 1 in 10,000)
- `RateLimiting` (attempts to sample at a given rate over a time window, default of 0.1 traces/second)

In addition to the Tracing and Context APIs, OpenCensus defines a tagging API. These are used by the Data Aggregation API (part of the stats package) in order to configure how data is aggregated and broken down in views. Since the focus of this text is primarily on distributed tracing, we won't dwell on this topic other than to distinguish it from OpenTracing span tags. Other important differences are that OpenCensus deliberately elides many of the details about interprocess propagation from the spec, instead delegating it to specific propagator plug-ins (such as the *go.opencensus.io/plugin/ochttp/propagation/b3* package).

So we've talked about how the tracing API is shaped, but what does it look like in practice? Example 3-3 offers a Java sample:

Example 3-3. Tracing API

```java
import io.opencensus.trace.AttributeValue;
import io.opencensus.common.Scope;
import io.opencensus.trace.Span;
import io.opencensus.trace.Status;
import io.opencensus.exporter.trace.zipkin.ZipkinTraceExporter;
import io.opencensus.trace.Tracer;
import io.opencensus.trace.Tracing;
import io.opencensus.trace.config.TraceConfig;
import io.opencensus.trace.config.TraceParams;
import io.opencensus.trace.samplers.Samplers; ❶


...

ZipkinTraceExporter.createAndRegister(
    "http://localhost:9411/api/v2/spans", "tracing-to-zipkin-service"); ❷

TraceConfig traceConfig = Tracing.getTraceConfig();
TraceParams activeTraceParams = traceConfig.getActiveTraceParams();
traceConfig.updateActiveTraceParams(
    activeTraceParams.toBuilder().setSampler(
        Samplers.alwaysSample()).build()); ❸

Tracer tracer = Tracing.getTracer(); ❹

try (Scope scope = tracer.spanBuilder("main").startScopedSpan()) { ❺
    System.out.println("About to do some busy work...");
    for (int i = 0; i < 10; i++) {
        doWork(i);
    }
}


...

private static void doWork(int i) {
    Tracer tracer = Tracing.getTracer();

    try (Scope scope = tracer.spanBuilder("doWork").startScopedSpan()) { ❻
        Span span = tracer.getCurrentSpan();

        try {
            System.out.println("doing busy work");
```

```
        Thread.sleep(100L);
    }
    catch (InterruptedException e) {
        span.setStatus(Status.INTERNAL.withDescription(e.toString()));
    }

    Map<String, AttributeValue> attrs = new HashMap<String, AttributeValue>();
    attrs.put("use", AttributeValue.stringAttributeValue("demo"));
    span.addAnnotation("Invoking doWork", attrs); ❼
    }
}
```

❶ OpenCensus handles the work of creating traces, so you only need to import an exporter to an analysis system.

❷ In order to export traces to an analysis system, you need to create and register the exporter. These options differ by analysis system.

❸ Notice that the sampling process is handled by OpenCensus—you'll still always sample in these test cases.

❹ There's no global tracer equivalent in OpenCensus (although some helper methods exist), so you need to grab a reference to a tracer.

❺ Similar to OpenTracing, OpenCensus supports try-with-resources patterns to automatically manage span life cycle.

❻ This span is implicitly a child of the span in main, since it's executed inside a scoped span.

❼ Notice that annotations are roughly equivalent to OpenTracing logs, but with slightly different usage semantics.

As you can see, OpenCensus provides a "batteries included" experience that Open-Tracing lacked. However, this part of its design is what makes it unacceptable for some use cases. The inability to replace parts of the SDK with differing implementations, for example, meant that it couldn't find purchase in certain vendor ecosystems. Bundling metrics and tracing APIs also proved a difficult pill to swallow for implementers who wanted to use only one part of the OpenCensus package. Tight coupling between the API and SDK made integration challenging for third-party library authors, who didn't necessarily want to have to ship the full SDK with their libraries. Ultimately, the biggest flaw was simply that the open source telemetry community was split between two separate projects, rather than one single and unified effort.

While OpenTelemetry is the new and current standard for tracing instrumentation, it isn't the only one. It's extremely likely that you'll continue to see OpenTracing and OpenCensus in the wild for years to come. In addition, you might encounter other technologies, instrumentation libraries, and propagation standards in the wild. We'll briefly discuss three of the most popular ones next.

Other Notable Formats and Projects

Distributed tracing isn't a completely new concept, it's worth repeating. Very large-scale distributed systems have created the need for some way to correlate and track a request across multiple processes or servers. With that in mind, we'd like to briefly discuss a few of the other popular systems you might see and give you some resources on how to use them.

X-Ray

X-Ray is an Amazon Web Services (AWS) product that provides distributed tracing for applications running in the AWS ecosystem. One advantage of X-Ray is its deep integration into the AWS client SDK, allowing for seamless tracing of calls to a variety of AWS managed services. In addition, X-Ray provides a suite of analytical tools for the trace data, such as a trace visualizer and a service map.

At a high level, X-Ray shares a lot in common with span-based tracing systems with a few differences in naming conventions. Rather than spans, X-Ray uses the term *segment* to refer to a unit of work being traced. Segments contain information about the resource running an application such as the hostname, request/response details, and any errors that occurred during operation. In addition, segments can have arbitrary annotations and metadata added by developers to assist in categorizing and analyzing them. In lieu of using individual spans to capture work done inside a single request, X-Ray introduces a concept known as the *subsegment*, which captures detailed timing information about downstream calls, be they remote or internal. All segments for a single logical request are rolled up into a single *trace*, which you should be familiar with by now. X-Ray uses a proprietary tracing header, `X-Amzn-TraceID`, which is propagated by the X-Ray SDK and all other AWS services. This single key contains all information about the trace, such as its root trace identifier, sampling decision, and parent segment (if applicable).

Functionally, X-Ray relies on a daemon process in conjunction with the X-Ray SDK to collect telemetry data. This daemon must be present or available to receive segment data from your services, which it can then forward to the X-Ray backend for trace assembly and display.

To learn more about X-Ray, see its developer documentation (*https://oreil.ly/l7Gli*).

Zipkin

Twitter developed Zipkin (*https://zipkin.io*) and released it to the wider open source community in 2012. It's notable for being one of the first popular implementations of Dapper-style tracing released under an open source software license, and many of the conventions that are supported by the wider distributed tracing world owe a debt to Zipkin for popularizing them. Overall, Zipkin includes a trace analysis backend, a collector/daemon process, and client libraries and integrations with popular RPC and web frameworks.

Much of the terminology used in Zipkin is portable to other tracing systems, owing to their shared heritage from the Dapper paper. A span is a single unit of work; a trace is a collection of spans; and so forth. One of the most enduring parts of Zipkin is the popularization of *B3 HTTP headers* as a defacto standard for passing trace context across the wire.[6]

These headers are effectively superseded by the W3C TraceContext specification, but it's likely that you'll see them in the wild—especially since they're supported by OpenTelemetry as well. The critical B3 headers are as follows:

X-B3-TraceID
: 64- or 128-bit hex string

X-B3-SpanID
: 64-bit hex string

X-B3-ParentSpanID
: 64-bit hex string (header absent if there is no parent)

X-B3-Sampled
: Boolean of "1" or "0," optional

Interoperability and Migration Strategies

In a sufficiently large organization, one of the most challenging parts of distributed tracing might be getting everyone to agree on a single standard. The relative ease of integrating tracing into a team's services has made it very attractive for SRE and DevOps practitioners to implement. This ease of integration, however, hasn't necessarily translated into ease of maintainability.

Over the past decade, distributed tracing has gone from a niche technology employed by a select group of large, modern software enterprises to a necessary component of modern microservice architectures. Part of this growth has involved changes in

---

6 Why are they called B3 headers? The original internal name of Zipkin at Twitter was "BigBrotherBird."

technology and tooling, with both proprietary and open source projects being announced, being adopted, growing, and eventually being eclipsed by newer projects which start the whole cycle over again. To combat this and be resilient in the face of future improvements and updates to the distributed tracing landscape, we need to develop ideas on how to maintain and upgrade distributed tracing systems.

The first thing to consider is whether you're looking for true interoperability between different tracing systems or trying to migrate and standardize around a single new system. We'll discuss the interop case first.

In general, traces are most useful when they can combine the entirety of a single logical request as it moves through your system. However, sufficiently complex systems (or sufficiently bifurcated organizations) might not have a desire or ability to create the necessary conditions to trace requests through the entire call stack. Just because that's the case today doesn't mean it will be the case tomorrow or the day after that, though. The primary obstacle to interoperability is usually a lack of information about the different systems used already, and more specifically, the method those systems use to propagate trace context. Your first step in achieving interoperability, then, should be to catalog the services that you're aware of and note a few things about them:

- If traced, the header format used for propagating trace context
- RPC framework(s) they use to communicate with other services, and if those frameworks are transparently passing headers
- Existing tracing instrumentation libraries (Zipkin, X-Ray, OpenTracing, OpenCensus, etc.) that are direct or second-order dependencies
- Clients for other services, such as databases

Documenting these tracing dependencies will reveal what parts of your system can communicate with each other and where you might see gaps in instrumentation (for instance, if you have an RPC framework that does not forward incoming headers, then you'd see a trace break at that point). With this information, you can begin to make other decisions, such as what trace context header format makes the most sense for your environment. Even if you don't have standard headers, there are approaches you can take in your instrumentation to support seamless context propagation. One popular method is to implement a *propagator stack* in your instrumentation library or RPC framework. This allows you to add new propagators while preserving support for existing ones. Example 3-4 illustrates creating this stack in OpenTracing.

Example 3-4. Creating a propagator stack in OpenTracing

```java
public final class PropagatorStack implements Propagator {
    Format format;
    List<Propagator> propagators;

    public PropagatorStack(Format format) {
        if (format == null) {
            throw new IllegalArgumentException("Format cannot be null.");
        }
        this.format = format;
        propagators = new LinkedList<Propagator>();
    }

    public Format format() {
        return format;
    }

    public PropagatorStack pushPropagator(Propagator propagator) {
        if (propagator == null) {
            throw new IllegalArgumentException("Propagator cannot be null.");
        }
        propagators.add(propagator);
        return this;
    }

    public <C> SpanContext extract(C carrier) {
        for (int i = propagators.size() - 1; i >=0; i--) {
            SpanContext context = propagators.get(i).extract(carrier);
            if (context != null) {
                return context;
            }
        }
        return null;
    }

    public <C> void inject(SpanContext context, C carrier) {
        for (int i = 0; i < propagators.size(); i++) {
            propagators.get(i).inject(context, carrier);
        }
    }
}
```

The propagator stack will stop extracting the span context once it finds its first match, but will inject headers for all registered propagators. You could theoretically modify this behavior to return multiple extracted contexts if you had multiple independent tracers in a given service. Standardizing tracing headers from the top down is usually the most successful strategy, however, rather than attempting to manage individual services' and teams' preferences.

When standardizing or migrating, the calculus changes somewhat. You may still find it useful to do much of the documentation work mentioned earlier, but in service of estimating the effort required to perform a migration. If your existing tracing system is largely home-brewed—perhaps it uses custom headers or trace/span identifier formats—you'll want to identify the number of services traced by that system versus the new one and see if you can create some sort of shim between your old code and the new code. Depending on the design of your existing tracing system, you may want to consider using OpenTelemetry as a standard API but rewrite parts of your library to meet its specification, plugging in those components in lieu of the reference SDK.

If you're already using OpenTracing or OpenCensus and simply want to migrate to OpenTelemetry, then you have several options as well. Do you want to use the Open-Telemetry SDK in lieu of your existing OpenTracing tracer? Then you'd need to use the OpenTelemetry bridge component to make it appear as an OpenTracing tracer to your existing instrumentation, and switch out the tracer in each of your services. You can achieve a more gradual migration by ensuring that you're using compatible header formats (W3C, B3, or one through a custom propagator) in your old and new instrumentation, then deploying new services with OpenTelemetry and leaving your old services as is for now. As long as your trace analyzer supports ingesting traces from both frameworks, you should see a single trace containing spans from both your old and new services.

Another migration strategy, especially useful if you're migrating to a new platform— for example, containerizing existing services in order to run them on Kubernetes—is to replace your existing tracing with a more black box approach as a prelude to reinstrumenting the logic. By using the tracing features built into service meshes, for example, you can trace requests between your containerized services without replacing any existing instrumentation or filling in any instrumentation gaps. Over time, you can extend the spans into the service code and rip out any existing instrumentation when it's convenient, while getting the immediate benefit of seamless traces that extend across all of your newly containerized services.

Why Use Open Source Instrumentation?

Regardless of your strategy, the best way to ensure that your tracing system is maintainable and extensible is using open source standards and frameworks. Proprietary, or home-brewed, tracing systems are almost always more difficult and costly to maintain than something with broad community support. To conclude this chapter, we'll discuss the rationale behind choosing open source instrumentation.

Interoperability

When implementing any sort of distributed telemetry, interoperability is a prime concern. You may have two services or two thousand, but unless there's a way to guarantee that the telemetry data from any arbitrary service is compatible with the telemetry data from any other service, you're going to have a bad time trying to understand performance across all of your services. Open source instrumentation addresses this by not only providing a single set of concepts and libraries for all of your services, but also allowing for telemetry capture that extends past the boundaries of your business logic.

The first case is the simpler one to understand—while it's certainly possible to create your own request tracing system through correlation identifiers, this approach can be brittle and difficult to maintain as you scale. One of the benefits of open source solutions is that they make many of these decisions for you! You don't have to sit down and decide whether you want a correlation ID based on a universally unique identifier (UUID) or a collision resistant unique identifier (CUID), for example. You can guarantee that each new service being instrumented is speaking the same language when it comes to context ID generation and propagation.

This also avoids frustrating migration strategies when you extend your traces out to new endpoints or frontends; you can guarantee that identifiers for traces are consistently generated, allowing for seamless extension. Contrast this with more log-based approaches to tracing such as Distributed Diagnostic Context (*https://oreil.ly/W-smF*), which can work great as long as your entire system is relatively homogenous. Extending these through a polyglot system can involve a lot of time massaging logs into the same format, and that's before you get into the challenges of retention and indexing that log data.

The second case for the superior interoperability of OSS instrumentation is how it integrates into *other* OSS software and libraries. Projects such as OpenTelemetry, by virtue of being vendor-neutral, are attractive instrumentation options for other OSS projects that wish to provide telemetry data to their end users. You can look at OpenTracing as an example of this: the OpenTracing registry (*https://opentracing.io/registry*) indexes hundreds of integrations and plug-ins that instrument other OSS projects, from database clients to distributed messaging queues to network libraries, and more. These integrations allow you to get started quickly instrumenting a new, or existing, service and ensure that instrumentation can be extended into your business logic. The registry's popularity led to OpenTelemetry adopting a similar registry (*https://opentelemetry.io/registry*). Keep in mind that OpenTelemetry is broadly backward-compatible with OpenTracing instrumentation, so be sure to check both!

Portability

As the observability space continues to mature, there will inevitably be a growing amount of projects and vendors who provide the ability to analyze distributed tracing data. With this in mind, it's critical that your instrumentation be portable between different analysis systems. In short, you don't want to have to rewrite your tracing code when you change the analysis tool you're using to ingest that data.

OpenTelemetry is an excellent example of this in practice. Your service emits telemetry data to a collector running as an agent, and those agents are able to export to a variety of backends. This gives you the ability to write instrumentation once and have it work with no configuration changes in a variety of environments, and even send that telemetry to multiple endpoints simultaneously simply by changing the configuration of the collector. For example, you could run a local analysis tool and have a local agent collecting telemetry data during development—then, with no changes to the code, have that same telemetry data go to a commercial analysis backend.

Ecosystem and Implicit Visibility

To echo some earlier points, the ecosystem of an open source community is going to be extremely valuable to your instrumentation journey. We won't belabor the basic value proposition of open source software in this text, but suffice to say many hands make light work.

Realistically, for as much as we harp on it, writing instrumentation and other "maintainability" code isn't a priority outside of its immediate utility. When you're writing a service, you'll absolutely use as much logging as you can get away with in order to figure out why things aren't working the way you expect them to, but how often do you go back in and delete "unnecessary" logging statements? I'd expect it's more frequently than you think! It's natural to think that the amount of telemetry you're adding is too much because development cycles tend to be very granular, especially initially. This also applies to modifying code; one of the quickest ways to understand the control flow of a program is to add some simple `print` statements in an `if` statement and see which get output for a certain input value or control flow. When debugging issues, we tend to create "windows" that look into the code at a specific, narrow angle. Many of those windows remain, but they're all too focused on specific, already existing problems to be much help in understanding overall performance.

So, how do we resolve these two ideas? On one hand, we want to build observable software. On the other, we're not sure what we should care about observing and don't do a great job of looking at the right thing, especially ahead of time. Open source instrumentation, again, helps address this tension. First, it provides a rich ecosystem of existing instrumentation that we can rely on to trace the important things in our lower-level dependencies (such as RPC frameworks). This existing instrumentation is generally lightweight and easy to add to our service, and satisfies much of the boilerplate associated with distributed tracing. Second, it allows for implicit visibility into our requests through this ecosystem. If you're using some sort of service mesh as part of your application, that service mesh is capable of creating and extending traces between all of your services, giving you implicit visibility into your entire backend system with no code overhead. If you start to combine this with other components, such as client-level tracing, RPC framework tracing, DB client tracing, and so forth, then you'll gain implicit visibility into your entire application.

Exploiting the OSS ecosystem is an excellent strategy to quickly bootstrap useful information about your system. However, there's more to distributed tracing than simply throwing a bunch of libraries at the problem and seeing what sticks—you'll want to move from implicit to explicit visibility into your requests and call stack. You'll want to create and use custom tags and attributes from your business logic in order to profile and understand what's going on in your code and application. In Chapter 4, we'll talk about some of the best practices for instrumenting your services and how you can supercharge your telemetry.

Best Practices for Instrumentation

The first step of any journey is the hardest—including the journey of instrumenting your applications for distributed tracing. Questions pile upon questions: What should I do first? How do I know I'm doing things right? When am I done? Every application is different, but this chapter offers some general advice and strategies to create best practices for instrumenting applications.

Best practices do not exist in a vacuum. The data your instrumentation generates will be collected by a trace analysis system, which will analyze it and process it. As the instrumenter, it's critical that you provide it with the best data possible!

We'll first discuss an application that lacks instrumentation in order to ground our discussion. Then, we'll talk about the first steps for instrumenting an existing application—looking at the nodes and edges—and some common ways to accomplish that. We'll go over best practices for creating spans and the sort of information you'll want to add to them. We'll discuss how you'd use tracing as part of application development to validate that your architecture is working the way you expect it to work. Finally, we'll give you some signals to let you know when you've hit "too much" instrumentation.

Tracing by Example

It's a truism that the best way to learn is by doing. To help make sense of how you should instrument a microservices application for distributed tracing, it stands to reason that you must first have a microservices application. We've built a sample application that we will use to illustrate some techniques and best practices. In this section, we'll describe how you can run the service on your computer in order to follow along with the examples provided, and demonstrate some basic principles of instrumentation that can be applied more generally to instrument your own services.

Installing the Sample Application

We've developed a small microservice application to demonstrate the important concepts required to instrument an application. To run it, you'll need an up-to-date version of the Go runtime (*https://golang.org*) and Node.JS (*https://nodejs.org*) installed on your computer. You'll also need to download a copy of the source code for the application, which can be found at this GitHub repository (*https://oreil.ly/microcalc*) —you can check it out using the Git version control software, or download and extract a zip archive of the files. Once you've got a local copy of the source files, running the software is fairly straightforward: in a terminal window, execute `go run cmd/<binary>/main.go` from the `microcalc` directory to run each service. To run the client application, you'll need to execute `npm install` in the `web` subdirectory, then `npm start`.

The application itself is a basic calculator with three components. The client is a web application for the browser written in HTML and JavaScript that provides an interface to the backend service. The next major component is an API proxy that receives requests from the client and dispatches them to the appropriate worker service. The final component, the operator workers, are services that receive a list of operands, perform the appropriate mathematical operation on those operands, and return the result.

Adding Basic Distributed Tracing

Before you add tracing, look at the code itself and how it functions. We'll look at the code in order—first, the web client, then the API service, and finally the workers. Once you have an understanding of what each piece of code does, it becomes easier to understand not only how to instrument the service, but why (see Figure 4-1).

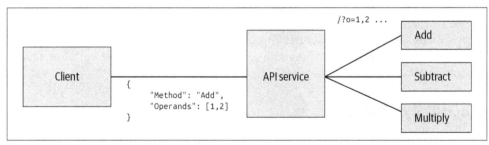

Figure 4-1. The design of MicroCalc.

The client service is very straightforward—a simple HTML and JavaScript frontend. The HTML presents a form, which we intercept in JavaScript and create a `XMLHttpRequest` that transmits data to the backend services. The uninstrumented version of this code can be seen in Example 4-1. As you can see, we're not doing anything terribly complicated here—we create a hook on the form element and listen for the `onClick` event that is emitted when the Submit button is pressed.

Example 4-1. Uninstrumented client service

```
const handleForm = () => {
    const endpoint = 'http://localhost:3000/calculate'
    let form = document.getElementById('calc')

    const onClick = (event) => {
        event.preventDefault();

        let fd = new FormData(form);
        let requestPayload = {
            method: fd.get('calcMethod'),
            operands: tokenizeOperands(fd.get('values'))
        };

                calculate(endpoint, requestPayload).then((res) => {
                        updateResult(res);
                });
    }
    form.addEventListener('submit', onClick)
}

const calculate = (endpoint, payload) => {
  return new Promise(async (resolve, reject) => {
    const req = new XMLHttpRequest();
    req.open('POST', endpoint, true);
    req.setRequestHeader('Content-Type', 'application/json');
    req.setRequestHeader('Accept', 'application/json');
    req.send(JSON.stringify(payload))
    req.onload = function () {
      resolve(req.response);
    };
  });
};
```

Your first step when instrumenting this should be to trace the interaction between this service and our backend services. OpenTelemetry helpfully provides an instrumentation plug-in for tracing `XMLHttpRequest`, so you'll want to use that for your basic instrumentation. After importing the OpenTelemetry packages, you then need to set up your tracer and plug-ins. Once you've accomplished that, wrap your method calls to `XMLHttpRequest` with some tracing code, as seen in Example 4-2.

Example 4-2. Creating and configuring your tracer

```
// After importing dependencies, create a tracer and configure it
const webTracerWithZone = new WebTracer({
  scopeManager: new ZoneScopeManager(),
  plugins: [
    new XMLHttpRequestPlugin({
      ignoreUrls: [/localhost:8090\/sockjs-node/],
      propagateTraceHeaderCorsUrls: [
        'http://localhost:3000/calculate'
      ]
    })
  ]
});

webTracerWithZone.addSpanProcessor(
    new SimpleSpanProcessor(new ConsoleSpanExporter())
);

const handleForm = () => {
    const endpoint = 'http://localhost:3000/calculate'
    let form = document.getElementById('calc')

    const onClick = (event) => {
        event.preventDefault(); ❶
        const span = webTracerWithZone.startSpan(
                            'calc-request',
                            { parent: webTracerWithZone.getCurrentSpan() }
);
        let fd = new FormData(form);
        let requestPayload = {
            method: fd.get('calcMethod'),
            operands: tokenizeOperands(fd.get('values'))
        }; ❷
        webTracerWithZone.withSpan(span, () => {
          calculate(endpoint, requestPayload).then((res) => {
            webTracerWithZone.getCurrentSpan().addEvent('request-complete');
            span.end();
            updateResult(res);
          });
        });
    }
    form.addEventListener('submit', onClick)
}
```

❶ Notice that we're starting a new span here. This encapsulates our entire logical request from client to server; it is the root span of the trace.

❷ Here we wrap our call to `calculate`, which will automatically create a child span. No additional code is required in `calculate`.

Run the page in `web` with `npm start` and click Submit with your browser console open—you should see spans being written to the console output. You've now added basic tracing to your client service!

We'll now look at the backend services—the API and workers. The API provider service uses the Go `net/http` library to provide an HTTP framework that we're using as an RPC framework for passing messages between the client, the API service, and the workers. As seen in Figure 4-1, the API receives messages in JSON format from the client, looks up the appropriate worker in its configuration, dispatches the operands to the appropriate worker service, and returns the result to the client.

The API service has two main methods that we care about: `Run` and `calcHandler`. The `Run` method in Example 4-3 initializes the HTTP router and sets up the HTTP server. `calcHandler` performs the logic of handling incoming requests by parsing the JSON body from the client, matching it to a worker, then creating a well-formed request to the worker service.

Example 4-3. Run method

```
func Run() {
        mux := http.NewServeMux()
        mux.Handle("/", http.HandlerFunc(rootHandler))
        mux.Handle("/calculate", http.HandlerFunc(calcHandler))
        services = GetServices()

        log.Println("Initializing server...")
        err := http.ListenAndServe(":3000", mux)
        if err != nil {
                log.Fatalf("Could not initialize server: %s", err)
        }
}
func calcHandler(w http.ResponseWriter, req *http.Request) {
        calcRequest, err := ParseCalcRequest(req.Body)
        if err != nil {
                http.Error(w, err.Error(), http.StatusBadRequest)
                return
        }

        var url string

        for _, n := range services.Services {
                if strings.ToLower(calcRequest.Method) == strings.ToLower(n.Name) {
                        j, _ := json.Marshal(calcRequest.Operands)
                        url = fmt.Sprintf("http://%s:%d/%s?o=%s",
```

```
                    n.Host,
                    n.Port,
                    strings.ToLower(n.Name),
                    strings.Trim(string(j),
                    "[]"))
        }
    }

    if url == "" {
        http.Error(w, "could not find requested calculation method",
    http.StatusBadRequest)
    }

    client := http.DefaultClient
    request, _ := http.NewRequest("GET", url, nil)
    res, err := client.Do(request)
    if err != nil {
        http.Error(w, err.Error(), http.StatusInternalServerError)
        return
    }
    body, err := ioutil.ReadAll(res.Body)
    res.Body.Close()
    if err != nil {
        http.Error(w, err.Error(), http.StatusInternalServerError)
        return
    }

    resp, err := strconv.Atoi(string(body))
    if err != nil {
        http.Error(w, err.Error(), http.StatusInternalServerError)
        return
    }

    fmt.Fprintf(w, "%d", resp)
}
```

Let's start at the edge of this service and find instrumentation for the RPC framework. In Example 4-4, since we're using HTTP for communicating between services, you'll want to instrument the HTTP framework code. Now, you *could* write this yourself, but it's generally a better idea to look for open source instrumentation for these common components. In this case, we can utilize the OpenTelemetry project's existing othttp package to wrap our HTTP routes with tracing instrumentation.

Example 4-4. Using the OpenTelemetry project's existing othttp package to wrap our HTTP routes with tracing instrumentation

```
std, err := stdout.NewExporter(stdout.Options{PrettyPrint: true}) ❶ ❷

traceProvider, err := sdktrace.NewProvider( ❸
    sdktrace.WithConfig(
```

```
        sdktrace.Config{
            DefaultSampler: sdktrace.AlwaysSample()
        }
    ), sdktrace.WithSyncer(std))

mux.Handle("/",
            othttp.NewHandler(http.HandlerFunc(rootHandler),
            "root", othttp.WithPublicEndpoint())
        )
mux.Handle("/calculate",
            othttp.NewHandler(http.HandlerFunc(calcHandler),
            "calculate", othttp.WithPublicEndpoint())
        )
```

❶ Handle errors and such appropriately. Some code has been deleted for clarity.

❷ First, we need to register an exporter to actually view the telemetry output; this could also be an external analysis backend, but we'll use stdout for now.

❸ Then, register the exporter with the trace provider and set it to sample 100% of spans.

What does this do for us? The instrumentation plug-in will handle quite a bit of "convenience" tasks for us, like propagating spans from incoming requests and adding some useful attributes (seen in Example 4-5) such as the HTTP method type, response code, and more. Simply by adding this, we're able to begin tracing requests to our backend system. Take special note of the parameter we've passed into our instrumentation handler, othttp.WithPublicEndpoint—this will slightly modify how the trace context from the client is flowed to our backend services. Rather than persisting the same TraceID from the client, the incoming context will be associated with a new trace as a link.

Example 4-5. JSON span output

```
{
        "SpanContext": {
                "TraceID": "060a61155cc12b0a83b625aa1808203a",
                "SpanID": "a6ff374ec6ed5c64",
                "TraceFlags": 1
        },
        "ParentSpanID": "0000000000000000",
        "SpanKind": 2,
        "Name": "go.opentelemetry.io/plugin/othttp/add",
        "StartTime": "2020-01-02T17:34:01.52675-05:00",
        "EndTime": "2020-01-02T17:34:01.526805742-05:00",
        "Attributes": [
                {
                        "Key": "http.host",
```

```
                    "Value": {
                            "Type": "STRING",
                            "Value": "localhost:3000"
                    }
            },
            {
                    "Key": "http.method",
                    "Value": {
                            "Type": "STRING",
                            "Value": "GET"
                    }
            },
            {
                    "Key": "http.path",
                    "Value": {
                            "Type": "STRING",
                            "Value": "/"
                    }
            },
            {
                    "Key": "http.url",
                    "Value": {
                            "Type": "STRING",
                            "Value": "/"
                    }
            },
            {
                    "Key": "http.user_agent",
                    "Value": {
                            "Type": "STRING",
                            "Value": "HTTPie/1.0.2"
                    }
            },
            {
                    "Key": "http.wrote_bytes",
                    "Value": {
                            "Type": "INT64",
                            "Value": 27
                    }
            },
            {
                    "Key": "http.status_code",
                    "Value": {
                            "Type": "INT64",
                            "Value": 200
                    }
            }
    ],
    "MessageEvents": null,
    "Links": null,
    "Status": 0,
    "HasRemoteParent": false,
```

```
        "DroppedAttributeCount": 0,
        "DroppedMessageEventCount": 0,
        "DroppedLinkCount": 0,
        "ChildSpanCount": 0
}
```

In `calcHandler`, we'll want to do something similar to instrument our outgoing RPC to the worker service. Again, OpenTelemetry contains an instrumentation plug-in for Go's HTTP client that we can use (see Example 4-6).

Example 4-6. API handler

```
client := http.DefaultClient
// Get the context from the request in order to pass it to the instrumentation plug-in
ctx := req.Context()
request, _ := http.NewRequestWithContext(ctx, "GET", url, nil)
// Create a new outgoing trace
ctx, request = httptrace.W3C(ctx, request)
// Inject the context into the outgoing request
httptrace.Inject(ctx, request)
// Send the request
res, err := client.Do(request)
```

This will add W3C tracing headers to the outgoing request, which can be picked up by the worker, propagating the trace context across the wire. This enables us to visualize the relationship between our services very easily, since spans created in the worker service will have the same trace identifier as the parent(s).

Adding tracing to the worker services is equally straightforward because we're simply wrapping the router method with the OpenTelemetry trace handler, as shown in Example 4-7.

Example 4-7. Adding the handler

```
// You also need to add an exporter and register it with the trace provider,
// as in the API server, but the code is the same
mux.Handle("/",
    othttp.NewHandler(http.HandlerFunc(addHandler),
    "add",
    othttp.WithPublicEndpoint())
)
```

The instrumentation plug-ins handle a great deal of the boilerplate that we need to be concerned with in this and other languages—things like extracting the span context from the incoming request, creating a new child span (or a new root span, if appropriate), and adding that span to the request context. In the next section, we'll look at how we can extend this basic instrumentation with custom events and attributes from our business logic in order to enhance the utility of our spans and traces.

Custom Instrumentation

At this point, we've got the critical parts of tracing set up in our services; each RPC is traced, allowing us to see a single request as it travels from our client service to all of our backend services. In addition, we have a span available in our business logic, carried along the request context, that we can enhance with custom attributes or events. What, then, shall we do? In general, this is really up to you, the instrumenter. We'll discuss this in more detail in "Effective Tagging" on page 80, but it's helpful to add custom instrumentation for a few things in your business logic—capturing and logging error states, for example, or creating child spans that further describe the functioning of a service. In our API service, we've implemented an example of this by passing the local context into a different method (ParseCalcRequest), where we create a new span and enhance it with custom events as shown in Example 4-8.

Example 4-8. Enhancing a span with custom events

```
var calcRequest CalcRequest
err = tr.WithSpan(ctx, "generateRequest", func(ctx context.Context) error {
        calcRequest, err = ParseCalcRequest(ctx, b)
        return err
})
```

In Example 4-9, you can see what we're doing with the passed context—we get the current span from the context and add events to it. In this case, we've added some informational events around what the function actually does (parsing the body of our incoming request into an object), and changing the span's status if the operation failed.

Example 4-9. Adding events to the span

```
func ParseCalcRequest(ctx context.Context, body []byte) (CalcRequest, error) {
        var parsedRequest CalcRequest

        trace.CurrentSpan(ctx).AddEvent(ctx, "attempting to parse body")
        trace.CurrentSpan(ctx).AddEvent(ctx, fmt.Sprintf("%s", body))
        err := json.Unmarshal(body, &parsedRequest)
        if err != nil {
                trace.CurrentSpan(ctx).SetStatus(codes.InvalidArgument)
                trace.CurrentSpan(ctx).AddEvent(ctx, err.Error())
                trace.CurrentSpan(ctx).End()
                return parsedRequest, err
        }
        trace.CurrentSpan(ctx).End()
        return parsedRequest, nil
}
```

Now that you have a basic handle on how to add instrumentation to an application, let's step back a bit. You might be thinking that "real" applications are obviously more complex and intricate than a purpose-built sample. The good news, however, is that the basic principles we learned and implemented here are generally applicable to instrumenting software of any size or complexity. Let's take a look at instrumenting software and how to apply these basic principles to microservice applications.

Where to Start—Nodes and Edges

People tend to start at the outside when solving problems—whether they're organizational, financial, computational, or even culinary. The easiest place to start is at the place that's closest to you. The same approach applies to instrumenting services for distributed tracing.

Practically, starting from the outside is effective for three major reasons. The first of these is that the edges of your service are the easiest to see—and, thus, manipulate. It's fairly straightforward to add things that surround a service even if it's hard to modify the service itself. Second, starting from the outside tends to be organizationally efficient. It can be difficult to convince disparate teams to adopt distributed tracing, especially if the value of that tracing can be hard to see in isolation. Finally, distributed tracing requires context propagation—we need each service to know about the caller's trace, and each service we call out to needs to know that it's included in a trace as well. For these reasons, it's highly useful to begin instrumenting any sort of existing application by starting from the outside and moving in. This can take the form of framework instrumentation or service mesh (or equivalent component) instrumentation.

Trade-offs of Outside-In Instrumentation

In general, changing code or infrastructure outside a process that you're instrumenting may require more effort than changing it for just that process. In addition, sweeping changes to your infrastructure or framework code are often more difficult to review, as they're less incremental. If it's logistically or organizationally difficult to approach instrumentation *outside-in*, you'll still get benefits from adding instrumentation to one service at a time at the cost of having *broken* traces. Make sure to check that other services are transparently forwarding the tracing headers that they'll be receiving in this case!

Framework Instrumentation

In any distributed application, services need to communicate with each other. This RPC traffic can take a variety of protocols and transport methods—structured data over HTTP, Protocol Buffers over gRPC, Apache Thrift, custom protocols over TCP sockets, and more. There must be some equivalency on both sides of this connection. Your services need to be speaking the same language when they talk!

There are two critical components when it comes to instrumentation at the framework level. First, our frameworks must allow us to perform *context propagation*, the transmission of trace identifiers across the network. Second, our frameworks should aid us in *creating spans* for each service.

Context propagation is perhaps the easier challenge to solve. Let's take another look at MicroCalc to discuss it. As shown in Figure 4-2, we're only using one transport method (HTTP), but two different ways of passing messages—JSON, and query parameters. You can imagine that some of these links could be done differently; for instance, we could refactor the communication between our API service and the worker services to use gRPC, Thrift, or even graphQL. The transport itself is largely irrelevant, the requirement is simply that we are able to pass the trace context to the next service.

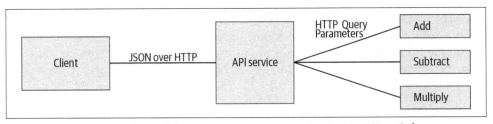

Figure 4-2. The protocols used for inter-service communication in MicroCalc.

Once you identify the transport protocols your services use to communicate, consider the critical path for your service calls. In short, identify the path of calls as a request moves through your services. In this stage of analysis, you'll want to focus on components that act as a *hub* for requests. Why? Generally, these components are going to logically encapsulate operations on the backend and provide an API for multiple clients (such as browser-based web clients or native applications on a mobile device). Therefore, instrumenting these components first allows for a shorter timeline to derive value from tracing. In the preceding example, our API proxy service meets these criteria—our client communicates directly through it for all downstream actions.

After identifying the service you'll instrument, you should consider the transport method used for requests coming into, and exiting, the service. Our API proxy service exclusively communicates via structured data using HTTP, but this is simply an example for the sake of brevity—in the real world, you'll often find services that can accept multiple transports and also send outgoing requests through multiple transports. You'll want to be acutely aware of these complications when instrumenting your own applications.

That said, we'll look at the actual mechanics of instrumenting our service. In framework instrumentation, you'll want to instrument the transport framework of your service itself. This can often be implemented as some sort of middleware in your request path: code that is run for each incoming request. This is a common pattern for adding logging to your requests, for example. What middlewares would you want to implement for this service? Logically, you'll need to accomplish the following:

- Check whether an incoming request includes a trace context, which would indicate that the request is being traced. If so, add this context to the request.

- Check whether a context exists in the request. If the context exists, create a new span as a child of the flowed context. Otherwise, create a new root span. Add this span to the request.

- Check whether a span exists in the request. If a span exists, add other pertinent information available in the request context to it such as the route, user identifiers, etc. Otherwise, do nothing and continue.

These three logical actions can be combined into a single piece of middleware through the use of instrumentation libraries such as the ones we discussed in Chapter 3. We can implement a straightforward version of this middleware in Golang using the OpenTracing library, as Example 4-10 shows, or by using instrumentation plug-ins bundled with frameworks like OpenTelemetry, as we demonstrated in "Tracing by Example" on page 61.

Example 4-10. Tracing middleware

```
func TracingMiddleware(t opentracing.Tracer, h http.HandlerFunc) http.HandlerFunc {
        return http.HandlerFunc(func(w http.ResponseWriter, r *http.Request) {
                spanContext, _ := t.Extract(opentracing.HTTPHeaders,
                                opentracing.HTTPHeadersCarrier(r.Header))
                span := t.StartSpan(r.Method, opentracing.ChildOf(spanContext))
                span.SetTag("route", r.URL.EscapedPath())
                r = r.WithContext(opentracing.ContextWithSpan(r.Context(),
                        span.Context()))
                defer span.Finish()
                h(w, r)
                span.SetTag("status", w.ResponseCode)
                }
        )
}
```

This snippet accomplishes the goals laid out earlier—we first attempt to extract a span context from the request headers. In the preceding sample, we make some assumptions, namely that our span context will be propagated using HTTP headers and not any sort of binary format. OpenTracing, generally, defines these headers to be of the following formats:

ot-span-id
  A 64- or 128-bit unsigned integer

ot-trace-id
  A 64- or 128-bit unsigned integer

ot-sampled
  A Boolean value indicating if the upstream service has sampled out the trace

Please note that these are not the only types of headers that can contain a span context. You can learn more about other popular header formats in "OpenTracing and OpenCensus" on page 43.

As we learned in Chapter 2, the span context is critical to propagating a trace throughout our services, which is why we first extract it from the incoming request. After extracting any incoming headers, our middleware then creates a new span, named after the HTTP operation being performed (GET, POST, PUT, etc.), adds a tag indicating the route being requested, then adds the new span to the Go context object. Finally, the middleware continues the request chain. As the request resolves, it adds the response code from the request to the span, which is closed implicitly through our call to defer.

Let's imagine that we stopped here. If you were to add this middleware to the API proxy service along with a tracer and trace analyzer, what would you see? Well, every single incoming HTTP request would be traced, for one. This would give you the ability to monitor your API endpoints for latency on every incoming request, a valuable first step when monitoring your application. The other win here is that you have now propagated your trace into the context, allowing for further function or RPC calls to add information or create new spans based off of it. Meanwhile, you will still be able to access latency information, per API route, and use that to inform you of performance issues and potential hotspots in your codebase.

There are trade-offs with instrumenting the framework, however. Framework instrumentation heavily relies on the ability to make code changes to your services themselves. If you can't modify the service code, you can't really instrument the transport framework. You may find framework instrumentation difficult if your API proxy acts simply as a translation layer—for example, a thin wrapper that translates JSON over HTTP to a proprietary or internal transport—in this case, the general principle would apply, but you may lack the ability to enrich a span with as much data as you would want. Finally, framework instrumentation may be difficult if you do not have components that centralize requests—for example, a client that calls multiple services directly, rather than through some proxy layer. In this case, you could use the client as the *centralization* point, and add your initial instrumentation there.

Service Mesh Instrumentation

When discussing the trade-offs of framework instrumentation, the first consideration we mentioned was "What if you can't change the code?" This isn't an unreasonable or outlandish hypothetical. There are a variety of reasons that the person instrumenting software isn't able to modify the service they're attempting to instrument. Most commonly this is a challenge for larger organizations to address, where the people monitoring the application are separated from the people making the application by geography, time zone, and so forth.

How, then, to instrument code that you can't touch? In short, you instrument the part of the code that you *can* touch and go from there.

You should first understand what a service mesh is—if you know, feel free to skip ahead a paragraph or so. A *service mesh* is a configurable infrastructure layer designed to support interprocess communication among services. It performs this, generally, through *sidecar proxies*, processes that live alongside each service instance and handle all of the interprocess communication for their associated service. In addition to service communications, the service mesh and its sidecars can handle monitoring, security, service discovery, load balancing, encryption, and more. In essence, the service mesh allows for a separation of *developer* concerns from *operations* concerns, allowing teams to specialize and focus on writing performant, secure, and reliable software.

Now that we're on the same page, let's talk about what *service mesh* instrumentation looks like. As indicated earlier, one of the critical features of the sidecar proxy is that all interprocess communication flows through the proxy. This allows us to add tracing to the proxy itself. As it happens, this functionality works out of the box in many modern service mesh projects such as Istio (*https://istio.io*), but at a more hypothetical level, the mechanics look remarkably similar to how framework instrumentation works. On incoming requests, pull the span context from the headers, create a new span using this context, and add tags that describe the operation—finishing the span when the request resolves.

The biggest advantage to this style of instrumentation is that you can get a complete picture of your application. Recall our discussion of framework instrumentation—we started at a centralization point, and then continued outward from there. By instrumenting at the service mesh, all of the services which are managed by the service mesh will be part of the trace, giving you much greater insight into your entire application. In addition, service mesh instrumentation is agnostic to the transport layer of each service. As long as the traffic is being passed through the sidecar, it will be traced.

That said, there are trade-offs and drawbacks to service mesh instrumentation. Primarily, service mesh instrumentation acts as a black box form of instrumentation. You have no idea what's happening inside the code, and you can't enrich your spans with data outside of the data that's already there. Realistically, this means you can achieve some useful implicit findings—tagging spans with HTTP response codes, for example, and presuming that any status code that represents a failed request (like HTTP 500) will be an error—but requires specialized parsing or handling to get explicit information into a span. The other flaw with service mesh instrumentation is that it's difficult for services to enrich the spans coming from the service mesh. Your sidecar will pass tracing headers into your process, yes—but you will still need to extract those headers, create a span context, and so forth. If each service is creating its own child spans, you can very quickly get into a state where your traces have become extremely large and begin to have a real cost for storage or processing.

Ultimately, service mesh instrumentation and framework instrumentation are not an either/or decision. They work best together! Not all of your services, realistically, will need to be instrumented out of the box, or potentially ever. Let's talk about why.

Creating Your Service Graph

Regardless of which methodology you use to begin instrumenting your application, you should consider the first milestone you'd like to achieve. What do you want to measure? We would argue that tracing is primarily a way to measure the performance and health of individual services in the context of a larger application. To understand that context, however, you need to have some idea of the connections between your services and how requests flow through the system. Thus, a good first milestone would be to build a service graph for your complete application or some significant subset of it, as Figure 4-3 illustrates.

This comparison should demonstrate the necessity of understanding your service graph. Even when services are simple, with few dependencies, understanding your service graph can be a critical component of improving your MTTR (mean time to recovery) for incidents. Since much of this is bound to unrelated factors, such as the amount of time it takes to deploy a new version of a service, reducing the time spent in diagnosis is the best way to reduce overall MTTR. A key benefit of distributed tracing is that it allows you to implicitly map your services and the relationships between them, allowing you to identify errors in other services that contribute to the latency of a particular request. When applications become more complicated and interconnected, understanding these relationships stops being optional and starts becoming fundamental.

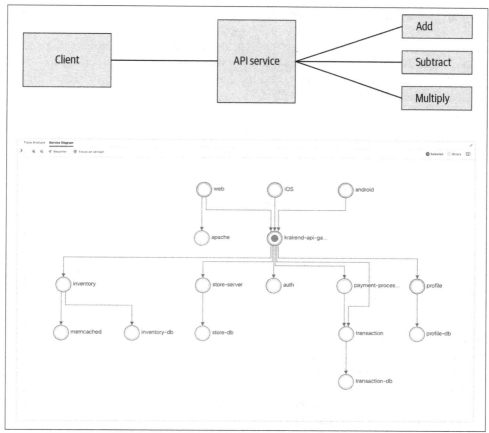

Figure 4-3. A comparison of MicroCalc versus a more complex microservice graph.

In the sample application, you can see that the dependencies between services are fairly straightforward and easy to understand. Even in this simple application, being able to build the entire graph is highly valuable. Let's imagine that you used a combination of techniques in order to instrument each of our services (API proxy, authentication service, worker services, etc.) and have a trace analyzer that can read and process the spans generated from our application. Using this, you can answer questions that would be difficult if you didn't have access to these service relationships. These can range from the mundane ("What services contribute most to the latency of this specific operation?") to the specific ("For this specific customer ID, for this specific transaction, what service is failing?"). However, if you limit yourself to merely tracing the edges of your services, you're in a bit of a pickle. You can only identify failures very coarsely, such as if a request failed or succeeded.

So, how do you fix this? You have several options. Certainly one is to begin adding instrumentation to the service code itself. As we'll discuss in the next section, there's an art and a science to creating spans that are useful for profiling and debugging traced code. The other is to leverage the edges you've traced, and mine them for more data. We'll present three more advanced mechanisms that use the concepts of framework and mesh instrumentation to fill in the gaps of your service mesh.

The first method is to increase the level of detail in our framework-provided spans. In our example HTTP middleware, we recorded only a small amount of detail about the request such as the HTTP method, route, and status code. In reality, each request would potentially have a great deal more data recorded. Are your incoming requests tied to a user? Consider attaching the user identifier to each request as a tag. Service-to-service requests should be identified with some semantic identifiers provided by your tracing library such as OpenTelemetry's SpanKind attributes or specific tags that allow you to identify the type of a service (cache, database, and so forth). For database calls, instrumenting the database client allows you to capture a wide variety of information such as the actual database instance being used, the database query, and so forth. All of these enrichments help build your service graph into a semantic representation of your application and the connections between it.

The second method is to leverage existing instrumentation and integrations for your services. A variety of plug-ins (*https://oreil.ly/OJHDX*) exist for OpenTelemetry, OpenTracing, and OpenCensus that allow for common open source libraries to emit spans as a part of your existing trace. If you're facing a daunting instrumentation journey, with a large amount of existing code, you can use these plug-ins to instrument existing frameworks and clients alongside higher-level instrumentation at the service mesh/framework layer. We list a sample of these plug-ins in Appendix A.

The third method is through manual instrumentation, which we covered in "Custom Instrumentation" on page 70, and the same principles apply. You'll want to ensure that a root span is propagated into each service that you can create child spans from. Depending on the level of detail required for a service, you may not need multiple child spans for a single service; consider the pseudocode in Example 4-11.

Example 4-11. A pseudocode method to handle resizing and storing of images

```
func uploadHandler(request) {
        image = imageHelper.ParseFile(request.Body())
        resizedImage = imageHelper.Resize(image)
        uploadResponse = uploadToBucket(resizedImage)
        return uploadResponse
}
```

In this case, what do we care about tracing? The answer will vary based on your requirements. There's an argument for having most of the methods being called here have their own child spans, but the real delineation here would be to restrict child calls to methods that are outside the scope of responsibility for a given team. You can imagine a situation where as our service grows we may factor the functions that parse and resize images out of this into another service. As we've written, you'll probably want to simply encase this whole method in a single span and add tags and logs based off the responses to your method calls, something like Example 4-12.

Example 4-12. Manually instrumenting a method

```
func uploadHandler(context, request) {
    span = getTracer().startSpanFromContext(context)
    image = imageHelper.ParseFile(request.Body())
    if image == error {
        span.setTag("error", true)
        span.log(image.error)
    }
    // Etc.
}
```

Any or all of these methods can be intermingled to build a more effective and representative service graph that not only accurately describes the service dependencies of your application but semantically represents the nature of these dependencies. We've discussed adding or enriching spans; next, we'll look at *how* to create these spans, and how to determine the most important and valuable information you should add to a span.

What's in a Span?

Spans are the building blocks of distributed tracing, but what does that actually mean? A span represents two things: the span of time that your service was working and the mechanism by which data is carried from your service to some analysis system capable of processing and interpreting it. Creating effective spans that unlock insights into the behavior of your service is one part art, one part science. It involves understanding best practices around assigning names to your spans, ensuring that you're tagging spans with semantically useful information, and logging structured data.

Effective Naming

What's in a name? When it comes to a span, this is a very good question! The name of a span, also known as the *operation name*, is a required value in open source tracing libraries, in fact, it is one of the *only* required values. Why is this the case? As we've alluded to, spans are an abstraction over the work of a service. This is a significant difference from the way you might think of a request chain, or a call stack. You should not have a one-to-one mapping between function name and span name.

That said, what's in a span name?

First, names should be aggregable. In short, you want to avoid span names that are unique to each execution of a service. One antipattern we see, especially in HTTP services, is implementers making the span name the same as the fully matched route (such as `GET /api/v2/users/1532492`). This pattern makes it difficult to aggregate operations across thousands or millions of executions, severely reducing the utility of your data. Instead, make the route more generic and move parameters to tags, such as `GET /api/v2/users/{id}` with an associated tag of `userId: 1532492`.

Our second piece of advice is that names should describe actions, not resources. To use an example, let's think back to MicroCalc. We could add a datastore, which could be blob storage, could be SQL, could be anything for any number of purposes, like a user database or a history of previous results. In lieu of naming a span based on the resource it's accessing, mutating, or otherwise consuming you'll be far better served by describing the action and tagging the span with the resource type. This allows for queries against your spans across multiple types, allowing for interesting analytical insights. An example would be the difference between the names `WriteUserToSQL` and `WriteUser`. You can imagine a situation where these independent components are switched out for testing (suppose we wanted to trial a NoSQL or cloud datastore for our users?); having this less proscriptive name would allow for comparisons between each backing store. Following these two pieces of advice will ensure that your spans are more useful down the line as you analyze them.

Effective Tagging

You're not required to tag your spans, but you should. Tags are the main way you can enrich a span with more information about what's happening for a given operation, and unlock a lot of power for analytics. While names will help you aggregate at a high level (so you can ask questions like "What's my error rate for looking up users across all services?"), tags will allow you to slice and dice that information to better understand the *why* of your query. Data with a high cardinality should be exposed in your span as a tag, rather than something else—placing high-cardinality data in a name reduces your ability to aggregate operations, and placing it inside of log statements often reduces its indexability.

So, what makes an effective tag? Tags should be *externally important*, which is to say, they should have meaning to other consumers of your trace data. While there are ways to use tags and traces in development, the tags you emit into a production tracing system should be generally useful to anyone trying to understand what your service is doing.

Tags should be *internally consistent* as well: using the same keys across multiple services. In our mock application, we could theoretically have each service report the same piece of information (a user ID, let's say) using different tag keys—`userId`,

UserId, User_ID, USERID, and so forth—but this would be difficult to create queries about in external systems. Consider building helper libraries that standardize these keys, or settle upon a format that comports with your organization's coding standards.

In addition to the consistency of tag keys, ensure that tag data is kept as consistent as possible within a tag key. If some services report the userId key as a string value, and others as an integer value, problems could arise in your analysis system. Furthermore, ensure that if you're tracking some numerical value, you add the unit of the tag to the key. For example, if you're measuring the bytes returned on a request, mes sage_size_kb is more useful than message_size. Tags should be *succinct* rather than verbose—don't put stack traces in tags, for example. Remember, tags are critical to querying your trace data and building insights, so don't neglect them!

Effective Logging

Naming and tagging of spans both assist in your ability to derive insights from your traces. They help you build a relational graph of sorts, showing you what happened (through names) and why it happened (through tags). Logs could be thought of as the *how it happened* piece of this puzzle, offering developers the ability to attach structured or unstructured text strings to a given span.

Effective logging with spans has two central components. First, ask yourself what you really should be logging. Named and tagged spans can significantly reduce the amount of logging statements required by your code. When in doubt, make a new span rather than a new logging statement. For example, consider the pseudocode in Example 4-13.

Example 4-13. Named and tagged spans

```
func getAPI(context, request) {
        value = request.Body()
        outgoingRequest = new HttpRequest()
        outgoingRequest.Body = new ValueQuery(value)
        response = await HttpClient().Get(outgoingRequest)
        if response != Http.OK {
                request.error = true
                return
        }
        resValue = response.Body()
        // Go off and do more work
}
```

Without tracing, you would want to log quite a bit here—for example, the incoming parameters, especially the value you care about inspecting. The outgoing request body would possibly be interesting to log. The response code would definitely be something you'd look to log, especially if it's an exceptional or error case. With a span, however, there's significantly less that's valuable as a log statement—the incoming parameter value, if it's generally useful, could be a tag such as `value:foo`, the response code would certainly be one, and so forth. That said, you might still be interested in logging the exact error case that's happening there. In this situation, consider making a new span for that external request instead. The rationale here is twofold: this is an *edge* of your application code, and, as discussed earlier, it's a good practice to trace the edges.

Another reason is that a log statement would be less interesting in terms of data than another span. HTTP GET may seem like a simple operation, and it often is when we think about using it. Consider what's happening behind the scenes, though—DNS lookups, routing through who-knows-how-many hops, time spent waiting on socket reads, and so forth. This information, if made available in a span through tags, can provide more fine-grained insight into performance issues and is thus better served by being a new span rather than a discrete log operation.

The second aspect to effective logging in your spans is, when possible, *write structured logs* and be sure your analysis system is capable of understanding them. This is more about ensuring the usability of your spans down the line than anything else—an analysis system can turn structured logging data into something more readable in a GUI, and provides options for performing complex queries (i.e., "show me all logs from Service X where an event was logged with a particular type of exception" or "are any of my services emitting logs at an INFO level?").

Security and Compliance Considerations

Attributes, tags, events, logs, and even span names can potentially contain personally identifiable information (PII). This data, depending on local and federal regulations, may be protected by law. You should pay careful attention to exactly what data is being added to your spans, especially if you are using a third-party analysis tool for your trace data. Your organization may also specify certain rules and regulations that pertain to the amount of time that diagnostic data may be retained for legal discovery or other purposes. Consult relevant legal advisers in your organization or locality for more information to determine exactly what can, and can't, be stored.

Understanding Performance Considerations

The undesirable side effect of creating these rich, detailed spans is that they all have to *go* somewhere, and that takes time. Let's consider a text representation of a *typical* span for an HTTP request (see Example 4-14).

Example 4-14. Typical span for an HTTP request

```
{
        context:
        {
                TraceID: 9322f7b2-2435-4f36-acec-f9750e5bd9b7,
                SpanID: b84da0c2-5b5f-4ecf-90d5-0772c0b5cc18
        }
        name: "/api/v1/getCat",
        startTime: 1559595918,
        finishTime: 1559595920,
        endTime:
        tags:
        [
                {
                        key: "userId",
                        value: 9876546
                },
                {

                        key: "srcImagePath",
                        value: "s3://cat-objects/19/06/01/catten-arr-djinn.jpg"
                },
                {

                        key: "voteTotalPositive",
                        value: 9872658
                },
                {

                        key: "voteTotalNegative",
                        value: 72
                },
                {

                        key: "http.status_code",
                        value: 200
                },
                {

                        key: "env",
                        value: "prod"
                },
                {

                        key: "cache.hit",
                        value: true
                }

        ]
}
```

This is less than 1 KB of data—about 600 bytes. Encoding it in base64 brings that up to around 800 bytes. We're still under 1 KB, so that's good—but this is just one span. What would it look like for an error case? A stack trace would probably balloon us up from sub 1 KiB to around 3–4 KiB. Encoding a single span is, again, fractional seconds—(`time openssl base64` reports `cpu 0.006 total`)—which isn't that much when you get down to it.

Now multiply that by a thousand, ten thousand, a hundred thousand…eventually, it adds up. You're never going to get any of this for free, but never fear, it's not as bad as it might seem. The first thing to keep in mind is that you don't know until you know —there's no single rule we can give you to magically make everything perform better. The amount of overhead you're willing to budget for and accept in your application's performance is going to vary depending on a vast amount of factors that include:

- Language and runtime
- Deployment profile
- Resource utilization
- Horizontal scalability

With that in mind, you should consider these factors carefully as you begin to instrument your application. Keep in mind that the stable use case and the worst-case performance profile will often look *extremely* different. More than one developer has found themselves in a hairy situation where some external resource was suddenly unexpectedly available for a long period of time, leading to extremely ungraceful and resource-intensive service crash loops or hangs. A strategy you can use to combat this is to build in safety valves to your internal tracing framework. Depending on your sampling strategy, this "tracing safety valve" could be a cutoff on new span creation if the application is in a persistent failing state, or a gradual reduction in span creation to an asymptotic point.

Graceful Degradation of Span Creation

Traditionally, distributed tracing has ameliorated persistent failure states and garbage data through per-process or per-application sampling strategies around span creation. New dynamic sampling approaches that move this decision out of the process allow you to collect 100% of the trace data from each of your services, but present some unique challenges in how you should handle span creation while in a persistent (non-recoverable) failure. You should consider the span creation rate (and size of those spans) during persistent failure of a service and use that to make a decision—in a low-throughput service where span count is measured in tens or hundreds a minute, you may be OK without a backoff.

Additionally, consider building in some sort of method to remotely disable the tracer in your application code. This can be useful in a variety of scenarios beyond the aforementioned unexpected external resource loss; it can also be helpful when wanting to profile your service performance with tracing on versus with tracing off.

Ultimately, the biggest resource cost in tracing isn't really the service-level cost of creating and sending spans. A single span is most likely a fraction of the data that's being handled in any given RPC in terms of size. You should experiment with the spans you're creating, the amount of data you're adding to them, and the rate at which you're creating them in order to find the right balance between performance and information that's required to provide value from tracing.

Trace-Driven Development

When tracing is discussed as part of an application or service, there's a tendency to "put it off," so to speak. In fact, there's almost a hierarchy of monitoring that is applied, in order, to services as they're developed. You'll start off with nothing, but quickly start to add log statements to your code, so you can see what's going on in a particular method or what parameters are being passed around. Quite often, this is the majority of the monitoring that's applied to a new service up until it's about ready to be released, at which point you'll go back in and identify some metrics that you care about (error rate, for example) and stub those in, right before the whole ball of wax gets shoved into your production deployments.

Why is it done this way? For several reasons—some of them good. It can be very difficult to write monitoring code when the code you're monitoring shifts and churns under your feet—think of how quickly lines of code can be added, removed, or refactored while a project is in development—so it's something that developers tend not to do, unless there's a very strong observability practice on their team.

There's another reason, though, and it's perhaps the more interesting one. It's hard to write monitoring code in development because you don't really know what to monitor. The things you do know to care about, such as an error rate, aren't really that interesting to monitor and often can be observed through another source, such as through a proxy or API gateway. Machine-level metrics such as memory consumption of your process aren't something most developers have to worry about, and if they do, those metrics are going to be monitored by a different component rather than by their application itself.

Neither metrics nor logs do a good job of capturing the things you *do* know about at the beginning of your service's development, such as what services it should be communicating with, or how it should call functions internally. Tracing offers an option, allowing for the development of traces as you develop your application that both offer necessary context while developing and testing your code and provide a ready-made toolset for observability within your application code. In this section, we'll cover the two high-level parts of this concept: developing using traces, and testing using traces.

Developing with Traces

No matter what language, platform, or style of service you write, they'll all probably start at the same place: a whiteboard. It's this surface that you'll use to create the model of your service's functions, and draw lines that represent the connections between it and other services. It makes a lot of sense, especially in the early prototyping phases of development, to start out in such a malleable place.

The problem comes when it's time to take your model and translate it into code. How do you ensure that what you've written on the board matches up with your code? Traditionally the usage of test functions is recommended, but this is perhaps *too small* of a target to really tell you anything useful. A unit test, by design, should validate the behavior of very small units of functionality—a single method call, for example. You can, of course, write bigger unit tests that begin to validate other suppositions about your functions, such as ensuring that method A calls method B calls method C…but eventually, you're just writing a test that exercises every code path for spurious reasons.

When you try to test the relationship your service has to antecedent and dependent services, it gets even more convoluted. Generally, these would be considered integration tests. The problem with integration tests to verify your model is twofold, however. The first problem is that if you begin to mock services out, you're not testing against the actual service, just a mock replacement that follows some preordained command. The second, and perhaps larger, problem is that integration tests are necessarily going to be limited to your test environment and have poor support for communicating across process boundaries (at least, without going through a bunch of hoops to set up an integration test framework or write your own).

If unit tests and integration tests won't work, then what will? Well, let's go back to the original point—it's important to have a way to validate your mental model of your application. That means you should be able to write your code in a way that allows you to ensure both internal methods and external services are being called in the correct order, with the correct parameters, and that errors are handled sanely. One common mistake we've observed, especially in code with significant external service dependencies, is what happens on persistent service failure.

You can see examples of this happening in the real world all the time. Consider the outages that occurred as a result of AWS S3 buckets becoming persistently unavailable for hours upon end several years ago. Having trace data available to you, both in test and production, allows you to write tools that quickly compare the desired state of your system with reality. It's also invaluable when trying to build chaos systems as part of your continuous integration/continuous delivery (CI/CD)—being able to find the differences between your steady-state system and the system under chaos will dramatically improve your ability to build more resilient systems.

Tracing as a part of your development process works similarly to tracing anywhere else in your codebase, with a few notable conveniences. First, recall our earlier discussion of how to start tracing a service ("Where to Start—Nodes and Edges" on page 71). The same principle applies to writing a new service and to instrumenting an existing one. You should apply middleware to each incoming request that checks for span data, and if it exists, create a new child span. When your new service emits outbound requests, it too should inject your current span context into the outgoing request so that downstream services that are tracing-aware can take part in the trace. The changes to the process tend to come between these points because you'll be faced with challenges around how much to trace.

As we'll discuss at the end of this chapter, there is such a thing as *too much* tracing. In production especially, you want to limit your traces to the data that matters for external observers and users when they view an end-to-end trace. How, then, to accurately model a single service with multiple internal calls? You'll want to create some sort of *verbosity* concept for your tracer. This is extremely common in logging, where log levels exist such as info, debug, warning, and error. Each verbosity specifies at minimum that the log statement must meet to be printed. The same concept can apply to traces as well. Example 4-15 demonstrates one method in Golang to create verbose traces, configurable via an environment variable.

Example 4-15. Creating verbose traces

```go
var traceVerbose = os.Getenv("TRACE_LEVEL") == "verbose"

...

func withLocalSpan(ctx context.Context) (context.Context, opentracing.Span) {
        if traceVerbose {
                pc, _, _, ok := runtime.Caller(1)
                callerFn := runtime.FuncForPC(pc)
                if ok && callerFn != nil {
                        span, ctx := opentracing.StartSpanFromContext(
                        ctx, callerFn.Name()
                )
                        return ctx, span
                }
        }
        return ctx, opentracing.SpanFromContext(ctx)
}

func finishLocalSpan(span opentracing.Span) {
        if traceVerbose {
                span.Finish()
        }
}
```

Setting trace verbosity isn't just limited to Go—aspects, attributes, or other dynamic/metaprogramming techniques can be utilized in languages with support for them. The basic idea is as presented, though. First, ensure that the verbosity level is set appropriately. Then, determine the calling function and start a new span as a child of the current one. Finally, return the span and the language context object as appropriate. Note that in this case, we're only providing a start/finish method—this means that any logs or tags we introduce will not necessarily be added to the verbose child, but could be added to the parent if the child doesn't exist. If this isn't desirable, then consider creating helper functions to log or tag through to avoid this behavior. Using our verbose traces is fairly straightforward as well (see Example 4-16).

Example 4-16. Using verbose traces

```
import (
        "github.com/opentracing-contrib/go-stdlib/nethttp"
        "github.com/opentracing/opentracing-go"
)

func main() {
        // Create and register tracer

        mux := http.NewServeMux()
        fs := http.FileServer(http.Dir("../static"))

        mux.HandleFunc("/getFoo", getFooHandler)
        mux.Handle("/", fs)

        mw := nethttp.Middleware(tracer, mux)
        log.Printf("Server listening on port %s", serverPort)
        http.ListenAndServe(serverPort, mw)
}

func getFooHandler(w http.ResponseWriter, r *http.Request) {
        foo := getFoo(r.Context())
        // Handle response
}

func getFoo(ctx context.Context) {
        ctx, localSpan := withLocalSpan(ctx)
        // Do stuff
        finishLocalSpan(localSpan)
}
```

In this example, we're creating a simple HTTP server in Golang and tracing it with the go-stdlib package. This will parse incoming HTTP requests for tracing headers and create spans appropriately, so the edges of our service are being handled. By adding the withLocalSpan and finishLocalSpan methods, we can create a span that's *local* to a function and only exists when our trace verbosity is set appropriately.

These spans could be viewed in a trace analyzer while performing local development, allowing you to accurately assess that calls are happening in the same way that you think they should be, ensuring that you can observe your service as it calls other services (or is called by them), and as a bonus allows you to use open source frameworks as a default choice for questions like, "What logging/metrics/tracing API should I be using?" as these can be performed through your telemetry API. Don't reinvent the wheel if you don't need to, after all!

Testing with Traces

Trace data can be represented as a directional acyclic graph. While it's usually represented as a flame graph, traces are simply directional acyclic graphs of a request, as illustrated in Figure 4-4. A directed acyclic graph, or DAG, may be extremely familiar to you if you have a computer science or mathematics background; it has several properties that are extremely useful. DAGs are finite (they have an end) and they have no directed cycles (they don't loop on themselves—those that do are called *cyclical references*). One other useful property of DAGs is that they are fairly easy to compare to each other.

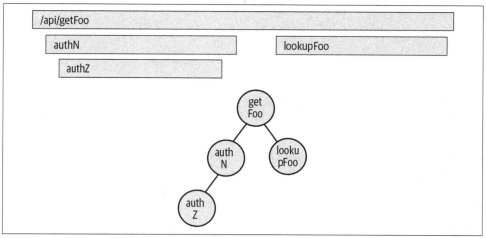

Figure 4-4. Comparison of a flame graph view of a trace versus a DAG view.

Knowing this, what are the possibilities? First, you may be asking, "So what?" As discussed earlier, integration testing and other forms of higher-level tests are sufficient and necessary to ensure the operation of our service as it is deployed. That said, there are several reasons you might want to consider adding trace comparisons to your testing repertoire. The easiest way to think about applied trace data as a form of testing is through simple diffs between environments. Consider a scenario where we deploy a version of our application to a staging or preproduction environment after testing it locally. Further consider that we export our trace data in some sort of flat file, suitable for processing, as shown in Example 4-17.

Example 4-17. Exporting trace data

```
[
    {
            name: "getFoo",
            spanContext: {
                    SpanID: 1,
                    TraceID: 1
            },
            parent: nil
    },
    {
            name: "computeFoo",
            spanContext: {
                    SpanID: 2,
                    TraceID: 1
            },
            parent: spanContext{
                    SpanID: 1,
                    TraceID: 1
            }
    },
    ...
]
```

In a real system, we might expect these to be out of order or otherwise not exist in a sorted state, but we *should* expect that the call graph for a single API endpoint will be the same between them.

One potential application, then, is to perform a topographical sort on each set of trace data, then compare by length or through some other diffing process. If our traces differ, we know we have some sort of problem because the results didn't match our expectations.

Another application of this would be to identify, proactively, when services begin to take dependencies on your service. Consider a situation where our authentication service, or search service, was more widely publicized to other teams. Unbeknownst to us, they start to take a dependency on it in their new services. Automated trace diffing would give us proactive insights into these new consumers, especially if there's some sort of centralized framework generating and comparing these traces over time.

Still another application is simply using tracing as the backbone of gathering service level indicators and objectives for your service, and automatically comparing them as you deploy new versions. Since traces are inherently able to understand the timing of your service, they're a great way to keep track of performance changes across a wide variety of requests as you iterate and further develop services.

Ultimately, a lot of this is speculative—we're not aware of anyone using distributed tracing heavily as a part of their test suites. That doesn't mean it isn't useful, but as a new technology, not every facet of it has been explored and exploited yet. Maybe you'll be the first!

Creating an Instrumentation Plan

For better or worse, most people come to distributed tracing and monitoring late in the development of an application or piece of software. Some of this has to do with the nature of iterative development—when you're creating a product or service, it can be difficult to understand what it is you need to know until you've spent some time actually building and running it. Distributed tracing adds a wrinkle to this as well because developers will often come to it as a solution to problems that are cropping up due to scale and growth, be it in terms of service count or organizational complexity. In both of these cases, you'll often have some large, presumably complicated set of services already deployed and running and need to know how you can leverage distributed tracing in order to improve the reliability and health of not only your software, but also your team. Perhaps you're starting greenfield development on some new piece of software and are adding distributed tracing out of the gate—you'll still need to create a plan for how to both add and grow tracing throughout your team and organization. In this section, we'll discuss how you can make an effective case for instrumentation of either new or existing services in your organization and how to get buy-in from your (and other) teams, signals that indicate when you've instrumented enough, and finally how to sustainably grow instrumentation throughout your services.

Making the Case for Instrumentation

Let's assume that you're already sold on the idea of distributed tracing by virtue of you reading this book. The challenge, then, becomes convincing your colleagues that it's as good of an idea as you think it is, because they're going to have to do some work as well to ensure that their services are compatible with tracing.

When making the case to other teams about the benefits, and costs, of distributed tracing, it's important to keep in mind many of the instrumentation lessons that we've discussed in this chapter. In short, instrumentation can be valuable even if it's fairly basic. If every service emits one span with some basic attributes that require no runtime overhead (i.e., string values that can be precalculated at service initialization) then the total added overhead to each request is simply the propagation of trace context headers, a task that adds 25 bytes on the wire and a negligible amount of cycles to decode afterwards.

The benefit—end-to-end tracing of a request—is extremely helpful for such a small price. This request-centric style of distributed tracing has found adopters at companies such as Google, which has used Dapper to diagnose anomalies and steady-state performance problems in addition to attribution for resource utilization.[1] Numerous other engineering teams and organizations, large and small, have adopted distributed tracing in order to reduce MTTR for incidents and other production downtime. In addition, distributed tracing is extremely valuable as part of a larger monitoring and observability practice, where it enables you to reduce the *search space* of data that you need to investigate in order to diagnose incidents, profile performance, and restore your services to a healthy state.

It can be useful to think of distributed tracing as a "level playing field" when it comes to service performance. Especially when interacting in a polyglot environment, or in a globally distributed enterprise, there can be challenges in ensuring that everyone is on the same page in terms of performance data. Some of these challenges are technical, but many are political. The proliferation of vanity metrics is particularly notable here; you can measure quite a few things about your software performance that don't matter, and you may already be doing so in order to achieve nebulous "quality" goals set for reasons beyond our ken. Distributed tracing data, however, provides critical signals by default in a standardized way for all of your services and does so without requiring synthetic endpoints or approaches to ensuring service health. This trace data can then be used to bring some peace and sanity to a possibly broken process. Of course, the first step to delivering that trace data is service instrumentation, so you'll need to start there.

It doesn't have to be difficult to instrument your services. Good tools—open source and proprietary—will ease the instrumentation burden. We detail these in Appendix A, with examples of automatic instrumentation as well as library integrations for popular frameworks that enable tracing—sometimes with no code changes required. You should be aware of your frameworks and shared code when making the case for instrumentation so that you can leverage these existing tools. In our experience, one of the most persuasive arguments for distributed tracing is to simply instrument some existing microservice framework already used by your organization and demonstrate how services using it can be traced by simply updating a dependency. If you have an internal hackathon or hack day, this can be a fun and interesting project to tackle!

No matter how you do it, the case for instrumentation ultimately comes down to the case for distributed tracing in general. As we've mentioned, there are plenty of interesting applications for tracing outside performance monitoring: tracing as part of your development cycle, tracing in testing other applications. You could use

---

1 [Sam16]

distributed tracing as part of your CI and CD framework, timing how long certain parts of your build and deployments take. Tracing could be integrated into task runners for creating virtual machines or provisioning containers, allowing you to understand what parts of your build and deploy life cycle take the most time. Tracing can be used as a value-add for services that provide some sort of API as a service—if you're already tracing the execution time of your backend, you could make some version of that trace data available to your customers in order to help them profile their software as well. The possibilities for tracing are limitless, and the case for instrumenting your software should reflect that.

Instrumentation Quality Checklist

When instrumenting an existing service or creating guidelines on how to instrument new services, it can be useful to have a checklist of items that are important to ensuring quality instrumentation throughout your entire application. We've included a recommended one in the book's repository (*https://oreil.ly/instrmntn-checklist*), but you're welcome to use it as a jumping-off point for your own.

Instrumentation Checklist

Span Status and Creation

- All error conditions under a given span appropriately set the span status to an error state.
- RPC framework result codes are mapped to span status (i.e., Internal Error, Not Found, etc.).
- All spans that are started are also finished, even in the case of unrecoverable errors if possible.
- Spans should only represent work that is semantically important to the request life cycle of a service; try not to create spans around endpoints only receiving synthetic traffic, like a /status or /health endpoint.

Span Boundaries

- Egress and ingress spans have appropriate labels (SpanKind is set).
- Egress and ingress spans have appropriate relationships (client/server, consumer/ producer).
- Internal spans are appropriately labeled and do not imply a remote call.

Attributes

- Spans include a version attribute for the service they represent.
- Spans that represent work by a dependency have an attribute for that dependency's version.

- Spans should include attributes identifying underlying infrastructure:
  — Hostname / FQDN
  — Container name, if appropriate
  — Runtime version
  — Application server version, if appropriate
  — Region or availability zone
- Attributes are namespaced where appropriate (i.e., to prevent collisions between key names where the semantic meaning of the key differs between services in a request).
- Attributes with numerical values should include the unit of measurement in the key name (i.e, payload_size_kb versus payload_size).
- Attributes should not contain any PII.

Events
- Useful and descriptive event messages that would be useful for upstream or downstream service users should be added:
  — Request-response payloads (sanitized)
  — Stack traces, exceptions, and error messages
- Long-running operations (such as waiting for a mutex) should be wrapped in events; one when the operation begins, and one when it ends.

Much of what's in our instrumentation checklist is drawn from other parts of this chapter, so we won't elaborate too much on it. A few notes to call out:

- Many open source instrumentation libraries or framework instrumentation libraries will, by default, instrument every incoming request or endpoint defined in your service code, including diagnostic endpoints. Generally, you'll want to implement a filter or sampler on your service to prevent spans being created from these endpoints unless you have some pressing need for it.
- Be very careful about exposing PII in your attributes and events; the costs for noncompliance can be severe, especially if you're transmitting trace data to a third party for analysis and storage.
- Version attributes are extremely valuable, especially when doing trace comparisons, as they allow you to easily diff a request across two or more versions of a service in order to discover performance regressions or improvements.

- Integrating your feature flags and other experiments with your trace data is a useful way to understand how those experiments are changing the performance and reliability of your service.

Feel free to adapt this checklist with specific information that makes it useful for your team, and include it on service rollout checklists.

Knowing When to Stop Instrumenting

We've touched on the costs of instrumentation several times in this chapter; let's take a deeper look. At a high level, instrumentation is a trade-off like anything else in software. You're trading some measure of performance for, hopefully, a much higher level of insight into the operation of your service at a level that's easy to communicate to others in your team or organization. In this section we point out a few notable antipatterns to watch out for when you're instrumenting. There's the risk that the trade-offs become too costly and lead you to stop instrumenting, or to oversample and lose resolution on your traces.

One antipattern is implementing *too high a default resolution*. A good rule is that your service should emit as many spans as logical operations it performs. Does your service handle authentication and authorization for users? Logically, break down this function—it's handling an incoming request, performing some lookups in a datastore, transforming the result, and returning it. There are two logical operations here —handling the request/response and looking up the data. It's always valuable to separate out calls to external services; in this example, you might only have a single span if the datastore is some sort of local database), but you may not need to emit a span for marshaling the response into a new format that your caller expects.

If your service is more complicated, adding more spans can be OK, but you need to consider how consumers of your trace data will find it valuable, and if it's collapsible into fewer spans. The corollary to this point is that you may want to have the ability to increase the verbosity of spans emitted by a service—refer back to "Trace-Driven Development" on page 85 for ideas on how to increase or decrease the resolution of your spans. This is why we say *default* resolution; you want to ensure that the default amount of information emitted is small enough to integrate well into a larger trace, but large enough to ensure that it contains useful information for consumers that might not be on your team (but might be affected by issues with your service!).

Another antipattern is *not standardizing your propagation format*. This can be challenging, especially when integrating legacy services or services written by a variety of teams. The key value of a trace is in the interconnected nature of a trace. If you have 20, 50, 200, or more services that are using a mishmash of tracing formats, you're going to have a bad time trying to get value out of your traces. Avoid this by standardizing your tracing practices as much as possible, and providing shims for legacy systems or between different formats.

One method to combat non-standard propagation formats is to create a *stack* of tracing propagators that can be aware of different headers (such as X-B3 or opentracing) and select the appropriate one on a per-request basis. You might find that it's less work to actually update existing systems to the new format rather than create compatibility layers—use your best judgment and your organization's existing standards and practices to figure out what's right for you.

The final advice, going back to the section title, is knowing when you should stop. Unfortunately, there's not a cut-and-dry answer here, but there are some signals you should pay attention to. In general, you should consider what your service's breaking point is without sampling any of your trace data.

Sampling is a practice where a certain percentage of your traces aren't recorded for analysis in order to reduce the overall load on your system. A discussion of sampling appears in "Sampling" on page 124, but we would advise that you don't consider the sample rate when writing instrumentation. If you're worried about the amount of spans created by your service, consider using verbosity flags to dynamically adjust how many spans are being created, or consider "tail-based" sampling approaches that analyze the entire trace before making a sampling decision. This is important because sampling is the best way to accidentally throw away potentially critical data that might be useful when debugging or diagnosing an issue in production. In contrast, a traditional sampling approach will make the decision at the beginning of a trace, so there's no reason to optimize around "will this or won't this be sampled"—your trace is going to be thrown away in its entirety if it is sampled out.

A sign that you need to keep going is if the inter-service resolution of your trace is too low. For example, if you're eliding multiple dependent services in a single span, you should keep instrumenting until those services are independent spans. You don't necessarily need to instrument the dependent services, but your RPC calls to each of them should be instrumented, especially if each of those calls are terminal in your request chain. To be more specific, imagine a worker service that communicates with several datastore wrappers—it may not be necessary to instrument those datastore wrappers, but you should have separate spans for each of the calls from your service to them in order to better understand latency and errors (am I failing to read, or failing to write?).

Stop tracing if the number of spans you're emitting by default begins to look like the actual call stack of a service. Keep instrumenting if you've got unhandled error cases in your service code—being able to categorize spans with errors versus spans without errors is vital. Finally, you should keep instrumenting if you're finding new things to instrument. Consider modifying your standard bug-handling process to not only include writing new tests to cover the fix, but to include writing new instrumentation to make sure that you can catch it in the future.

Smart and Sustainable Instrumentation Growth

It's one thing to instrument a single service, or a demonstration application that's meant to teach you some concepts about tracing. It's another, altogether more challenging task to figure out where to go from there. Depending on how you start your instrumentation journey, you may quickly find yourself in untested waters, struggling to figure out how to provide value from tracing while simultaneously growing its adoption within your organization or team.

There are several strategies you can employ to grow instrumentation inside your application. These strategies, broadly, can be grouped into technical and organizational solutions. We'll first address the technical strategies, then talk about the organizational ones. There is some overlap between the two—as you might expect, technical and organizational solutions work hand in hand to enable each other.

Technically, the best way to grow instrumentation throughout your application is to make it easy to use. Providing libraries that do the *heavy lifting* required to set up tracing and integrate it into your RPC frameworks or other shared code makes it easy for services to integrate tracing. Similarly, creating standard tags, attributes, and other metadata for your organization is a great way to ensure that new teams and services adopting tracing have a road map to quickly understand and gain value from tracing as they enable it. Finally, look at adopting tracing as part of your development and testing process—if teams are able to start using tracing on a day-to-day basis, then it becomes part of their workflow, and it'll be available once they deploy their services to production.

Ultimately, the goal of instrumentation growth should be tied to the ease of adopting instrumentation. You're going to find it challenging to grow the adoption of tracing if it's a lot of work for individual developers to implement. Every major engineering organization to adopt distributed tracing (including Google and Uber) has made tracing a first-class component of its microservice architecture by wrapping its infrastructure libraries in tracing code. This strategy allows for growing instrumentation quite naturally—as new services are deployed or migrated, they'll automatically gain instrumentation.

Organizationally, there's a bit more to talk about. All of the technical solutions presented earlier aren't going to be worth much without organizational buy-in. How, then, should you develop that buy-in? The easiest option, and one we've seen be incredibly successful, is simply a top-down mandate to use distributed tracing. Now, this doesn't necessarily mean you should start emailing your VP of Engineering, and in many cases, this isn't the most effective strategy. If you have a platform team, SRE team, DevOps team, or other infrastructure engineers, these teams can be a successful place to look for the impetus to grow tracing throughout your software. Consider how problems are communicated and managed in your engineering organization. Who has performance management as part of their portfolio? These can be allies and advocates for the initial implementation of tracing across all your services.

If your SRE team is using tools such as launch checklists, add tracing compatibility to the checklist and start to roll it out that way. You should also consider how your tracing is performing when you're performing postmortems on incidents—were there services that weren't traced that should have been? Was there data that was critical to resolving the incident that wasn't present in the spans? Instrumentation beyond the basics can also be a defined goal for your teams that's measured like any other aspect of code quality. It's also useful to track improvements to instrumentation rather than simply adding new services—effective instrumentation is just as important as ubiquitous instrumentation.

Ensure that a process exists for end users of your traces to suggest improvements, especially to shared libraries, in order to drive continuous improvement. Pay careful attention to existing instrumentation code during refactors, especially refactors that modify instrumentation itself. You don't want to lose resolution on your traces because someone removed spans accidentally! This is an area where building tests around your instrumentation is valuable, as you can easily compare the state of your traces before and after changes, and automatically warn or notify developers of unexpected differences.

Ultimately, instrumentation is a critical part of distributed tracing, but it's only the first step. Without instrumentation, you're not going to have the necessary trace data to actually observe and understand requests as they move through your system. Once you've instrumented your services, you'll suddenly be presented with a fire hose of data. How can you collect and analyze that data in order to discover insights and performance information about your services in aggregate? Over the next few chapters, we'll discuss the art of collecting and storing trace data.

CHAPTER 5

Deploying Tracing

Understanding how to instrument code so that your application generates quality telemetry is no small feat, so congratulations on making it this far! However, that telemetry won't amount to much without the rest of a tracing deployment to consume those spans and use them to provide value to you and other developers. We'll spend this and the following chapter looking underneath the hood of tracers and consider some of the common components in those implementations as well as some of the trade-offs required. While not many readers are likely to be considering building new tracing solutions from scratch, a high-level understanding of what's going on will help you to choose the best tracer for your organization and to maximize the value that it can bring.

Distributed tracing can offer a lot to organizations where individual teams work independently. Tracing problems across the many layers of your application helps you quickly identify which service is the performance bottleneck or is responsible for a regression. However, this independence can also be an obstacle to getting started with distributed tracing: if you're responsible for deploying tracing across your organization, you'll need to get these teams to work together.

You'll get the most value from tracing if it's deployed consistently across your organization and your application. However, you'll face two sets of challenges in doing so. First, you need to overcome some organizational barriers: getting data from some teams may require those teams to instrument their services, change configuration, or maybe just redeploy their services. You may also need them to follow conventions about tags or at the very least propagate tracing context.

Second, you'll need to make sure you have the right infrastructure in place. While this can be partially outsourced to a vendor, some parts of the tracing system will still run on your infrastructure or could affect the performance of your application. And even if do you manage to offload most of the work, understanding trade-offs in tracing system design can help you evaluate different vendors and perhaps get some insight into how their pricing reflects the underlying costs of processing, storing, and analyzing traces.

Organizational Adoption

If your organization is building a distributed application, chances are that organization is not small. Successful adoption of distributed tracing will require work not just from you and your team, but from many teams across your organization—and perhaps even *outside* of your organization.

In this context, you're looking not just to get the most value from distributed tracing early on, but to get the most *demonstrable* value. That is, you'll need to produce evidence of the value of tracing *for your organization*. To do so, you'll need to be thoughtful about where and how you deploy it. Though it's often considered a tool for "end-to-end understanding," tracing can also provide value for individual teams; showing an example of this is the best way to convince other teams to adopt it as well.

In addition, deploying tracing at scale will also require considerable computing and storage resources. We will cover the costs of these resources in more detail in Chapter 6, but when thinking about how to deploy tracing, it's important that you choose a tracing solution that can meet your organization's needs not just in terms of features, but in how those features perform at scale. It's also important to make sure that the incremental cost of doing so doesn't outpace the incremental value offered by tracing.

Start Close to Your Users

There's no better way to ensure that tracing has business value than to start close to the users of your application. How do they interact with your application? Through a mobile app? A single-page web app or a more traditional one? Through a specialized device? Perhaps your organization only provides an API to your users, in which case, that API is as close as you'll be able to get. In any case, if you measure performance close to your users, you can be sure that you are measuring something that matters. In our experience, we've seen both large and small organizations fail to take this approach and instead choose a service to instrument because it was *easy*. Unfortunately, while the instrumentation was indeed easy, it didn't help build evidence that tracing should be a priority for the organization and it didn't help to surface challenges that developers faced as they continued to roll out tracing.

It is possible to start *too* close to your users for your initial foray into tracing. For example, if your mobile app is on a slow release cadence, it might take too long yo get the initial version of tracing deployed or be too slow to iterate on instrumentation. Web apps or nightly builds of mobile apps can make good choices. Get as close to your users as you reasonably can, but make sure you can still move quickly.

You should also consider specific types of requests or transactions that are important to your users and your business. For example, it might be tempting to choose an asynchronous request type that's used to record some analytics about user behavior: this might seem easy (it's a simple request and changes to it do not receive much scrutiny) and low risk (changes are unlikely to negatively impact users). However, you also have far less to gain by starting with this type of request. Instead, start with a type of request that represents an important user conversion. For example, if your application is part of an ecommerce solution, start with the point at which a purchase is made.

Start Centrally: Load Balancers and Gateways

If you can't start with a mobile app, web app, or other client of your application, choose a part of your backend systems that is still relatively close to your users: ingress load balancers or API gateways.

Ingress load balancers, especially HTTP (or "level 7") load balancers, are good candidates for quickly getting started with tracing. Load balancers are designed to efficiently pass through traffic, and it's relatively easy for them to generate spans in addition to other metrics and logs they might already be emitting.

Many widely used load balancers have support for tracing built in or have existing plug-ins that make adding tracing easy. For example, Envoy supports several tracers out of the box; Linkerd ships with support for the OpenCensus collector; NGINX supports an OpenTracing plug-in that can be used with several tracing systems.

HTTP load balancers can add a number of interesting tags automatically, including the request path, method, and protocol as well as status codes indicating the success or failure of the request. These tags can be valuable data sources when using distributed tracing to understand application performance.

Note that TCP (transmission control protocol, or "level 3/4") load balancers provide significantly less value since they do not have access to HTTP (or other application-level) request data. We have seen few examples where instrumenting TCP load balancers provides value as part of a distributed tracing solution.

API gateways also provide an opportunity to gather rich telemetry that is relatively close to the user and also broad in scope. Teams who manage API gateways often feel a lot of pain that can be alleviated with tracing and will be willing allies. In particular, they are often held accountable for the performance of the APIs that sit beneath the gateway or, at the least, get paged frequently when those upstream systems perform poorly.

If a gateway service can emit spans for the endpoints it serves *and* for its view of the services for which it's acting as a gateway, these spans can be used to attribute slow performance to other backend services (and their respective teams). This is important because API gateways frequently make calls to several upstream systems, including authorization and other common services, in addition to the services providing the business logic for API requests that they are serving. An immediate effect of this approach is that the team that owns the gateway service can more confidently identify which other teams need to improve performance. This is an example of how tracing can benefit even a single team: by tying the performance of a service to the performance of its dependencies, even very short traces can provide value.

When starting a tracing deployment with either ingress load balancers or API gateways, these initial traces can help inform your next steps in that deployment. For example, if a particular upstream service is frequently a bottleneck for request latency, that service would be a logical next step for instrumentation (and that instrumentation hopefully will provide results that directly impact user-perceived latency).

Leverage Infrastructure: RPC Frameworks and Service Meshes

Finally, a third approach to starting with tracing in a larger organization is to leverage the infrastructure that connects services. If your organization has a standard framework for making RPC calls or you use a service mesh, you can get at least half the work done for a broad (though not deep) integration with tracing very quickly.

As we discussed in Chapter 4, RPC frameworks and service meshes provide standard ways of connecting services, and often provide support for security, service discovery, load balancing, and (relevant to the current topic) generating telemetry. Many frameworks and service meshes already support tracing out of the box or can be easily extended to do so. As with ingress load balancers, they may also be able to add some additional information to those spans, possibly including request information and error codes. RPC frameworks and service meshes can also facilitate propagating context *between* services: they can make sure that span and trace IDs are included among the headers or other metadata.

Extracting context is another story, however. Since many of these frameworks are not part of handling requests on the server side, you'll need to find another way to do this. If there is already common code used across your organization as part of handling requests, then you can plug in additional middleware at that point to extract trace context. Without any common request-handling code, however, you will need to make some changes to the services themselves to extract context from requests as they arrive. If you don't have either of these options, you'll be left with a lot of single-span traces and not much to say about getting better end-to-end visibility.

In addition to instrumenting your framework, choose one service to start with and make sure that context is being propagated properly through that service. At the very least, the team that owns that service will be able to understand how the performance of requests it handles relates to its upstream services. As with the previous approach, even without deep instrumentation into all of your organization's services, a broad integration with tracing can help inform the next steps for rolling out tracing.

What About Service Orchestration?

We have discussed load balancers, service mesh, and other infrastructure, but you may be wondering why we don't mention Kubernetes or other orchestration tools as part of deploying tracing. (After all, users of Kubernetes certainly need distributed tracing, right?) While it might be possible in the future, today orchestration systems don't have much to offer directly to speed the adoption of distributed tracing. (Of course, you might use Kubernetes or other platforms as part of the infrastructure on which the components of a tracing solution run, but here we're talking about collecting telemetry.)

The fundamental reason for this is that most orchestration platforms, including Kubernetes, focus on making sure that the right code is running in the right places rather than on how individual requests are handled. When they do help with things like service discovery, they aim to get out of the way as quickly as possible. This is all to say, these platforms focus on the *control plane* rather than the *data plane*.

In many ways, orchestration tools like Kubernetes complement observability tools like distributed tracing. Distributed tracing provides an understanding of what is happening in a distributed system, while orchestration tools provide a means to control these systems and effect change. Once you know what service deployment is causing a problem, Kubernetes will help you to quickly roll it back.

Make Adoption Repeatable

After you've shown that one team can be successful with tracing, the next step is, well, to help a second team do so. Take what you've learned from that first team and use it to make the next steps easier. This can mean both choosing which teams to go to next and knowing how to approach them. For example, did any other teams get pulled in to help address performance problems with the first roll-out of tracing? (Were any other teams implicated in those problems?) Are there other teams that are facing similar problems to those addressed by tracing in the initial roll-out?

Also consider what worked and didn't work for that first team. If there was a particular type of request for which tracing offered a lot of value, look for an analogue of that type of request. If particular tags were invaluable, make sure that those are included for each new service. If particular use cases came up a lot, consider how to automate anything necessary for new teams to take advantage of those.

If you didn't instrument any of the frameworks or standard libraries used across your organization as part of your initial deployment, now is a good time to start planning that work. With the evidence you gathered in support of tracing, it should be easy to make the case for the organization to invest in tracing.

One thing that we didn't worry about with your first deployment was how to standardize the process; this might be the time to start. As we discussed in Chapter 4, tracing is most effective when there are standards around how operation names appear and the types of tags that are included in spans. While this wasn't necessary for the first team to adopt tracing (and in fact, wouldn't have provided any value), this may become important for the second team—and certainly for the third, fourth, and fifth teams—to get the most value from tracing. It's also a good time to consider adding tracing to launch checklists so that all new services will be built and deployed with tracing enabled.

While the goal of the initial roll-out was to prove the value of tracing, moving forward it should be to reduce the friction for each subsequent team and to help make sure that tracing is used consistently from team to team.

Tracer Architecture

As you roll out tracing across your organization, the tracer you use must be prepared for greater and greater load. Whether you are deploying an open source tracer or adopting a proprietary solution, understanding what's going on underneath the hood will help you deploy and scale up your tracing solution smoothly. Though the architecture will vary from implementation to implementation, this section presents a high-level view of the major components of most tracers.

Figure 5-1 shows a simplified view of a tracer architecture. While some components may be combined in some implementations, the work of the tracer can be logically divided as follows:

In-process libraries
 Application code generally creates spans not by making network requests, but instead by using an SDK. As discussed in previous chapters, this SDK may be used as part of explicit instrumentation or may use reflection or other features of dynamic languages to automatically create spans.

Sidecars and agents
 Some parts of the tracing system run near the application and help to forward data quickly to the rest of the tracer.

Collectors
 As opposed to sidecars or agents, which are generally stateless, collectors may temporarily store spans, filter them, compute aggregate statistics about them, or prepare them for storage and analysis.

Centralized storage and analysis

This is where the real magic happens: where traces are assembled from their constituent spans and where global statistics about application performance are computed. It also provides the user interface that lets developers search traces and that visualizes those traces.

We'll cover each of these components in turn.

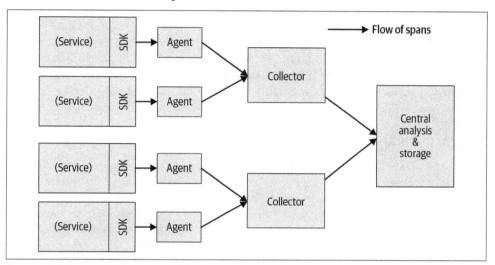

Figure 5-1. Simplified tracer architecture.

In-Process Libraries

While applications could send spans over the network to a tracing system as they are generated, there's a lot to be gained from buffering them and sending them in batches: some repeated parts of the spans need only be sent once, and sending batches can reduce network overhead. We can't expect every service to reimplement this functionality, so nearly all tracers provide some form of buffering as part of their SDKs.

In addition, these libraries handle discovery of other components of the tracer as well as network errors by retrying attempts to send spans (and reporting those errors appropriately). They may also offer a number of performance optimizations that are important for high-volume services: optimizations in how spans are buffered (including how those buffers are synchronized) and improvements in performance achieved through continuously streaming many spans over a single network connection (reducing network overhead, latency, and local memory consumption).

Depending on your position within your organization and the service in question, deploying new tracing libraries might be a breeze or a Sisyphean task. For the services that are deployed weekly (or even daily), adding a new dependency might be a relatively easy task. If you are part of a platform team, doing so might involve a little more work, including making the case for the change, creating the pull request in an unfamiliar codebase, getting approval, and deploying the change. In any case, the actual process will depend on the language, platform, and package (or dependency) management system.

On some platforms, especially those that use interpreters, just-in-time compilers, or dynamic linking, it's possible to deploy in-process libraries with no code changes (and no recompilation). For example, Java's Special Agent offers a means to dynamically link relevant instrumentation and tracer libraries into the Java virtual machine (JVM) by inspecting the bytecode of modules that have already been loaded. In those cases, redeploying services with new configurations may be sufficient. (Note that services on these platforms make excellent candidates for your initial roll-out of tracing!)

Sidecars and Agents

The terms *sidecar* and *agent* can be used to mean a number of things, so if you see them, take a closer look to be sure you understand what functions that tracer component is implementing. In many cases, these are relatively stand-alone components that, while deployed close to your application, are isolated enough to have little opportunity to interfere with application performance. A common motivation for creating this type of component is to move as much functionality as possible from the in-process library to a sidecar, alleviating the need to reimplement this functionality for every language or platform. Some of this functionality may include discovering other tracer components and handling network errors.

Depending on how you've set up your infrastructure, this might take the form of a host-level daemon (for example, using `systemd`) or a sidecar container running alongside your service container. One important consideration will be budgeting for the resources required to run these sidecars: though it's likely to be a small amount of CPU per service instance, the total cost can quickly add up as you deploy tracing for every service in your application.

Even in a containerized environment, you might consider running only one sidecar per host (for example, using a Kubernetes DaemonSet). This will potentially save on some resources (since you will need to run fewer sidecars) and can help collect better telemetry throughout the service life cycle (running within the same Kubernetes Pod can mean that your tracing sidecar can't observe service shutdown, since it is shut down at the same time). On the other hand, running only one sidecar per host can mean that one noisy service instance on that host can generate so much telemetry that the tracing sidecar is overwhelmed and data from it—and other service instances —is dropped.

Historically, the term "agent" was used to describe processes that interacted more directly—or even were part of—your service instances, often plugging into the runtime of the service itself. While most modern tracing systems use the terms "client" or "SDK" for this sort of functionality, you still might see it in some cases. One reason that many of these systems stopped using this term was that it can be associated with plug-ins that would significantly impact performance, in some cases so much so that it could only be used in staging or QA environments and never in customer-facing production environments. Java's Special Agent was named because it offers many of the advantages of a more traditional agent (primarily that it's easy to install) without the runtime overhead.

Collectors

Span data is often emitted in a format that's not optimized for storage or analysis. At the same time, not all data will be kept in most tracing deployments: most of these spans will not offer enough value, and, as we'll describe in Chapter 6, the costs of doing so are quite high. As such, it's important to perform some translation, sampling, and aggregation of spans. For these reasons, and generally to provide a level of abstraction between the application and the rest of the tracing components, many tracers include a component called a *collector*. What distinguishes a collector from a sidecar or agent is that it's usually running further away from application services and may even run on dedicated hosts or virtual machines (VMs). The function of a collector varies from implementation to implementation, but we will cover some common cases here.

Most in-process libraries and sidecars transmit spans in a way that minimizes performance impact on the service process itself. This usually means minimizing the amount of computation required by the service (since CPU is often the scarcest resource). However, this is often not the most efficient way to transmit spans from the point of view of network consumption, nor is it usually a convenient format for querying, storing, or analyzing spans. One common function of a collector is to translate incoming spans into a format more amenable to these processes. For example, a simple translation would be to compress spans using a generic compression algorithm. Another more domain-specific compression technique would be to create dictionaries of commonly appearing strings (for example, common service and operation names and common tags) and then forward those dictionaries and spans that reference them.

Collectors may accept spans in a number of different formats and translate spans into a single, uniform format. Others may forward spans to multiple tracer systems and possibly even forward spans to these systems in different formats. In cases where the in-process library or sidecar is shared across multiple tracer implementations (as in the case of OpenTelemetry), the collector may be the first component to introduce a tracer-specific format.

Collectors are also often responsible (at least in part) for sampling spans: that is, in implementations where only a subset of spans are processed, collectors are responsible for selecting which spans should be forwarded to other tracer components. There are a number of different ways that spans can be sampled, including uniformly randomly, based on attributes of those spans or other information. In some cases, sampling can be performed either in-process or in a sidecar, but since there is often a need to change the parameters controlling how spans are sampled, moving this functionality to a smaller set of centrally controlled processes can make managing this configuration easier. In other cases, spans must be buffered for a longer period of time before they can be sampled, requiring more memory than would typically be available in a sidecar.

Collectors may also be responsible for computing some aggregate statistics about spans. For example, the spans that are *not* sampled may be accounted for in various ways, including the total number of spans received from a given service, the number of spans where an error occurred or with a given tag key and value, and information about the latency of some or all spans (including median and standard deviation), or even as a histogram.

Computation of these statistics might be too expensive to do within the service process or in a sidecar. These statistics will also be more accurate if they are computed before significant sampling takes place. In all cases, the goal of computing these aggregates is to preserve *some* information about as many spans as possible, while reducing the total amount of data that must be forwarded to other tracer components.

Collectors may be deployed in a number of different ways, depending on what functionality they provide. In some cases, they may require significant resources to store, index, or otherwise process spans. When they do, they'll often be deployed on dedicated hosts (to isolate them from the rest of the application). If they perform significant sampling, it might be beneficial to deploy them on the same network as the application because this can reduce network costs, especially if other tracer components are *not* deployed on the same network (and even if they are still on dedicated hosts).

On the other hand, if a tracer implementation performs few of the kinds of functionality described in this section, this functionality may be built into the sidecar and agent. This is often the case when they store very little state (and especially when that state is specific to a service instance). Doing so simplifies tracer deployment, since there is one less component to deploy.

Centralized Storage and Analysis

Finally, tracers must take these spans (and any other information computed from them) and provide some value to developers. This work is usually performed not just by one component but by a set of components. Together they are responsible for gathering *all* of the tracing telemetry from your application, storing it, analyzing it, and visualizing it in useful ways. The number of components and their function will vary widely based on the tracing implementation you choose. Likewise, how you deploy these components of a tracer will also vary significantly based on this choice.

Tracers may store spans and other data in a variety of ways. Tracers may include databases of spans or traces as well as time series data (including request rates and latency). These storage systems will typically provide at least a few different indices on these spans and time series. They may also include temporary storage of spans that is used during the ingestion process (for example, as a message queue). Tracers will also include components which can search these storage systems, in response to developer queries or automated analyses. In many cases, tracers are used as part of an incident management process, and in those cases, they must be able to answer questions about requests that have occurred in the last few minutes—if not the last few seconds. As such, the process of receiving, storing, indexing, and analyzing traces must also be completed in minutes or seconds after a request is completed. Due to the volume of data, the tracer components that ingest and store data often require significant effort to deploy and maintain.

The most important aspect of these tracer components is that they *centralize* the functionality described earlier: since the whole point of traces is to provide cross-service visibility, some components of the tracer must bring together data from across all services. In most tracer implementations, the in-process libraries, sidecars, and collectors all have only a narrow view of the application, perhaps from one service instance or from a handful of them. It's the role of these centralized storage and analysis components to take whatever data has been forwarded to them and build a unified view of the application and its behavior.

Incremental Deployment

As you begin your journey toward adopting distributed tracing, think about which aspects of the implementation could present the biggest challenges for your organization. Perhaps your organization uses a large number of languages and frameworks; perhaps teams in your organization make similar technology choices, but manage releases using very different processes; perhaps some tracing use cases are much more important than others; or perhaps your organization operates at a scale much larger than most other organizations. Consider what makes your organization different than others, and how these differences might impact choices related to tracing.

Despite all of these potential variations, we can unilaterally endorse the use of open source APIs, SDKs, and libraries. A great deal of effort has gone into building these tools in ways that minimize potential performance impact on your application, while at the same time maximizing your options for other choices about tracer implementations. A number of different open source and commercial tracer implementations work with projects like OpenTracing, OpenCensus, and OpenTelemetry; they make a great choice even if you decide that your best path forward is to build a new tracer from scratch!

Using an open source API and SDK will also enable you to compare tracer implementations very early in the process: the functionality offered by different tracers can vary a lot. As you are making the case for tracing within your organization, make sure that you are using results of specific implementations. As part of that comparison, also make sure that you test at scale: you don't want to find out several months into your project that your favorite tracer can't handle traffic from your production workload.

Also, remember that—at least from your organization's point of view—the adoption of distributed tracing will continue for some time. Make sure that the initial investment in terms of instrumentation and implementation makes sense for both the short- and long-term value that your organization will be deriving from it.

Data Provenance, Security, and Federation

So far, when we've discussed instrumenting your application and deploying a tracer, we made a simplifying assumption that all of the code was under your control. In fact, that code runs in a variety of environments, including not only your datacenter or virtual private cloud but also the phones and computers of your users and the environments managed by any service providers that you might leverage as part of your application. If telemetry is generated by code that runs outside of your control, you should ask additional questions about the quality of that data.

Frontend Service Telemetry

One powerful aspect of distributed tracing is its capacity to tie performance from your frontend services (that is, your mobile app and web clients) together with performance from your backend services, providing a complete view of how your application is working. Capturing telemetry from frontend services lets you measure performance from as close to your users as you can get. However, because of its source, frontend telemetry must be given special treatment in a couple of ways, and in the context of our current discussion, it's important to ask how much you can and should trust it.

Frontend telemetry can be suspect first because of the quality of the platforms themselves. Mobile devices and desktops are notoriously prone to inaccurate clocks; that is, the time reported by a mobile device may be seconds or even minutes different from that reported on your backend servers. This leads to a kind of clock skew where a span reported by a frontend service might look as if it doesn't start until *after* its child span (as reported by a backend service). The top trace in Figure 5-2 shows an example of how this might appear; in the example span A is generated by a frontend service, and the other four spans come from a backend service, including spans B and C, which are child spans of A. While A starts before C (as it should), it appears to start after B, which should not be possible.

There are two common methods to address this problem. First, tracing solutions can attempt to measure this clock skew using adaptations of the Network Time Protocol.[1] This involves recording timestamps both on the tracing library (running as part of the frontend service) and within the tracing implementation, and comparing these timestamps to estimate the clock skew. This skew can then be removed from frontend spans by adding or subtracting it from the timestamps that appear in the span. In our experience, this method is effective most of the time. However, when it does fail (usually due to one of the many uncertainties of running code on a mobile device), the results can be very confusing, and can offer results that are even less accurate than the original timestamps. (It's important to call out when this is happening so that developers can disable it and restore the original timestamps.)

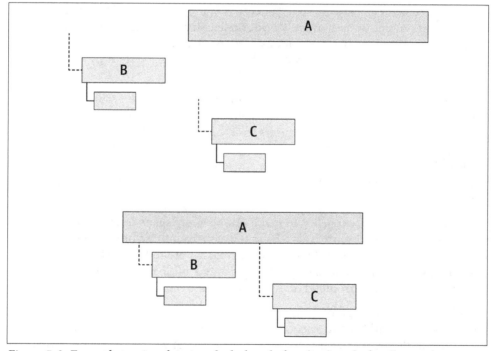

Figure 5-2. Example tracing showing clock skew before (top) and after (bottom) correction.

---

1 [Mil17]

A second method to address clock skew between frontend and backend services is to leverage the causal relationships between client and server spans. By definition a client span *must* start before its associated server span starts. And while it's not always the case, in many applications server spans end before their associated client spans end. Given this, the timestamps in frontend spans can be adjusted to maintain these invariants. Unlike an estimate of clock skew, these adjustments yield more predictable results. However, these adjustments are quite coarse: they don't establish exactly when a frontend span should start, they only put an upper bound on it. As such, it's difficult to distinguish how much network time is consumed by the request as opposed to the response.

In our work on implementing tracing solutions, we've used a combination of these two techniques: we use clock skew estimation to try to build a precise model of performance, but use causal relationships as a check to make sure that these estimates make sense. The bottom trace in Figure 5-2 shows what that same trace might look like after timestamps in A have been corrected.

Frontend telemetry can also be suspect because of the actions of malicious users. That is, these users might try to manipulate your telemetry to disguise performance problems or distract you from other work by creating spans that indicate spurious issues. Malicious users might also try to overwhelm your tracing system by instigating a denial-of-service attack against it.

One course of action that we've observed is to simply ignore the problem. The cost of generating sufficient false telemetry is high enough—and the impact of that telemetry sufficiently low—to discourage any users from carrying out such an attack. Figure 5-3 (A) shows what this might look like: spans are sent directly over the internet to tracing backends, in parallel with requests made to other application backends. Depending on how you are using spans from frontend services, this may be appropriate for your organization.

One variation of this approach is to make sure that any spans from frontend services (that is, from untrusted sources) can be segregated from those originating from backend services. That way, even if your tracing system were to be attacked in some way, you could still be confident that spans originating from *backend* services were accurate (and simply ignore frontend ones until you could put another solution in place).

OpenTelemetry's concept of a "public endpoint" (as discussed in Chapter 4) is another way of marking this sort of trust boundary. By setting that attribute, you're indicating to the tracing system that you don't completely trust the context that was propagated to this point.

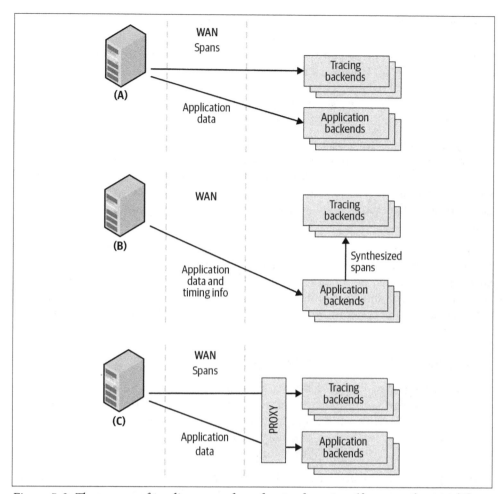

Figure 5-3. Three ways of sending spans from frontend services (for example, a mobile app) to tracing backends.

An alternative to trusting frontend services is to synthesize these spans on the backend. That is, rather than sending spans directly from frontend services, those frontend services send enough data (for example, span start and end times) to the backends that the backends can reconstruct those spans and forward them to the tracing implementation. Figure 5-3 (B) shows what this might look like. (Not shown in the figure are spans sent from the application backends to the tracing system.) This might mean extending the API provided by the application backends, but because such an API is much narrower than a generic tracing API, it limits the kinds of false information that an attacker can provide and also increases the cost of doing so (since the attack must be customized to your application).

This approach also has a couple of other advantages: you might be able to save on the number and size of network requests from frontend services; you can also more easily upgrade the format of your frontend telemetry, since it will only require a backend deployment to do so. However, taking this approach means that when your backends are down, you will receive neither any backend telemetry nor any frontend telemetry. It is also a lot more work, since you are in some ways reimplementing part of the frontend tracing SDK.

Finally, the most secure way to accept spans from frontend services is (perhaps unsurprisingly) to authenticate these requests. For example, you can set up an authenticating proxy that can validate the users from which spans are being sent, as shown in Figure 5-3 (C). In fact, you probably already have one of these proxies, so authenticating telemetry might just be a question of setting up a new route in its configuration.

This approach has a couple of drawbacks: it doesn't work if your application accepts anonymous traffic and it is still possible for an attacker to send spurious data through such a proxy (though it's much harder to do so at scale). And of course, if an attacker compromises your authentication system, they could leverage that to confuse or over-whelm your tracing system…but in that case, you've probably got bigger problems to consider.

Server-Side Telemetry for Managed Services

In some cases, you may now be able to let others take on some of the work of deploying tracing for you: some managed service providers are now starting to emit telemetry describing the services that they provide. This means that you need to manage neither these services nor their telemetry. While this practice is still in its infancy, it's an important step forward for observability.

Managed service providers, whether they offer data storage, data analysis, or integration with other services, are a great way to quickly implement parts of your application or even extend it. And while these service providers probably have an obligation to provide some sort of baseline performance, there can still be variations in this performance that affect your application (positively or negatively). Even if not, it can still be useful to understand how managed service performance is related to the performance of the rest of your application.

Even without the cooperation of service providers, you can instrument your application to provide some visibility into how these services are performing by adding client-side spans to your application. The span labeled GET /<key> shown in Figure 5-4 is an example of this. It's tagged kind: client to indicate that it represents time waiting for an external request to complete. Without any managed service spans, this would be the bottom span in this trace: you'd have no indication of what's happening within this request.

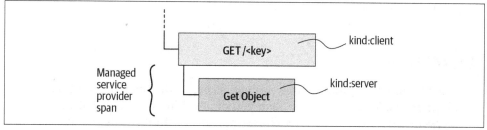

Figure 5-4. An example trace that includes a span from a managed service provider.

However, with managed service spans, you would also see the span labeled `GetObject` (which is also tagged as `kind: server`), as shown in the figure. This can then be used as part of the approaches described in Chapter 8 and Chapter 9, for example, using the difference between the client and service spans to measure the impact of the network on request latency. In fact, this trace looks like any other trace you'll see in this book. Depending on the level of visibility that the service provider is comfortable with, you might also glean some information about how the request was handled.

As with frontend spans, there can be some concerns about trusting the data that comes from devices beyond your organization's control. Since you have an explicit relationship with this service provider, you can probably trust it not to intentionally pollute your data. However, it still would be worthwhile to identify these spans in some way: should a problem occur, doing so will enable you to isolate data from external sources.

There are still several challenges that need to be addressed to make it easy to integrate managed service spans. For example:

- How are spans transmitted to the tracing backends? (Directly from the service provider or not?)

- How is tracing context propagated to the managed service? (As part of request metadata?)

- What naming and other conventions are used for operation names, tags, and other span data?

Ultimately, these are all questions about how to federate tracing. And while these problems existed before (for example, when integrating several open source projects), they are more acute when the software is not only written by different organizations but also *managed* independently. In part, efforts like OpenTelemetry can help address these problems. However, they will also require some standardization (or at least coordination) of tracing solutions as they concern not just the format of the telemetry data but also how it is ingested.

Managed service telemetry is still very new and only available for a handful of services. If you see it, thank your provider…and take advantage of it!

Summary

Properly instrumenting your services is the first step in distributed tracing, and doing so will generate a lot of data, more than you or any other developer has time to look at. Success in distributed tracing requires something to sift through that data and find the insights you need to understand and improve application performance; that's the role of the rest of the tracer implementation.

In this chapter, we considered some of the human factors at play in deploying tracing within a larger organization, as well as a high-level architecture of many tracer implementations. A major factor driving the design of tracers is managing infrastructure costs—computing, network, and storage. We'll dive into these costs and how different tracers handle them in more detail in the next chapter.

CHAPTER 6

Overhead, Costs, and Sampling

Defining the right set of spans to trace to understand your application can be a challenge—though a challenge worth rising to—but once you've done so, you'll find yourself faced with another challenge: managing the torrent of spans as they're emitted from your application. Even when your application is generating data at the right volume, it's still important to understand the impact on the performance of your application and the cost of your computing infrastructure. The first tenet of distributed tracing—like all observability tools—should be to "first, do no harm." Tracing can be implemented in a way that has negligible impact on your application, but managing the cost of the infrastructure can be more difficult.

Not all spans have equal value. Many spans represent run-of-the-mill requests that are (hopefully) bountiful within your application. While it's useful to measure the performance of these requests and perhaps to have a few examples, chances are that just a handful will be sufficient. On the other hand, spans related to a rarely occurring bug or to a small but important user can provide critical insight into what's happening and why.

Above all, it's important that the set of spans representing a single request are preserved as an atomic unit. If only a part of a request is available, then tracing has failed in its goal of providing end-to-end information about what's happening. This means than while many spans might appear to be low value because they represent ordinary cases, they provide context for other less-ordinary spans within the same request.

If not all spans have equal value, then selecting the right spans is crucial to managing costs and making sure you are getting a return on your investment in tracing.

In this chapter, we will make a few assumptions about the architecture of a tracing solution to aid our discussion. Most tracing solutions include most or all of the components shown in Figure 5-1, though they may be implemented in different ways.

First, most tracing solutions include some sort of SDK that enables application developers to create and annotate spans. Some solutions may also include an agent that runs close to application services as a sidecar process or on the same host. A set of collectors begin the aggregation process, while finally spans are analyzed and stored by some central service.

Application Overhead

The first place the cost of tracing can show up is in the performance of the application itself. Ideally, tracing SDKs would have no effect on your application's performance, but without some care, tracing can have an impact on both your application's latency and its throughput.

Latency

Latency, or the time required to process a request, is of utmost importance to application owners: reducing latency is one of the primary metrics that lead developers to look to distributed tracing. However, gathering the data required to build traces can also contribute to latency. Understanding that impact is an important part of choosing the right granularity for spans.

Creating and finishing spans as well as adding tags and logs all can generate latency. High-performance tracers perform only the absolutely necessary work on application threads and move the remaining work to a background thread. Still, building spans often requires additional function calls, allocation, or updates to shared data structures. For example:

- Creating a span might require allocating a new object, adding a reference to the string representing the name of the operation, reading a value from a performance timer, and possibly updating some thread-local state.

- Logging an event may require serializing a data structure into a generic format that can be sent over the network.

- Finishing a span might require reading a value from a performance timer, updating a field in an object, and storing that object in a shared buffer.

Allocating additional objects can certainly have an impact, especially if tracing instrumentation is added to a performance-critical piece of code. In a garbage-collected language, this allocation may trigger a collection which can have further negative impact on latency.

Logging has the greatest potential for impact here as it often involves the greatest amount of data. Best practices for logging mean that an event should be structured: application authors should log each event with a well-defined structure, including field names:

```
span.LogEvent({'request_id': req.id,
        'error_code': 404,
        'message': 'document not in corpus'});
```

However, these events must be converted to a generic format that can be sent over the network to downstream tracer systems. Usually this means that each event is serialized into a single string, often JSON. This requires additional allocation and time to convert integers and other binary data into appropriate representations.

One strategy for reducing the cost of this serialization is to defer this work or move it to a background thread. While attractive, this can have unintended consequences if any of the parameters passed as part of the event are subsequently modified. Consider Example 6-1, where incremental progress is logged as part of a span.

Example 6-1. Incremental progress logged as part of a span

```
status = {progress: 0.1, complete: false};
span.LogEvent({'message': 'work started', 'status': status});
doSomething();
status.progress = 0.2;
```

If the event is not serialized until after the last line of that example, the data that later appears as part of the trace will not reflect the state of the application when LogEvent was called.

Some tracers distinguish between an ordinary event and one which might be serialized out of band. However, application developers often miss this subtle distinction, and many tracers opt for a simple interface where all events may be serialized out of band. As such, many tracer APIs force users to express each field of an event as a scalar value. If that's not the case, best practice is to avoid passing shared, mutable data structures when logging with tracers.

In a multithreaded application, using a shared buffer can become a source of contention as many threads try to add spans to that buffer. This can be mitigated by either batching spans locally before adding them to a shared buffer or by using a lock-free data structure as the implementation of that buffer.

While tracing can contribute to application latency, following best practices usually means that its impact is quite small and might even be too small to be measured. For example, if spans are only created as part of network calls, the latency changes will be in the noise: one additional function call, allocating a handful of bytes, and performing an atomic compare-and-swap instruction are all orders of magnitude faster than making a round-trip RPC, even within a single datacenter. When combining these best practices with reusable buffers and lock-free structures, and moving work to a background thread, most developers can safely ignore the latency impact of tracing even in user-facing production systems.

Performance Impact of Other Kinds of Tracing

Throughout this book, we focus on *distributed* tracing, but there are many other kinds of tracing that developers use to understand applications performance. Kernel tracing and browser tracing are two examples. Many of these techniques and the associated tools focus on a single process, diving deep into the performance of that process. They often provide extremely fine-grained performance data, even down to the level of an individual function or line of code. To provide that level of resolution, these tools integrate tightly with the language complier or runtime and may have significant impact on performance. If enabled in user-facing or large scale deployments, this could result in poor user experience or additional infrastructure costs.

When developers first learn about distributed tracing and how it's being using in production systems, they may be surprised to learn how little effect it has on performance. This is largely due to the granularity of instrumentation: since distributed tracing focuses on events such as interprocess communication, the overhead is negligible when compared to the duration of the events themselves.

Throughput

Tracing can also affect application performance by reducing *throughput*, the number of requests that a fixed amount of infrastructure can handle in a fixed period of time. This can result in increased infrastructure costs, since additional computing power is required to handle the same number of requests. Throughput is often an important concern for high-volume services, where these costs can be significant.

As described in "Latency" on page 118, one of the primary ways that latency impact is managed is by moving work to a background thread. This thread (or threads) is then responsible for serializing span data so that it can be sent downstream. It is also responsible for buffering spans to reduce per-span network overhead as well as retrying failed network requests. As in other contexts, buffering has its trade-offs. A larger buffer trades off-network overhead for increased memory usage. In addition, larger buffers introduce a delay between when events occur in the application and when they can be observed in a tracing tool. Best practices indicate that application events should be reflected in observability tools within one minute: any more delay can mean that developers and operators can't adequately understand whether the changes they are making (for example, rollbacks) are having the desired effects.

For mobile clients, power is another critical resource, and many devices will periodically power down mobile data radios to save power. Tracer SDKs should be careful not to buffer spans for too long in case the radio is powered down in the meantime (and sending those spans would cause it to be powered up again).

Given these concerns about memory and power, and the fact that other parts of the tracing pipeline may also introduce additional delay, most tracer libraries buffer spans for at most a few seconds, usually less than a second. Network costs may also be reduced by maintaining long-lived connections to downstream tracer systems, for example by streaming spans to backends, effectively reducing the delay to nothing while also keeping memory impact low.

Tracers may compress span data to reduce the network costs, though this is another example of trading computing resources for network ones. Often, spans emitted from a single process will share many operation names, tag keys, and even some tag values. For example, a service will generally only serve a static number of endpoints, which in part determine the unique operation names found in the spans emitted by that process. Often spans will include a tag indicating the language or platform, the host, or the datacenter, all of which will be shared by all spans emitted by that process. If these strings are sent only once as part of a request containing many spans, a significant amount of bandwidth can be saved. Tracers may also use a generic compression technique, such as gzipping the entire span buffer, before sending it over the wire. In all of these cases, tracers may incur slightly more computational overhead in exchange for lowering network usage.

Finally, tracer SDKs and agents may also reduce the impact on throughput by only emitting a subset of spans that could be generated. We'll discuss this as part of sampling strategies later in this chapter.

Tracing Overhead at Google

Google's distributed tracing system, Dapper, was built to measure latency in a high-volume distributed system. Many first-time tracing users believe that tracing cannot be used in a production system because the overhead on the application will be too high.

Despite its enormous scale, Google deployed Dapper as part of every web search request. As described in its technical report,[1] it measured the effects on latency and throughput at a variety of different sampling rates. Even when each server is handling tens of thousands of requests per second, Google found that the latency and throughput impact of sampling 1 in 16 requests was within the experimental error. Dapper often sampled more aggressively—not because of the impact on application overhead, but because of the infrastructure costs associated with storing these spans. When running on hundreds of thousands of servers concurrently, even with 1-for-16 sampling, Dapper generated far too much data to store at a reasonable cost.

---

1 [Sig10]

Infrastructure Costs

While the effect of tracing on the application itself can be minimized relatively easily, the cost of the network and storage required to collect, store, and eventually analyze traces is a more significant design and engineering challenge.

We'll walk through a simplified—and in many ways, naive—model to help make these costs more concrete. This is not meant as a guide for analyzing the cost of tracing your application, since it bakes in many assumptions about the size and implementation of an application. Hopefully, however, it gives a sense of the relative scale of the different ways that tracing can affect your infrastructure costs.

Assuming an individual span (including tags and logs) is 500 bytes in size, we can start to estimate these costs by computing the approximate data rate required to trace your application. You can do so based on the number of end-user requests (that is, the number of interactions that your users have with your application) and the number of services in your application (including browser or mobile apps and backend services such as an authentication service, a user database service, or a payment service). For example, if your application serves two thousand end-user requests each second and consists of 20 services, it would generate 20 MB of span data every second or 72 GB every hour.

Network

Tracing solutions aim to move span data away from applications as quickly as possible, both because this helps minimize the impact on the application and because it makes these spans available for analysis (and therefore the source of insights for tracing users) more quickly. As discussed earlier, tracers can trade off some network costs by incurring additional computation, but there are a number of additional design choices to be made in how these spans are collected.

Not all network costs are the same. Network transfer within a datacenter or virtual private cloud (VPC) is typically free, and is usually only limited by the capacity of an individual machine (often around a few GB per second). Sending data out of a VPC, on the other hand, can quickly incur large costs. Sending data within a region or a continent might cost as little as $0.01 per GB, but costs quickly rise when sending data across continents or public networks—by a factor of 10 or even 20. Assuming a cost of $0.10 per GB, a tracer that sends every span over the internet would incur about $173 in network fees per day for our small example application.

As a basis for comparison, even a conservative estimate of the infrastructure required to run the application itself is less than this amount. For example, if we assume that each instance of a service can serve 500 requests per second and that every service participates in every request, 80 VM instances are required. At $0.04 per hour (on-demand prices) these instances would only cost about $77 per day. Again, we are making a number of assumptions about the behavior of an application (and your application's performance might vary by an order of magnitude), but this example shows that the network costs required to send all spans over the internet are on the same scale as the computing costs required to run an application. This is far beyond what most organizations are willing to spend.

Where spans are stored can have a huge impact on cost. Storing them close to the application can reduce these costs, but this can complicate global analysis of traces. Most tracers take a sample of spans to reduce these costs.

Storage

No matter where spans are stored, tracers must store them somewhere. As a baseline, assume you use a simple block storage system (such as AWS S3 or Google Cloud Storage), and your provider charges $0.02 to store 1 GB for a month. Assuming that storing spans for one month is sufficient, the cost of using this solution for storing spans generated by our example application would be about $35 per day.

However, these storage solutions are among the simplest—and cheapest—solutions. Making use of spans requires much more than just storing them: providing functionality to search spans, bulk access for analysis of similar or related spans, and aggregating metrics about groups of spans all require some way of indexing spans once they are stored. These indices of course also require storage and other resources, so this estimate must be seen as the lower bound on what a naive implementation would cost. As in the case of networking resources, most tracing solutions implement some form of sampling to reduce storage costs.

Tracing Costs at Google

Most of the sampling implemented with Dapper was aimed at reducing network and storage costs. The default sampling rate in the process itself was 1 in 1024, and spans were typically reduced by another factor of 10 before traces were stored durably.

Even at these sampling rates, Dapper stored traces in regional repositories to reduce network costs. At the time when Dapper was originally deployed, most requests were handled by a collection of services running within a single region, so all of the spans for a given trace would be generated in a single region. The team was frugal with which attributes could be used to search for spans. While they originally implemented two different indices (one for service and one for host), they found that usage patterns didn't justify the cost of maintaining these indices separately. They later combined these two into a single composite index to bring costs in line with value.[2]

---

2 [Sig10]

Sampling

So far in this chapter, we've discussed the many different costs that a tracing solution might incur. We concluded that if every span of every request was captured, stored, and indexed, the cost of tracing could be greater than the cost of running the application itself.

It is paramount, therefore, that a tracing solution reduce the amount of telemetry data in some way. Tracers use several strategies to do so, but the most widely used and effective is to collect and process a subset of spans by *sampling* them. Almost all significant application behavior will surface in more than one request, so as long as the tracing solution can capture at least one example of each interesting behavior, users can use those examples to find and address bugs and performance problems.

Minimum Requirements

The first and most important consideration when determining how to sample spans is to make sure that the tracing solution is building complete traces. By complete, we mean that if a tracer chooses to capture a given request, it must collect *every* span from that request. Failing to do so means that users will be left with as many questions as they started with.

The trace in Figure 6-1 shows three spans as part of an example of an incomplete trace. These three spans are labeled A (the root of the trace), C (missing parent span B), and E (missing parent span D). From these, the user can possibly infer that the latency is due to C or E, but the three configurations in the figure show there are several possibilities for why C and E were invoked. Their closest common ancestor might be A, B, or D, and each of these possibilities might lead to users taking different actions to understand the causes of slowness. Furthermore, additional spans as children of C or E that did not appear in the trace might describe the ultimate cause of the latency.

Sampling consistently across a distributed system is difficult because, like in many challenges in a distributed system, it requires coordination. Either sampling decisions must be made globally or the tracer component associated with each service must come to the same sampling decision, often by sharing some information about the request. This must be done in an extremely efficient way since it must be done for every request handled by the application.

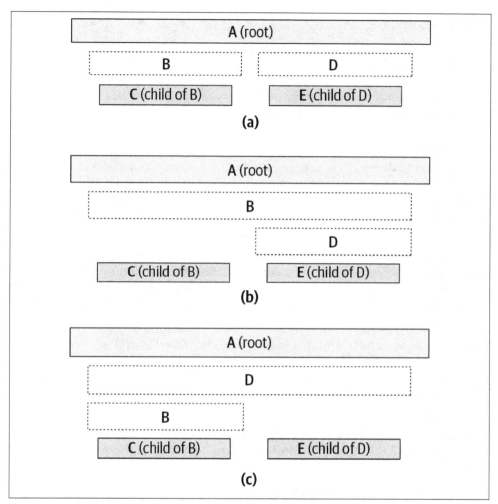

Figure 6-1. An incomplete trace.

Because the cost of sending spans over the network between datacenters is high, sampling decisions must be made in—or very close to—the application: at the very least, the decision must be made before spans leave the datacenter or VPC. This poses an especially large problem for applications that span (no pun intended!) regions or even cloud providers.

Strategies

As sampling is nearly ubiquitous in tracing solutions, it can be useful to classify each solution by the methods and kinds of data it uses to sample traces. Which traces are sampled affects which kinds of analysis can be performed and of course the results of those analyses. Consider which sorts of use cases are most important to you as part of choosing a tracing solution and sampling approach.

Up-front sampling

A simple way to determine which spans to keep is to make sampling decisions before any spans have been generated for a given request. This is often called *up-front* or *head-based* sampling, as the decision is made at the beginning or "head" of the request. In some cases, it is referred to as *unbiased* sampling when sampling decisions are made without even looking at the request.

In its original instantiation, Dapper followed this strategy by flipping a coin at the beginning of each request and passing the result of that coin flip to every other service that participated in the request. With this strategy, each service knows at the moment it begins processing a request whether to capture spans as part of handling that request.

Solutions can vary their sampling rates based on some features of a request. For example, the tracer for a lower-throughput service or endpoint might be configured to use a higher sampling rate. In this case, as a user of a tracing solution, you are essentially writing a set of rules that govern how data is sampled.

Sampling rates can also be varied dynamically to achieve a desired output rate: this enables you to budget for a given amount of infrastructure (mostly network and storage) and to make the most of that infrastructure, regardless of the actual throughput of the application.

Up-front sampling is a strong approach for use cases that only consider traces in aggregate (especially high-throughput services) and for which there is little diversity within the population of traces. Up-front sampling was chosen as part of the implementation of Dapper as Google search requests are both plentiful and relatively homogeneous.

While up-front sampling is both simple and efficient, it suffers from two deficiencies. First, requiring that sampling decisions are passed to every service that participates in the request means there is a high degree of uniformity in the application code. It also requires that the root span of each request can be determined with high confidence. If the result of each coin flip is not propagated properly or if it is inadvertently ignored, incomplete traces will result. At Google, a unified codebase (with a small set of languages and a single RPC framework) was sufficient. In addition, Google also runs a standard set of frontend servers, making it easy to determine where traces should start for nearly all requests.

Second, up-front sampling means that sampling decisions are made with no information about what will happen in the course of handling the request. The parameters of the request itself can be used to inform that decision, but important signals such as the duration of the request or even if the request succeeded are, obviously, not known until after the request has completed. This can be mitigated to some extent by performing the sampling in two stages. A first pass of sampling is made within each service instance to reduce the amount of data to a more manageable level. This partially sampled data can then be forwarded to a centralized solution which—with the advantage of a now complete picture of each request and its response, including latency and response code—can make a second sampling decision. However, if *any* sampling occurs within the service instances themselves (that is, in the first pass), requests with interesting behavior that occur infrequently will be lost. In the next section, we will consider a solution where sampling decisions are made only in a central location.

Response-based sampling

To address many of the shortcomings of up-front sampling, many tracers make each sampling decision based on features of the response or on information derived from the request as a whole, including the response. For example, part of the response may indicate that the request failed. This failure may be used as a trigger to sample this request (since failed requests may be especially valuable in tracking down issues). This strategy is sometimes called *tail-based* sampling since the sampling decision is made at the end or the "tail" of the request.[3]

In addition to errors, response-based sampling may also use the duration of the request as part of making sampling decisions. For example, tracers may set a threshold and keep all (or a significant portion of) traces whose duration exceed that threshold. Response sizes or other application-specific features of responses may also be used as part of making those decisions.

Response-based sampling is significantly harder to implement than up-front sampling. Unlike up-front sampling, whether a span is going to be sampled may not be known until seconds (or more) after the part of the request corresponding to that span has finished. For example, a deeply nested span may be ready seconds before the root span of its trace has finished—and seconds before a sampling decision for that trace can be made. In that case, that child span must be temporarily stored in some

---

3 "Tail-based" can be an especially confusing term for those with a statistics background, as "tail" can refer to the narrow part of an asymmetric distribution. In that case, "tail-based" would mean sampling requests that have a higher latency compared with other requests.

way. This can consume resources from the application (if it's stored locally) or additional network bandwidth (if it's not).

Centralized sampling decisions

Since the purpose of tracing is to construct a *global* view of your application, it shouldn't be surprising that sampling techniques require *global* knowledge of your application. Even passing a single bit from service to service, as in the case of up-front sampling, is a form of global coordination. It follows that as more information is centralized, more sophisticated sampling methods can be applied.

A naive approach where we first centralize all spans and then perform any sampling would, as discussed, be quite expensive. However, we can achieve similar results by first centralizing only *portions of spans*, making sampling decisions using that centralized data, and then communicating those sampling decisions back out so that they can be implemented in a distributed fashion.

The first step in implementing this hybrid approach is to make sure that the spans which are selected are still available at the time that sampling decisions are made. This requires that spans are buffered for at least as long as the duration of the longest request your application is expected to handle. For example, if your application handles interactive search queries that may take as long as 30 seconds, then this buffer must be large enough to hold at least 30 seconds' worth of spans (and probably more) to account for the time it takes to make and communicate the sampling decisions themselves. In other applications, a buffer of five or even 10 minutes might be more appropriate. For the purposes of illustration, assume that the tracer will buffer spans for one minute.

For example, consider two spans that are part of the same trace: span A represents handling an HTTP request and span B represents a database query performed as part of handling that request. In addition, assume that significant additional computation occurs after that database query. Figure 6-2 shows what this trace might look like.

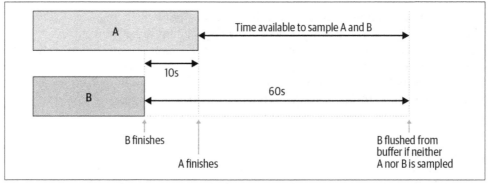

Figure 6-2. A trace with a timeline of buffer events.

In Figure 6-2, span A doesn't finish until 10 seconds after span B finishes. If a property of span A (for example, the response code of the HTTP request) is used to select A as part of the sample, that decision cannot be made until at least 10 seconds after span B finishes. It follows that span B must be kept in the buffer for at least 10 seconds.

Typically, such a buffer is implemented as an in-memory cache in which spans are appended to the buffer as they arrive. Memory is fast and cheap enough to store these spans for a short period of time. Once the size of the buffer reaches its limit, the oldest span is overwritten each time a new span is added. Though these spans could be written to local disk, the additional value of storing them durably is relatively low, and the cost of doing so is usually large enough to make this approach prohibitively expensive.

As the number of spans that are generated in one minute can be quite large, it should be clear that we cannot implement this buffer inside of the service process: the amount of memory required would be large enough to have a significant impact on the service itself. Sometimes the buffer is implemented as a sidecar process or, more commonly, in a separate container or on a dedicated virtual machine (shown in Figure 6-1 as a "collector"). As discussed earlier, for high-throughput applications, this buffer would also need to be located close to the application—within the same datacenter or VPC—to keep network costs under control.

A key part of this approach is to make sure that all spans that are part of a trace can be easily identified. In fact, this was already a requirement, since the spans that make up a trace will arrive from many different sources and as they are collected and analyzed, spans must be sorted into their respective traces. As part of propagating context between processes, each span must have a *TraceID* or other means to identify which trace it belongs to. Tracing solutions can use TraceIDs to indicate which spans should be sampled. Since TraceIDs are much smaller than the spans themselves, and because the number of sampled spans is typically much smaller than the total number of spans, this technique can dramatically lower infrastructure costs. Figure 6-3 shows how part of the flow of spans from collectors to the central analysis and storage components can be replaced with TraceIDs. If some or all trace IDs are forwarded to the central analysis component, these can be sent back to other collectors to ensure that sampling decisions are made consistently.

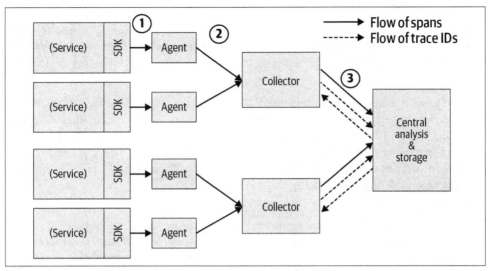

Figure 6-3. An updated collection architecture showing propagation of TraceIDs.

Selecting Traces

Once a tracing solution offers a way to make sampling decisions based on a wide range of request characteristics, we are left with a choice: which characteristics should we use? Since the decision to sample a trace begins with the decision to sample a span (which will eventually become part of that trace), we should choose span characteristics that lead to valuable traces.

As we've mentioned, one approach is to select traces which indicate problems—those traces that are slow or have errors—since these often offer the most actionable information. However, there are a few problems with this approach. First, it is also useful to have healthy requests, which can serve as a baseline for understanding problematic requests. Second, what constitutes "slow" may depend on the operation that the span represents: we might expect certain more expensive operations to generally be slower than others, meaning that fast operations will rarely or never be sampled. Third, though a given span may be tagged with an error, an operation further up the stack may recover from that error, meaning that the trace as a whole is not that interesting.

Rather than selecting spans which are slow relative to all other spans, many tracing solutions focus on spans which are slow relative to other spans for the same service and operation. Similarly, spans that indicate errors at the root of a trace or as the top-level span for a given service are more likely to be of value. As such, tracing solutions may build models of performance for each service and operation, and then select spans (and build traces) relative to these models. In organizations with a few services per team and at most dozens of operations per service, this approach often provides a lot of value to users.

Tracing solutions that take this approach, however, must put some safety mechanisms in place to handle intentional or unintentional misuses of these fields. For example, in our experience building and managing tracing solutions both in-house and as a commercial product, we've seen many examples of other kinds of data leaking into the operation field. In one case, a developer set the operation to the URL of the request, which included a user ID. This led to hundreds of thousands of "operations" and an attempt by the tracing system to capture representative slow traces for every one of them. Obviously, this was both expensive and offered little value to users.

For implementers and power users of metrics tools, this will be a familiar problem: maintaining state for each element of a high-cardinality set is expensive. As a result, tracing solutions that attempt to find interesting examples for each service and operation should include a safeguard such as choosing only the most commonly occurring operations, up to some limit. In fact, once such a safeguard is implemented, it can be applied to arbitrary tags, enabling the tracing solution to capture representative samples for a wide range of traces.

Once you've chosen what sorts of characteristics make a span (and therefore, a trace) interesting, you're left only with the choice of how frequently to sample them. This choice can largely be driven by costs: set a budget for infrastructure costs, then configure your tracing solution to periodically sample as many traces as can fit into that budget.

In addition, you may also consider selecting traces based on some external events, such as when a new release is pushed out or when some production configuration is changed. Service failures are often caused by changes to one or more parts of an application, and ensuring that you have traces to help explain what's happening during these failures can be invaluable. The moment when a failure is known to have occurred—for example, when an alert fires—is also an excellent opportunity to capture a number of traces.

As with all biased sampling, it's important that tracing tools account for bias when computing statistics about latency, error rates, or other aspects of application performance. For example, if your tracing solution biases toward slower requests, it's critical that these requests get *less* weight if they are used to compute the average latency for your service.

Off-the-Shelf ETL Solutions

Can off-the-shelf extract-transform-load (ETL) tools be used to implement the ingestion portion of a tracing solution? While it is certainly possible to do so, most generic ETL tools are built to process data that is much more homogeneous. As we've discussed, not all spans provide the same value: spans which are slow or have errors may provide important clues to improving performance. Likewise, ordinary spans that are part of the same trace as a slow span (or a span that failed) may also provide helpful context. In addition, the true value of a span might not be known until sometime after it is collected by a tracing solution, seconds or even minutes later. Many ETL tools expect that each piece of data can be processed independently or that collections can be processed uniformly, and therefore are not a good fit for distributed tracing.

Unsurprisingly, generic ETL solutions also offer less flexibility for trading off different sorts of resources (for example, network versus storage). In our experience, using a generic solution for the collection typically will require an order of magnitude more infrastructure resources than a solution built specifically for tracing.

On the other hand, once spans have been sampled and grouped together into traces, there are many opportunities to use off-the-shelf tools to analyze and store them. Though detailing it is beyond the scope of this book, many of the use cases described in Chapters 7 and 8 can be implemented using off-the-shelf tools.

Other Approaches to Reducing Data Volume (and Therefore Costs)

One of the main challenges in building a tracing solution is managing costs: sifting through spans to find information that will be valuable to users without doubling your storage or network bills. Though we have focused on sampling as the main technique for reducing data volume—and therefore managing costs—there are other techniques that tracing solutions can also take advantage of.

It might typically be considered out of scope for a tracing solution, but gathering statistics about spans is a powerful way to derive some information from a set of spans without recording every detail of that set or even of a single span. The rate that a given operation occurs at, the frequency of specific tag values, or a histogram of latency for a class of spans can all be represented efficiently (often requiring less space than a single span) and can offer powerful insights into what's happening in an application.

Similarly, once a trace has been sampled, you need not store every detail of that trace. Often just knowing which operations were on the critical path (and how much each contributed) or the presence of certain interesting tags can be valuable. If this information can be extracted before traces are stored durably—and the trace itself discarded—storage costs can be significantly reduced.

Summary

Like other observability tools, distributed tracing tools must minimize the impact they have on application performance. Fortunately, there are straightforward ways of doing this: even at scale, tracing can be implemented in a way that has very little overhead on the application itself, meaning that it's safe for you to use tracing in your production environments. This is important because it is difficult to reproduce many failures and other issues outside of production in distributed systems—and increasingly, in almost any modern application. Using tracing in production will enable you to find these issues much more quickly,

While the impact on the application is small, the cost of processing and storing trace data can be large. The value of traces is often in the details they provide, whether following requests across services or in the tags and events associated with spans. A trace can become much larger than the request and response that it describes, so storing every trace would be expensive from an infrastructure point of view. However, not all trace data offers the same value. Traces representing slow or failed requests may offer a lot more value. Sampling a subset of traces (and discarding the rest) is a commonly used technique to make sure you are collecting the right traces while keeping costs under control.

As either an implementer or a user of a tracing solution (or both), you should be aware of different sampling techniques, including when sampling decisions are made and, most importantly, what information is used to inform those decisions. Different techniques will offer different performance trade-offs and provide better support for different sets of use cases.

Since tracing takes a request-centric view of observability, it offers an opportunity to serve as the backbone for other types of telemetry, including metrics and logs. Tracing can help ensure you are maximizing the value of all of your observability tools by putting telemetry data in context. In Chapter 7, we'll focus on what you should expect from observability tools in general and how tracing relates to—and can amplify the benefits of—these other tools.

A New Observability Scorecard

Engineers at organizations like Google and Twitter originally promoted observability as a method not just for *monitoring* their production systems but for being able to *understand* the behavior of those systems using a relatively small number of signals. Borrowed from control theory, the term *observability* formally means that the internal states of a system can be inferred from its external outputs. This became necessary within these organizations as the complexity of their systems grew so large—and the number of people responsible for managing them stayed relatively small—that they needed a way to simplify the problem space. In addition, as part of site reliability engineering (SRE) organizations, many of the engineers that were responsible for observability were not working on the software directly, but on the infrastructure responsible for operating it and making it reliable. As such, a model for understanding software performance from a set of external signals was appealing and, ultimately, necessary.

Despite a formal definition, observability continues to elude the understanding of many practitioners. For many, the term is equated with the tools used to observe software systems: metrics, logging, and (as will come as no surprise to the reader) distributed tracing. These three tools became known as the "three pillars of observability," each a necessary part of understanding system behavior. Though often implemented as separate tools, they are usually used in conjunction as part of an observability platform.

Metrics, logging, and tracing tools are built around three different corresponding data sources, and are often compared based on what can be effectively or efficiently derived from each of those data sources. In the end, however, users are more interested in what they can learn from an observability tool than where the data came from.

Users turn to observability tools to understand the relationships between causes and effects in the distributed systems. That is, they are usually more interested in what can be accomplished with a tool than how it works or where the data comes from. In this chapter, we'll look at the three pillars of observability in turn, consider their limitations, and build a framework for assessing observability tools in general.

The Three Pillars Defined

Before examining the trade-offs and alternatives, it's useful to understand these three observability tools as they are most often deployed today.

Metrics

Metrics, broadly defined, are collections of statistics about services that enable developers and operators to understand the gross behavior of those services and how they are being used. Examples include request rate, average duration, average size, queue size, number of requests, number of errors, and number of active users.

These values are usually captured as time series, so that operators can see and understand changes to metrics over time. Changes can then be correlated to other coincident events, which in turn can indicate what corrective actions to take.

In today's production environments, metrics are typically aggregated every minute or even six to twelve times per minute. To enable operators to react quickly enough to maintain three—or even four or more—"nines" of uptime, metrics must be aggregated and visualized within at most one minute but ideally even more quickly.

Metrics and Service Level Indicators

The authors of *Site Reliability Engineering* describe how to measure the level or quality of service provided by a service or application in terms of service level indicators (SLIs).[1] As a quantitative measure of service levels, SLIs are a subset of metrics and, like other metrics, will typically be measured as a time series. Examples of SLIs include some the examples given in this chapter, including request duration (or latency) and error rate.

Of course, there are many other types of metrics and often the same tools will be used to measure both SLIs and non-SLI metrics. This can lead to some confusion on the part of users of these tools: while SLIs should be measured and compared with your service level objectives (SLOs), other metrics are not things that you should be optimizing (unless doing so helps you meet one of your SLOs). As such, we encourage readers to label dashboards and the metrics clearly as SLIs in cases where they are, in fact, indicators of service levels.

---

1 [Bey16]

To help developers and operators understand more about changes to metrics, developers add *labels* as they record metrics. Typically in the form of a key-value pair, each label describes the circumstances of the change to the metric more specifically. For example, request latency may be labeled with the version of the service handling the request, the host on which the request is handled, or the datacenter in which the host was running.

Using labels, a metric such as latency can broken down into submetrics, one for (say) each host. This can enable an operator to pinpoint problems, for example, by establishing that an overloaded host is responsible for slow requests.

Types of metrics: Counters and gauges

Most metrics fall into two categories: counters and gauges. *Counters* are values which describe, well, the number of events of a particular type that have occurred. Examples include the number of requests and the number of bytes transferred. From a developer's point of view, the primary operation associated with a counter is to *increment* it.

Counters can be manipulated in several ways. For example, it's easy to aggregate changes to a counter from multiple sources, simply by adding them together. From a counter, it's also easy to compute a rate of change by considering the values of a counter at different points in time. For example, though recorded as a counter, the number of requests is usually visualized as a rate, such as requests per minute or requests per second.

Gauges are metrics that describe the state of a part of your software as a numeric value and at a particular moment in time. Examples include the duration of a request, the size of a queue, or the current number of active users. From a developer's point of view, the primary operation associated with a gauge is to describe its current value (or *set* it).

Gauges are somewhat more challenging than counters to aggregate, as doing so necessarily discards information. When combining gauge values from several sources, metrics systems capture statistics about them, including average, minimum, and maximum.

Gauges' values may also be combined using histograms. The range of values can be divided into discrete buckets, and the number of instances in each bucket can be recorded. This effectively turns gauges into counters (or, more precisely, into a *set* of counters), which can then be easily combined by simply adding together the counts for each bucket. Histograms are useful in that other statistics may be derived from them. For example, using bucket counts, a metrics tool can estimate the 99th-percentile value of a gauge.

Metrics tools

The challenges of implementing metrics tools stem largely from how to aggregate data. What is the window across which values are aggregated? How are the windows from different sources aligned?

Logging

Logging can describe any activity where systems capture events as text or structured data and either print these events out or store them for future use and analysis. In the context of observability, logging usually means *centralized* logging, where event data from each service instance is transmitted to a single system so that it can be analyzed and searched uniformly.

To support this collection and analysis, log entries must have a timestamp that indicates when the event occurred. Aside from that, however, there is usually little standard structure to logs. While there are standard schema for some specific use cases (for example, web server logs), as an observability tool, log structure will depend on how it's used by the application and how logs are created by developers.

Example 7-1 shows an example of logging in Java (using Log4j).

Example 7-1. Java logging example

```
import org.apache.logging.log4j.Logger;
import org.apache.logging.log4j.LogManager;

...
Logger LOGGER = LogManager.getLogger();
LOGGER.info("Hello, world!");
```

Similarly, Example 7-2 shows an example of logging in Go.

Example 7-2. Go logging example

```
import "log"
import "bytes"

...
buf bytes.Buffer
logger = log.New(&buf, "logger: ", log.Lshortfile)
logger.Print("Hello, world!")
```

Logging conventions

Partly due to the volume of data produced through logging, there are a few conventions in common use. First, most logging systems support some notion of a "level" or "severity." Typical examples of levels include "informational," "warning," and "error."

These can be used as part of an automatic or manual filtering process. For example, a logging tool may only keep info-level logs for a few hours, but might store errors forever.

A second common convention is to add some correlation ID or other means to create links between related log entries. In a distributed system, this is often used to trace requests as they pass from one service to another. For example, all logs related to a single end-user request may include a unique identifier for that request.

Defined in the broadest sense, even a summary of logging tools would be far beyond the scope of this section or chapter: logging is used for a wide range of use cases, such as revenue tracking, security auditing, and business metric tracking. To give a sense of what these tools look like as part of an observability suite, we'll briefly describe a common implementation using Elasticsearch, Logstash, and Kibana (often called an "ELK stack").

In an ELK stack, log data is generated by many different sources—including server logs, event APIs and streaming publish-subscribe (pub-sub) systems, to name a few—and fed into Logstash. Logstash transforms these log entries by providing additional structure and normalizing data across different sources. The results are then forwarded to Elasticsearch where they are indexed so that they can be searched easily. Finally, Kibana is an analysis and visualization tool used to build dashboards based on the data stored in Elasticsearch.

The primary challenge of implementing a logging tool is storing the data in a way that is cost-effective and will allow the data to be searched efficiently. Most log entries will be of little value, but finding the log which contains a rare error or a suspicious transaction will have tremendous value. A specific type of search is to find all of the logs associated with a single request.

Distributed Tracing

After the previous chapters, hopefully you have some sense of the purpose, scope, and implementation of distributed tracing. For the purposes of this chapter, it's useful to define distributed tracing as it was implemented as part of Google's Dapper project.[2] Using this definition, distributed tracing consists of collecting request data from the application and then analyzing and visualizing this data as traces.

Tracing data, in the form of spans, must be collected from the application, transmitted, and stored in such a way that complete requests can be reconstructed. In Chapters 5 and 6, we discussed the high-level architecture of distributed tracing implementations and some challenges of these implementations. As with centralized

---

2 [Sig10]

logging systems, many of these challenges are associated with transmitting and storing large amounts of data. In some ways, tracing is a specialized form of logging that attempts to address these costs by tightly coupling the collection process to application request handling. As tracing tools are often focused on use cases around performance analysis, they build in some common fields that describe the timing of application events (for example, request duration).

As visualization tools, distributed tracing tools often show requests using a flame graph (or, when presented upside down, an icicle graph) or a tree showing the timing relationships between spans.

The current practice of distributed tracing being part of distributed systems software development stems largely from the Dapper project at Google and the subsequent OpenZipkin and Jaeger projects (from Twitter and Uber, respectively). Many other organizations have deployed the open source tools OpenZipkin and Jaeger.

All of these tools combine some SDK or agents with a collection pipeline and a storage system (usually off-the-shelf) to store and process the data. In the case of Dapper, this storage system was BigTable, while OpenZipkin and Jaeger can be deployed using Cassandra, Elasticsearch, or even (for OpenZipkin) MySQL.

Though not billed as "distributing tracing," many application performance management (APM) tools provide functionality that overlaps with distributing tracing and may include traces as part of that. However, because they take a simpler approach to data collection, they often fail to provide good results for large distributed systems. In particular, they may not be able to pass through context or may need to use a very small sample to avoid adversely affecting performance (leading to broken traces or other missing data).

The challenges of implementing and deploying a tracing solution depend largely on the use cases you are considering. As Dapper was focused primarily on long-term performance optimization, the primary challenges were related to managing the costs associated with transmitting and storing traces, largely due to Google's scale. In organizations with more heterogeneous development environments, just getting span data from the application in a way that can be used to generate complete traces can be a significant challenge.

Fatal Flaws of the Three Pillars

As we've considered each of these types of tools in turn, we've discussed some challenges in implementing each in ways that are effective and efficient. However, it's useful to consider the challenges and limitations of these tools in a more systematic and holistic way. Doing so will enable us to better understand the trade-offs in building, operating, and using these tools. It will also challenge the notion that they are really three separate and independently defined categories of tools.

Design Goals

When designing an observability solution as a whole, there are three areas that we should consider. These areas are broader than any specific use cases and instead focus on how value is derived from a solution and how that value relates to cost. For any solution, we should be able to assess how it performs in each of these areas:

- Does it account for every transaction? If so, then the impact of every transaction can be measured using the solution.
- Is it immune to cardinality issues? If so, the solution allows users to analyze arbitrary subsets of transactions.
- Does its cost grow proportionally with business value? If so, as the volume of business grows, the cost of the observability solution grows proportionally.

Accounting for every transaction

An observability solution accounts for all of the data if even the rarest events can be observed. This includes, for example, infrequent errors or the behavior of the smallest of customer segments. Solutions that sample transactions may miss these rare but still valuable events.

Immunity from cardinality issues

An observability solution is immune to cardinality issues if users can ask questions about and compare behaviors for arbitrary subsets of the data. *Cardinality* means the number of different elements in a set, and in the context of observability, *cardinality* refers to the number of different labels (or equivalently, tags) present on data points. *Cardinality issues* means the challenges of managing and querying data with many different labels. For example, can a user compare performance data between service instances running on two different hosts? When there are dozens of hosts? Hundreds? Thousands? Can performance data be further broken down by software version? Can we compare performance across customer segments or even among individual customers? Solutions that aggregate data before these questions are asked may miss opportunities to answer them; if the data is not aggregated, it may incur high resource costs.

Cost growing proportionally with business value

An observability solution's cost grows proportionally with business value if its cost per transaction stays constant even as the number of transactions increases. In the case of modern distributed systems, including microservice- or serverless-based architectures, developers may add new observability data sources as they add new services or functions; each of these will create more data and therefore cost more, even as the number of transactions stays fixed. However, in doing so, the observability solution now consumes a larger portion of the value of each such transaction.

Assessing the Three Pillars

With these design goals in hand, we can succinctly evaluate each of the three pillars of observability, as shown in Table 7-1.

Table 7-1. Fatal flaws of the three pillars, summarized

	Metrics	Logs	Distributed tracing
Accounts for every transaction	✓	✓	-
Immune to cardinality issues	-	✓	✓
Cost grows proportionally	✓	-	✓

Fatal flaws in metrics

It is straightforward to build a metrics tool that accounts for every transaction: statistics like count, mean, and standard deviation can be easily computed in a distributed fashion. Moreover, the cost of doing so is modest since the amount of data that must be transmitted and stored is small and, in fact, constant with respect to the number of transactions.

However, the cost of processing and storing metrics increases with the cardinality of the dataset. That is, as the number of different labels grows, and more importantly, as the number of *combinations* of different labels grows, the cost of managing these statistics increases significantly: the number of values that must be maintained grows exponentially with the number of different labels.

For example, suppose that a metrics tool is capturing request counts from five different hosts, and that each request is labeled with all of the following:

- Its hostname
- The response class (no error, not authorized, bad request, server unavailable, or internal error)
- The client host from which the request was issued (say that there were also five)

Using these labels, metrics can then be used to answer questions such as:

- Which host served the most requests?
- Which host served the most internal errors?
- Which client host made the most bad requests?

To answer all of these (and other arbitrary) questions about request counts, a metrics tool must aggregate $5 \times 5 \times 5 = 125$ different counters. This small example might not seem prohibitively costly, but in real-world use cases, there might be dozens of different dimensions across which a user might want to examine behaviors and hundreds or thousands of different values for each of these dimensions. Tracking millions or billions of different combinations is prohibitively costly. As a result, most metrics solutions limit the number of different label combinations that you can track. While these solutions can be powerful tools for understanding *when* something has gone wrong, they are not as useful for understanding *why* something has gone wrong.

Fatal flaw in logging

Centralized logging solutions account for every transaction by definition: they record every event as a log entry. Moreover, they are generally immune from cardinality issues as the cost of storing each new event is proportional only to the size of that event (and not the number or content of previous events). Unlike metrics, there is no hidden cost in adding labels, tags, or other structure to individual logs. While there is some cost in maintaining indices of log data (to enable users to find relevant entries), search engines such as Google have developed a number of techniques for searching extremely large datasets efficiently using arbitrary queries. Many of these techniques can be applied to log data.

However, while this cost is predictable, it is not small in aggregate nor is it scalable for an organization adopting microservices, serverless, or other distributed architectures. For logging to explain problems with an individual transaction, it must surface *all* of the logs associated with that transaction. That means, even for a fixed number of transactions, adding to a system's complexity (for example, by adding a new service) will increase the cost of logging even if the number of transactions remains constant.

As a result, developers are often discouraged from adding verbose logging to applications, and in most cases logging may be severely curtailed or even disabled in production environments to save on cost. This is particularly problematic as there can be significant value in some of these production logs since many performance problems only emerge at scale or in the context of hard-to-predict customer behavior.

Fatal flaws in distributed tracing

Because distributed tracing tools are built from the ground up to support distributed applications, maintaining complete records of individual transactions (including across services) is a primary capability. As such, it's easy to control costs simply by changing the fraction of transactions for which traces are transmitted and stored. Dapper showed that sampling an extremely small portion of transactions—as few as 0.1% or even 0.01%—still has tremendous value for understanding performance and driving optimization work. If new services are added in a way that significantly increases the number of spans, the sampling rate can simply be turned down. And like logging, there are no issues with adding high-cardinality tags or other annotations to spans.

However, this sampling has a critical downside: it's no longer possible to reconstruct a complete picture of application performance from these samples. Nor is it possible to examine types of transactions that occur rarely. For example, if an operator is trying to understand 99.9th-percentile latency performance, the chances of 1-in-10,000 sampling finding helpful examples is vanishingly small.

As such, distributed tracing is often used as a tool to *explain* gross performance problems rather than determining when they are occurring. And while it can be quite valuable for high-volume applications with relatively homogeneous users (like Google), it doesn't offer many advantages over centralized logging for lower-value applications, nor does it help provide visibility into small user segments or infrequently occurring errors.

Three Pipes (Not Pillars)

The reader may be asking some questions about our framing of the problem at this point: for example, why define distributed tracing as a technique that must use some form of sampling? Why require that metric time series be computed in advance and stored as separate streams? You are absolutely correct to be asking such questions! While implementers of these tools have each focused on optimizing for specific use cases, in fact, they are not really three separate tools but three different *techniques* for collecting and managing telemetry data.

If we instead view these three techniques as *pipes*—three ways of transmitting and storing data—rather than three separate pillars, there are many opportunities to answer interesting and valuable questions at a reasonable cost. While it is far beyond the scope of this chapter to describe the design of a unified observability platform, the following examples show how metrics, logging, and distributed tracing *data* can be used to provide functionality usually associated with one of the other pillars:

- Logs may be visualized as traces. In cases where each entry is tagged with *transaction* or *request identifier* (sometimes called a *correlation ID*), it's straightforward to describe a query to find all of the logs associated with an individual transaction. If the logs also contain request latency (or if pairs of logs can be used to infer latency) then they can be visualized as a flame (or icicle) graph.

- Time series may be derived from spans. For example, the durations of spans may be extracted either as they are generated or after the fact and then displayed as a time series of latency. (If sampling is used, then the results must be scaled appropriately.) Other metric time series can also be derived from tags as they occur in spans.

- Logs may also be extracted from spans. In cases where volume is sufficiently low, span annotations can be extracted and centralized with other logs.

- Metric time series may be computed from logs. For example, Facebook's Scuba database ingests (and stores) millions of events per second and then lets users query and view metrics derived from these events as time series.[3]

- Changes to metric counters or gauges can be added as span annotations. While metrics are usually aggregated very close to the source to reduce the cost of transmitting and storing them, associating changes to spans offers additional possibilities in how they are analyzed.

While these three different ways of organizing observability data present many tradeoffs, we shouldn't ask users to commit to these tradeoffs as part of selecting tools: these are the concerns of tool implementers. At the same time, as users of observability tools we will ultimately pay for these choices. As we will discuss in the next section, we must first approach the problem from the point of view of the outcomes we want to achieve. Only then can we adequately assess which tools are required and how well they are performing.

Observability Goals and Activities

The fragility of the three pillars is perhaps unsurprising. It is a trio of convenience: there is no fundamental law of nature that requires there to be *exactly three* observability tools. Despite this, the three pillars are often used as a checklist for infrastructure teams whose responsibility is to provide tools to the rest of their organizations. Unfortunately, it is quite possible to deliver suitable implementations of all three pillars but still leave gaps in the observability platform. That is, developers and operators may not be able to understand the behavior of their applications and services despite having metrics, logging, and tracing tools, because even together, those tools often do not achieve the primary goals of observability.

Two Goals in Observability

There are ultimately only two goals in using any observability tool:

- Improving baseline performance
- Restoring baseline performance (after a regression)

By *improving* baseline performance, developers hope to improve user experience, lower infrastructure costs, or both. For user-facing applications, performance often

---

3 [Abr13]

means request latency, though it might also include other, longer transactions. This sort of optimization is a process usually undertaken over the course of days, weeks, or even months.

Observability tools are critical for improving baseline performance first in measuring that performance (that is, in establishing the baseline) and then by directing developers toward the parts of their software where they can be more effective in improving performance. With a monolithic application, developers may simply use a CPU profiler to understand which parts of the application are taking the most time. In a distributed system, it's often unclear when slow parts of a request are actually impacting user experience. We will consider examples in Chapter 9 that show how distributed tracing is critical in determining how to plan and execute work in improving baseline performance.

In contrast to the planned work behind improving baseline performance, *restoring* baseline performance is, almost by definition, unplanned. Regressions in performance, including application outages, can result in a loss of revenue, negatively impact the brand, and degrade user trust. As such, regressions occurring in production systems must be corrected as soon as possible. Depending on your organization's service level goals, you may have only minutes to detect, understand, and mitigate performance regressions.

Observability tools are also critical in restoring baseline performance. Often problems in one service may not be detected in that service itself but still negatively affect the performance of other services. (This can be true when both services are managed by the same organization or when they are managed by two different ones.) As we discuss in Chapter 9, distributed tracing is also critical in effectively and quickly responding to performance regressions.

Two Fundamental Activities in Observability

While improving and restoring baseline performance might feel like very different kinds of goals, they are both based on the same two fundamental activities:

- Measuring the impact of performance on users
- Explaining variation in those measurements

To some users of monitoring tools, especially infrastructure- and network-monitoring tools, it might come as a surprise to see such a narrow definition of what we care about: that we focus only on the impact on *users*. There are hundreds of other types of measurements that could describe the behavior of a production software system: from host, storage, and network utilization, to queue sizes, open connections, and garbage collector overhead and many other types of performance.

In the case of improving baseline performance, if you are *not* working on something that will improve the performance as observed by your users (or reduce cost), well, you are wasting your time. And if you just got woken up at 3 a.m. for something that is *not* impacting your users, you should have a few words with the rest of your team about what constitutes an urgent alert!

While we're strict about measuring performance impact *on users*, we're less so about what exactly "performance" means in this context. Generally, any behavior of the software that users might notice is worth measuring: not just request latency but quantitative user experience and even correctness can all be considered types of performance.

Focusing on user impact is closely related to the mantra of "alerting on symptoms rather than causes." And of course, your tools should measure all these other potential causes, but as a user of observability tools, you need concern yourself with them only inasmuch as they assist you in the second fundamental activity: explaining variations in user-impacting performance. The danger of looking too closely at all of these other metrics is that many of them may describe problems that will distract you from more important work: in any production system of reasonable scale, there are always dozens—if not hundreds—of things going wrong, but (hopefully) only a small fraction of them are impacting your users at any given time.

As a concrete example of this kind of distraction, consider the giant dashboards that can be seen in operations centers or on the monitors of many on-call engineers. Filled with rows and rows of time series, these dashboards capture many signals that might tell an operator what is going wrong.

Even—and perhaps especially—during a user-impacting incident, these dashboards often will show many graphs that are changing simultaneously: when something is going wrong, it will often affect many different aspects of performance. However, these graphs are merely showing *correlated* failures and not bringing you any closer to the cause of the problem. While there may be one or two people on your team who can look at these sorts of dashboards and infer the root cause of the problem, it doesn't bode well for the team if these people ever go on vacation.

Worse, many members of your team may look at these dashboards and assume that they are exhaustive: that they include *every* possible explanation for the cause of a problem. After all, they were built by smart, experienced people! This can lead to the assumption that, if the dashboard can't explain the problem, it must be a "networking glitch" or another problem that can't be explained, and therefore shouldn't be investigated. Unfortunately, today's software systems are too complex and too dynamic for developers—even seasoned ones—to anticipate every possible cause.

While variation in performance is often first described as a time-dependent phenomena ("our service started slowing down at 5:03 p.m." or "error rate jumped at 11:30

a.m."), time is merely a proxy for some other precipitating event, whether that be a new release of your service, a change in one of your service's dependencies, or another change to the environment.

It's critical that observability tools measure performance in ways that let these events be distinguished from each other. This is the root of the requirement around cardinality discussed earlier: the ability to compare performance across releases, hosts, clients, or other dimensions that can impact that performance.

The number of signals that can *explain* performance variation is orders of magnitude larger than the number of ways that performance can impact users. While a typical application might only measure a handful of ways that users can be affected, there can easily be thousands or even tens of thousands of explanations for why users are being impacted. The problem is not a signal-to-noise problem (where there is a lack of information) but a too-much-signal problem: there are just too many data sources, each of which will probably help to explain a performance problem at some point, even if they are not helpful in explaining today's problem.

We seem to still be rather far from the point where tools can automatically pinpoint the root cause of a performance problem. As such, the role of an observability tool in explaining variation is often to help *narrow the search space*. This can take the form of providing suggestions as to what likely causes might be. It can also mean allowing developers and operators to interactively query data in such a way that they can form hypotheses and then build evidence to support or repudiate them.

Explaining performance variation leads us to the purpose of an observability tool: to take action to improve performance. The type of variation will lead to the type of action to be taken. If slow requests are associated with a new release, that release should be rolled back; if slow requests are all occurring on the same compute node, a new node should be provisioned to augment or replace the old one. Ultimately, being able to explain variation in performance will enable you to control the impact on your users.

A New Scorecard

With these goals and activities in mind, we are now in a better position to think about the trade-offs of metrics, logging, and distributed tracing and to judge the efficacy of an observability platform in general. We will do so looking at how solutions address each of the activities described earlier.

First, to help users measure the impact of performance on users (or put another way, to measure symptoms), observability tools should be judged on the following characteristics:

- Statistical fidelity
- Cardinality limits
- Volume limits
- Time limits

While no tool can provide perfect fidelity with no limits (and at reasonable cost), striking the right balance between these is critical to providing value.

Second, to help users explain variations in these measurements, observability tools must be able to help quickly narrow the search space of possible explanations. While there is no fixed set of ways to do that, there are some high-level approaches that observability tools can take to facilitate this:

- Providing context
- Prioritizing by impact
- Automating correlation

These are more qualitative than the ways we can judge how well observability tools measure impact. They are outlined later in this chapter and will be described in more detail in the context of specific use cases in subsequent chapters.

Statistical fidelity

By fidelity, we mean that when summarizing the behavior of a large population of requests, observability tools maintain enough information to understand the overall "shape" of the behavior, often shown using histograms.

Statistics like mean and standard deviation are great tools for summarizing behaviors that follow normal or other simple distributions. However, software measurements like latency are rarely normal—they often have long tails—and are often multi-modal. For example, request latency will often have multiple modes based on whether required data can be found in a cache. When trying to understand or improve latency, it's important to understand whether the current objective would be best served by increasing the number of cache hits or improving the latency of a cache miss.

Histograms provide a simple visual way of capturing these discrete behaviors and understanding their relative frequency. Histograms can also be used to derive statistics such as different percentiles.

High-Percentile Latency

While they are certainly more difficult to measure than other statistics (such as count, mean, or standard deviation), high-percentile measurements are critical for understanding and improving performance, particularly in the case of request latency. As such, it's best practice to measure not just mean latency, but also the latency of the slowest requests, such as the 95th, 99th, or even 99.9th percentile.

In a distributed system, the combinatorics of fanning out a request across hundreds of services means that, while only 1% of requests to an individual service may be slow, the chances of these slow requests impacting users may be much higher.

More qualitatively, those users experiencing the slowest 1% of requests can act as bellwethers for the rest of your user-base. These are often expert users who are pushing the limits of your system. As the data volume grows or the complexity of user interactions increase, many more users may experience larger latencies.

Cardinality limits

The ability to break down performance across different dimensions is at the core of explaining variation. As such, an observability solution must be able to ingest and analyze data with many different labels or tags that represent these dimensions. While there will likely be some limits on the cardinality of the data, observability solutions should be measured on their capacity to use labels, tags, and other metadata to explain variation in performance.

Volume limits

An observability solution's volume limits are defined by how many events can be captured every minute and how much detail can be captured with each event. In cases where not all events are captured, what mechanisms are used to select events (that is, to sample them)? The processes used to select events can affect which are available for subsequent analysis as well as what statistics inferences can be drawn from the sample.

Time limits

Not all observability can (or should) be kept forever. The amount of history that an observability solution stores is sometimes called its *horizon*. Depending on the use case, different horizons may be appropriate. In the case of validating a new release, hours or maybe days of data will be sufficient. Measuring the impact of a quarter-long optimization project will obviously require a longer horizon. Infrastructure capacity planning might require a year or more of data to account for a business's seasonality.

The other important aspect of time is how soon a request is reflected in measurements and analysis. As part of restoring baseline performance for a highly available service, it's critical that measurements be made within a minute or less. For other use cases, processing data as part of a daily or weekly batch may be sufficient.

Provide context

Many (maybe even most) software problems are caused not by a failure of a single component but by an unanticipated interaction between two or more components. One of the most common cases is where one component fails gracefully but another component, one that depends on the first, does not handle this failure properly.

As such, observability solutions must put failures and other performance problems in context. What was the original request that led to the problem? What sequence of actions led to the current state? A distributed trace is one example of this sort of context, but context can span multiple requests or even hosts. For example, an operator trying to understand why one service instance is overloaded would benefit from understanding that several other instances have recently crashed (leading a load balancer to redirect traffic).

Prioritize by impact

As mentioned earlier, the complexity of distributed systems means that there will always be many things going wrong, including many requests (or parts of requests) that are slow. An observability solution should help prioritize both the problems and their potential causes by the impact they are having on users.

One example is to prioritize performance problems based on their contributions to the *critical path* of requests. The critical path is the parts of a request that, if sped up, would improve the latency experienced by an end user. Since, by definition, speeding up parts of a request that are *not* on the critical path would have no impact on end users, it's not worth spending time on them.

Automate correlation

Human operators have important knowledge about the behavior of software systems as well as insights into their failures, but the number of signals that are emitted from distributed systems is far too large to sift through manually. An observability solution can help human operators focus on what matters by promoting signals which correlate with performance issues and, conversely, by filtering out signals which have no correlated changes. For example, if the rate of errors observed during a slow roll-out is much higher for the new version, then showing the difference in performance based on version can be invaluable. (On the other hand, showing a breakdown by host might lead to incorrect conclusions.)

The Path Ahead

In this light, when making choices about observability tools, we should not ask simply "Is this a good metrics tool?" (or a good logging tool or a good tracing tool) but instead "Is this a good *observability* tool?" Doing so means accepting broader definitions of each of these tools and of distributed tracing in particular. Unlike metrics and logs, distributed tracing starts from the assumption that we are trying to observe a *distributed* system. It is critical that any observability tool used in a distributed system provide a holistic view of the application, and there is an opportunity for distributed tracing to play a much larger role in how applications are developed and run.

As we consider use cases and potential future work in subsequent chapters, we will continue to take a broader view of tracing: not just as it was deployed as tools like Dapper at Google, but as a tool that takes advantage of multiple sources of information and combines them in ways that are timely and cost-efficient for developers and operators. This will mean leveraging metric data to understand possible causes outside of the application or deriving metrics from traces to show operators when application behavior is changing. It will also mean leveraging log data as another source of information for tracing and showing users specific events data as part of explaining what happened.

While the three pillars of observability offer an easy way to categorize existing tools, breaking free of this paradigm offers many more possibilities for how we approach observability problems. As we consider a range of use cases in the next few chapters, consider how these different data sources—individually and especially when combined—can help connect cause and effect in production systems.

CHAPTER 8

Improving Baseline Performance

In any other production system—whether it's a software system or a factory—the process by which the product is created has a profound impact on the cost of production and on the product itself. In modern software applications, production costs are mostly related to computing resources and other infrastructure, including the costs of buying and running servers in a private datacenter or renting them from a cloud provider. How that software is delivered also affects user experience. In this chapter, we consider how to reduce costs and improve user experience using distributed tracing.

In particular, we focus on improving *baseline* performance: that is, how the software performs over the course of weeks, months, or quarters. Understanding baseline performance will enable you to plan engineering work over the next few weeks or months effectively, maximizing your chances of having a positive impact. (In contrast, the following chapter will focus on approaches to *restoring* performance to that baseline when something has gone wrong.)

In the previous chapter, we discussed distributed tracing in the context of the "three pillars of observability." In particular, we said that software developers and operators have the most to gain from distributed tracing and other observability tools when those tools take advantage of all three forms of performance telemetry: metrics, logs, and traces. As such, the approaches in this chapter will consider distributed tracing as a means for not merely viewing traces, but for analyzing and visualizing telemetry using tracing data as a way to put that telemetry in the context of application requests. While we will start with looking at individual traces as a way of understanding application performance, we will quickly progress to approaches that automate many manual steps and take advantage of hundreds or thousands of traces.

Before we can start to analyze performance data, however, we must first establish how we measure performance, including the statistics tools required to do so for a large volume of requests.

Measuring Performance

For user-facing applications, it's critical to measure performance as it affects users. As such, request *latency* is a critical measure for these applications, and moreover, latency should be measured as close to the user as possible. Measuring latency in the user's browser or mobile app is better than measuring it at the load balancer: this will enable you to see the effects of the network on performance. Even better would be to measure latency between a user's interaction and when new results are rendered on their screen: this lets you see the impact of multiple requests to your backends as well as any computation done in the client.

Economic Value of Lower Latency

Numerous studies have shown that even barely perceptible increases in latency can have significant effects on revenue and other kinds of user conversions. Experiments performed by Google showed that increasing the time to load a page of search results by half a second reduced the total number of searches by 20%, and conversely, if Google made a page faster, it would see a roughly proportional increase in the amount of usage.[1] Research by Akamai showed that even an increase in latency as little as 100 milliseconds could reduce ecommerce conversion by as much as 7%.[2] Pinterest showed that a 40% reduction in visitor wait time resulted in a 15% increase in conversion to sign-up.[3]

While it may be easy to focus on reducing infrastructure costs when thinking about the economic value of software performance, improving user experience is not just good for users, but has real—and measurable—business value as well.

In measuring performance, you should also consider *which* users' performance you care about. Are you interested in improving performance for your average users? For your power users? Perhaps for a specific customer segment? This choice will affect how you go about measuring performance.

If you are interested in improving performance for most users or are working to reduce costs, targeting *median latency* might be a good place to start. Working to improve median latency can not only improve performance for many users, it's also a good place to start if you are looking to reduce overall costs. Because many requests tend to cluster around the middle of the distribution, reducing the amount of

---

1 [May10]

2 [Aka17]

3 [Med17]

computation required for each of these requests can have a big impact on overall compute requirements.

If you want to improve performance for the subset of your users that are having the worst experience, measuring *high-percentile latency* (as discussed later) will get you pointed in the right direction. It may seem counterintuitive to spend your time improving latency for only (say) 1% of requests. However, there are several important reasons to consider doing so:

- If you are responsible for a service in the *middle* of your application, 1% of the requests that your service is handling can affect many more than 1% of end users. This occurs most often when requests from users are fanned out (directly or indirectly) across many instances of your service. The chances of a slow request affecting a given user increase with the number of instances serving that part of the request, since the slowest such instance will determine the overall latency observed by that user.

- Users experiencing high-percentile latency often serve as bellwethers for the rest of your users. The slowest requests are usually hitting parts of your application that are already performing at or near their limits. As request volume increases, more and more requests will suffer from similar problems; though you are improving only 1% of requests today, they will represent a larger portion of requests in the near future.

- Our experience has shown that users experiencing high latency tend to do so because they are using larger datasets or are issuing more complex queries. These also tend to be high-value users, including those responsible for an outsize portion of your revenue.

Though not always considered part of "performance," the *portion of user requests that fail* (or have some unrecoverable error) is also important to measure. (If you require that all "performance" measures be expressed in terms of "faster" or "slower," then consider failed requests to be infinitely slow.) Requests fail for any number of reasons in distributed systems, including software bugs in service (locally or further down the stack), user errors, network failures, and underprovisioned services. In many ways, understanding errors is the bread and butter of distributed tracing: isolating them requires understanding the dependencies between services and how they interact with each other.

The two other "golden" metrics of application performance, *traffic rate* and *saturation*, cannot be associated with individual requests in the same way that latency or the presence of errors can be. (An individual request can certainly be part of what causes traffic to spike, but it's difficult to blame that request more than any other.) These metrics typically play a larger role in applications that are more focused on throughput than on latency: this is true of many batch-processing systems and some high-volume delivery systems (including video processing). In these applications, if the throughput falls below a given threshold then user experience may suffer, but most optimization is focused on maintaining that throughput while reducing costs. Note, however, that traffic rate and saturation can also be important signals in explaining and improving latency and error rates; we will consider how they can be integrated into distributed tracing to do so.

Whatever measures of performance matter for your business, organization, or users, once you've determined what they are, measuring and setting goals for them is critical to prioritizing your work. Though mostly beyond the scope of this book, establishing SLIs is a way of formalizing performance measurements in a way that can be measured precisely by determining:

- What you are measuring (for example, median or 99th-percentile latency)
- What you are measuring it for (for example, which service, endpoint, or operation)
- Over what time period you are measuring it (for example, the last five minutes)

If integrated into your distributed tracing solution, SLIs can also help to make automated decisions about data collection and sampling and even guide you toward the root causes of performance problems. Before we look at that, however, let's introduce a few concepts from statistics.

Percentiles

Throughout this chapter and the next, we will frequently refer to *high-percentile latency* or in some cases, *99th-percentile latency*. (If you are familiar with percentiles, feel free to skip this section.) Like statistics such as average and maximum, percentiles are a way of summarizing the performance of a large set of requests. Unlike average or maximum, however, percentiles offer a much more powerful way of comparing sets (or "populations") of requests. Two common places where you may have seen percentiles and similar statistics are academic tests that were "graded on a curve" or measures of the height or weight of young children.

Percentiles can be defined as follows: each percentile gives the value of some measurement (in our case, often latency) for which a given portion of the population lies below that value. For example, if the 50th-percentile latency is 100 milliseconds (ms), then 50% of the requests considered were faster than 100 ms. Similarly, if the 90th-percentile latency was 1 second, then 90% of the requests considered were faster than 1 second (see Table 8-1).

Table 8-1. Example request latencies and statistics

Request latency (ms)
87
89
91
93
102
138
174
260
556
5000

Selected statistics (ms)	50th percentile
120	Average
659	90th percentile
1000	Maximum

Given the request latencies shown in Table 8-1, we can compute the average, 50th and 90th percentiles, as shown. (Note that we've chosen to use a definition of percentiles that interpolates between values.)

Percentiles provide more flexibility than just looking at an average value. Simply put, looking at the average only works well when the average is representative of the data as a whole. In measuring software performance, it's not uncommon for values to be widely distributed. And when a few values are *very* widely distributed, they can have an outsize impact on the average. In our simple example, because there is one extremely large value, the average is larger than all of the values but that one. The 50th percentile (or median) is often more robust to outliers than the average.[4]

Percentiles are also useful when looking to understand and improve the performance of the slowest requests. It can be tempting to look at the *maximum* latency; however, the maximum will often be determined by how timeouts are configured or even by some aspect of the telemetry or monitoring system. For example, if you are investigating a request that took exactly 60 seconds, chances are you will find that some part of the request repeatedly failed until the entire request was aborted (meaning that you are not really debugging a slow request but a failed one). Looking at requests that are

---

4 You can assess how wide a distribution is using its standard deviation; however, most latency distributions are not *normal* distributions. As we'll discuss in the next section, looking at the whole distribution can be even better than just looking at a single percentile, including the median.

among the slowest 1%, 5%, or 10% (depending on your overall request volume) will usually offer better candidates for improving latency.

Beware: Computing with Percentiles

In addition to being less familiar to many engineers and developers, using percentiles also presents some challenges for *implementers* of distributed tracing and other observability tools.

Averages and maximums can be measured on separate hosts (or even in separate datacenters) and then easily combined: averages by weighting them appropriately, and maximums simply by taking the largest.

Unlike statistics such as average and maximum, however, there's no straightforward way of combining separate measurements of the 50th (or any other) percentile. Users should be careful when observability tools claim to do so.

Computing percentiles for small datasets can be confusing and often misleading. In our work, we've come across developers from time to time who are trying to measure 99th- (or even 99.9th-) percentile latencies for datasets with only dozens of examples. In trying to keep our example in Table 8-1 small, we are ourselves guilty of this: in our example of 10 points, the 90th percentile is determined by only two points (the two largest)!

When a percentile (or any statistic, for that matter) is determined by only a few points, noise in the measurement of those points can carry over into that percentile. In addition, differences in how different tools compute percentiles (for example, using interpolation or the nearest point) can also make it difficult to compare results. In those cases, it's easy to make incorrect conclusions. Try to avoid computing percentiles that will be determined by only a handful of points.

Histograms

Though slightly more expensive in terms of network and storage costs, *histograms* provide much more detail than just a handful of statistics. This is especially important in software performance where the behavior of a service is often much more complex than just a single Gaussian or "bell" curve. While they might at first seem unfamiliar if you are more used to reading time series graphs, they will quickly become a go-to tool for improving performance.

Unlike a time series graph, where the unit of measurement—in our case, latency—is on the vertical axis, in a histogram the unit of measurement is on the horizontal axis (see Figure 8-1).

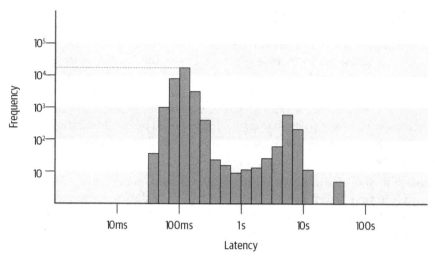

Figure 8-1. Example of a histogram.

Each bar in the histogram represents a subset of the overall population: for example, the requests with a latency between 100 and 150 ms. The height of the bar indicates the size of that subset; this is sometimes labeled "frequency." In the example, there are around 10,000 requests with latencies between 100 m and 150 ms. Like many latency histograms, the example is plotted on a log-log scale. A logarithmic horizontal axis lets us see a much wider range of latencies (from only a few milliseconds up to a minute) while a logarithmic vertical axis lets us see patterns in even small subsets of requests.

While the 99th- and other high-percentile latencies are more robust to outliers than statistics like the maximum, they can still fail to reveal many aspects of application performance. For the requests in Figure 8-1, the 99th-percentile latency is around 3 seconds. However, this would still be the case even if the cluster of requests between 100 and 150 ms slowed down to around 1 second instead. Likewise, it would still be the case even if the cluster of requests around 5 seconds had occurred at 10 seconds instead. Ultimately, the 99th percentile is really just showing a simple division of your requests: 99% of them are faster and 1% are slower. It says nothing about how requests are distributed within these two sets.

The *shape* of a latency histogram, however, describes the performance of your service or application in far more detail. In several of the analyses later in this chapter and in the following chapter, we'll show how to use them to divide requests into meaningful classes and then to understand the reasons behind the performance differences between those classes.

Defining the Critical Path

In any distributed system of reasonable complexity, there are always many services and RPCs that are slow. So many, in fact, that even the hardest-working developers would not be able to track down all of these issues and fix them before more were introduced. And indeed they shouldn't! Most of these issues have no impact on users and so fixing them is of little value to your business or organization. Before working to address latency of any particular service, you should be confident that doing so will affect performance as observed by users. (In Chapter 7 we referred to this as "prioritizing by impact.")

A common method for understanding which services are impacting user-visible performance is to first determine the *critical path* of each slow request. Originally developed as part of project management, the critical path (when applied to requests in a distributed software system) describes the parts of processing the request that, when taken together, determine the overall duration of the request.

In the terms of distributed tracing, the critical path of a trace is a subset of spans of that trace or even parts of those spans. One definition says that span A is part of the critical path at time t if and only if two conditions are true:

- A's parent is blocked on A's completion at time t
- A is *not* blocked on any child span's completion at time t

This is a convenient way of thinking about the critical path; in a way, it describes the "bottom edge" of a trace. In some cases, however (and as we'll describe later), there is some ambiguity when there are multiple concurrent child spans. To avoid this ambiguity, we define the critical path as follows. Span A is part of the critical path at time t if and only if *reducing the length of A at time t reduces the overall latency of the request.*

Figure 8-2 shows an example trace with the critical path shaded. You can see that the length of the critical path is the same as the length of the overall request, and in this case, the length of the longest span as well. In this example, span A contributes to the critical path at several points, including at the beginning and end of the request. Spans B, D, and E are each entirely on the critical path. Span C is partially on the critical path, but only before and after D.

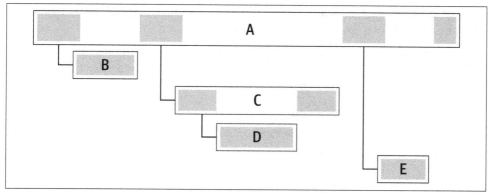

Figure 8-2. Example trace with critical path.

If you were looking to reduce the latency of this request, you should look at spans B, D, or E or at the parts of spans A and C that are not blocked on one of the other spans.

Figure 8-3 shows a second trace. In this example, two of the spans represent the same work, but as perceived by the client (`client A`) and the server (`server A`).

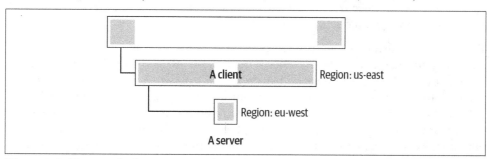

Figure 8-3. Trace with client span on the critical path.

Looking at the time where `client A` is on the critical path, you might be asking "Why is the client doing any work here?" In this case, the delay is most likely due to network latency, though different tracing tools may show this in different ways. As a user you must often consider: is the latency being caused by the service directly? Or is it a delay caused by something external (like the network)? Or is it caused by contention for some other resource (for example, the CPU or a lock)? Additional metadata on spans can help shed light on these cases, as discussed later.

Figure 8-4 shows a third trace with the critical path shaded. In this case, span A has two child spans (B and C) that represent concurrently executing work. At time t, A could be said to be blocked on either of the child spans (and neither of those two are blocked on any other spans), so by the first definition of "critical path" either one could be considered to be on the critical path.

In this case, however, reducing the length of B would *not* reduce the overall length of the request; only reducing C would have that effect. When there are multiple child spans that describe work that is being executed concurrently, the longest such request is the only one on the critical path.

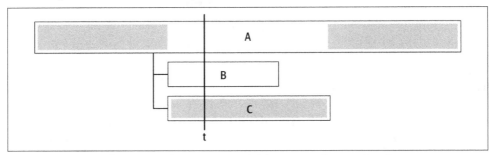

Figure 8-4. Example trace with concurrent child spans and critical path.

Note that the definition only says that *some* reduction of the length of a span on the critical path will reduce the overall latency of the request, but not that *any* reduction will result in an equal reduction in overall latency.

For example, consider a span that is on the critical path and is 1 second in duration. Reducing its length by 500 ms doesn't necessarily reduce the time of the entire request by 500 ms. In the trace shown in Figure 8-4, when the length of span C is reduced to less than the length of B, it will no longer be on the critical path (and therefore reducing its duration will no longer reduce overall latency). Remember that as part of optimizing the work represented by an individual span, you may change which spans appear on the critical path altogether (and therefore need to change your plans for further optimization work).

Understanding Causal Relationships

When using the span-based model of distributed tracing popularized by Google's Dapper, spans contain explicit references to their parents. From this information, a tree can be built showing where spans started relative to each other. However, some assumptions about the relationships between spans still need to be assumed.

When a child span starts, is the parent truly blocked on the work represented by the child? Or is this an asynchronous request with other work continuing concurrently? Understanding the difference will partly depend on the developers who are looking at traces to understand that code that generated them.

In addition, using conventions about how concurrent work is represented using spans can also help. For example, whenever two or more threads (or workers, etc.) are processing concurrently, use a separate span for each of them *that is distinct from their parent*. This means that if one thread makes an asynchronous call and then continues processing, *two* child spans should be created. Doing so will make it easier to understand whether the original thread ever blocks on the asynchronous call and enable automatic trace analysis to better understanding what's happening.

Approaches to Improving Performance

With these concepts in hand, we'll now consider a number of different approaches to improving baseline performance. Since our focus is on distributed tracing, we will consider ways to isolate performance problems to a single component within a distributed system. We'll assume that you are familiar with conventional approaches to software optimization and that, if tasked with improving the speed or efficiency of a single function, class, or module, you can do so using debuggers, profilers, and other tools. Our goal with these approaches is to help you identify that function, class, or module, so that you can then apply those tools.

Individual Traces

The most basic use of distributed tracing is to consider individual requests and look for unexpected behavior, common antipatterns, or other opportunities for improvement.

The first questions you should ask when looking at optimizing an individual trace are:

- Are there any operations on the critical path that could be optimized?
- Could queries on the critical path be cached?
- Could the functionality offered by request be refactored to split expensive operations from commonly needed ones?

As we've noted, asking any of these questions without understanding the critical path could mean a lot of effort expended with little improvement to what your users are experiencing.

When optimizing a trace such as that shown in Figure 8-2, you should also consider the relative lengths of these spans. In this case, since D is more than twice as long as E, a 20% improvement to D will offer more than twice the benefit of a 20% improvement to E. (Similarly, caching the result of D could yield as much as twice the benefit of caching the result of E, assuming equivalent cache hit rates.) Focus your optimization work on the spans that make up the largest parts of the critical path.

Understanding the performance impact of refactoring requires some additional explanation. To make our example more concrete, imagine in Figure 8-2 that span B represents some authentication operation, span C some computation that determines what's changed since the user last logged in, and span E a lookup of the user's display preferences. Often, when you are maintaining an API endpoint, both the underlying performance and uses of that endpoint will change over time. In this example, perhaps the original use case required these operations to be bundled together (or perhaps bundling them reduced network overhead), but now the endpoint is being invoked frequently just to perform the lookup of the display preferences. In that case, those preferences could be returned much more quickly if the endpoint is refactored into two parts: one that determines what's changed and one that returns those preferences. Sometimes, as in cases like this, "optimization" simply means doing less.

Another example of one of the most common problems discovered when starting with distributed tracing is shown in Figure 8-5. The trace on the left shows a root span with six subspans (labeled A through F). These spans represent sequential calls to other services, possibly including queries of one or more remote databases. It's often the case that these calls are independent of each other (that is, no one of them depends on the results of any of the others), and that the calls or queries can be performed concurrently. If they are performed concurrently, as shown in the trace on the right side of the figure, the overall latency of the request can be greatly reduced.

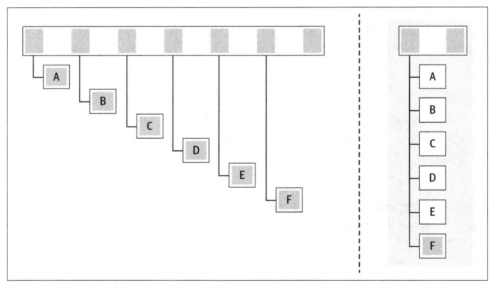

Figure 8-5. Trace showing sequence of independent subspans (concurrent on right).

Sometimes several subspans are each implemented efficiently when considered in isolation, but when considered as part of some larger request, they do redundant work;

Figure 8-6 shows an example. Both spans labeled A on the left side represent the same computation. (Taken together these two A spans represent a majority of the critical path.) This code can be refactored to perform that computation only one time —with the results passed down to each of the two subspans—reducing the total time required to process the request, as shown on the right side of the figure. Doing so reduces the total amount of work performed during the request: this is an example where tracing can improve both latency *and* throughput.

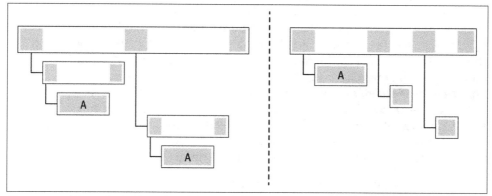

Figure 8-6. Trace showing redundant work performed in two subspans (refactored on right).

A final example of an individual trace that can offer an opportunity for optimization comes not from optimizing the code itself but from changing the configuration of that code. Recall that Figure 8-3 shows a trace where there is a large difference between the duration of a client span and a server span for a single RPC, and that this difference can often be a result of network latency. Sometimes this network latency is unavoidable, but at other times it can be a result of a misconfiguration. For example, one service might be calling another service but routing requests to an instance in another datacenter instead of a local one or, similarly, it might be querying a database replica in the wrong region. This frequently occurs when service configuration is heedlessly copied from one datacenter to another.

The example shows that you can discover this by inspecting the tags on each of the spans found in the trace. If the `region` tag differs between the client and server spans, that's a good indication that there might be an opportunity to reduce overall latency.

Biased Sampling and Trace Comparison

In Chapter 6, we discussed sampling and how it can be used as a mechanism to control costs. In summary, collecting all traces (and all spans) is not necessary to understanding or improving application performance—and is usually prohibitively expensive. Traces may be sampled in a way that biases toward those with valuable information, usually by selecting those that represent slow requests or requests with errors. Here we will consider sampling in the context of improving performance indicators that matter to your business, organization, or users: your SLIs. Moreover, once the right traces are selected, you can compare them to quickly identify the root causes of issues.

While looking at a single trace can be a good approach to improving median latency, improving the performance of the *slowest* requests is best done by considering at least two requests: one close to the median latency and one that has a high-percentile latency. Sampling requests uniformly at random, however, is unlikely to yield many examples of slow requests, especially if the distribution of requests looks like that shown in Figure 8-1. That is, if the latency of requests was uniformly distributed, then uniform sampling would be a reasonable approach, but since latency is almost never uniformly distributed, sampling should be biased to make sure that infrequent—but still valuable—traces are collected. For improving slow requests, make sure that a sufficient number of 99th-percentile (or even 99.9th-percentile) latency requests are sampled. Note that this might even mean that these requests are sampled just as frequently as median requests, even if they are many times less likely to occur.

Similarly, it is important to bias trace samples toward requests with errors. Services typically try to keep the portion of errors to a fraction of a percent, so again, uniform sampling is unlikely to pick up a reasonable set of examples.

There are other, more application-specific, features that might also be good candidates for driving sampling bias. For example, if you are running an experiment with only 0.1% of your users, biasing toward that set of users is important in understanding the performance of code running that experiment.

Once you have a sample of traces (as few as just two), you can then compare them to understand what is causing the slow ones to be slow. Typically it's not the case that every subspan is proportionally longer in the slow request, but that one or two subspans are much longer.

Figure 8-7 shows two traces for an /api/update-inventory request, one on the top that takes 186 ms and one on the bottom that takes 1.49 seconds (in both cases as observed by the client). Looking at the spans that contributed to the critical path, most of the spans in the two traces are approximately the same length. The exception is the write-cache operation, which takes more than *28 times longer* in the top example. Further investigation would be required to understand why this operation takes longer in some cases, but comparing these two traces has more or less eliminated any other theory as to why the trace show at the top is slow.

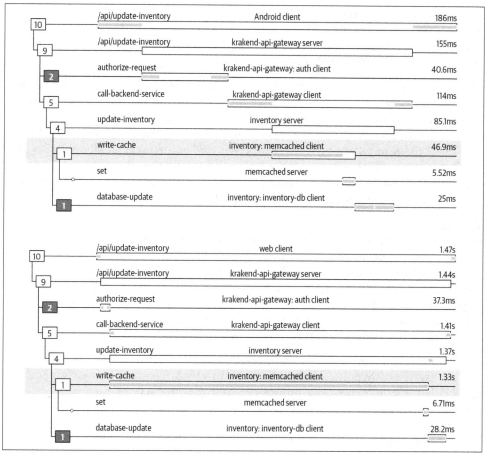

	/api/update-inventory	Android client	186ms
10			
9	/api/update-inventory	krakend-api-gateway server	155ms
2	authorize-request	krakend-api-gateway: auth client	40.6ms
5	call-backend-service	krakend-api-gateway client	114ms
4	update-inventory	inventory server	85.1ms
1	write-cache	inventory: memcached client	46.9ms
	set	memcached server	5.52ms
1	database-update	inventory: inventory-db client	25ms
10	/api/update-inventory	web client	1.47s
9	/api/update-inventory	krakend-api-gateway server	1.44s
2	authorize-request	krakend-api-gateway: auth client	37.3ms
5	call-backend-service	krakend-api-gateway client	1.41s
4	update-inventory	inventory server	1.37s
1	write-cache	inventory: memcached client	1.33s
	set	memcached server	6.71ms
1	database-update	inventory: inventory-db client	28.2ms

Figure 8-7. Two traces, showing fast and slow responses for an example API request.

Trace Search

In addition to automated sampling based on latency, errors, or other features of spans, users may also want to search for spans in a manual, ad hoc way. For example, users may be working to eliminate specific classes of errors. Or users may be testing new code using their own user accounts and want to search for the traces associated with those accounts. For traces that are generated as part of a CI/CD pipeline, they may be tagged with build labels or deployment information so that users can find traces associated with failures quickly. Being able to search for specific traces is important when you, as a user, have a hypothesis that you want to validate or refute. To support these use cases, it's necessary to index traces in such a way that a relevant trace can be found easily and efficiently.

There is ample work on indexing structured data like traces; however, in many cases, these indexes can become almost as large as the trace repository itself. Since storage is one of the major costs associated with distributed tracing, understanding how to balance the needs of users with this cost is important.

The Dapper work at Google showed that a single index based on service and then host and time was able to meet many of the needs of our users.[5] This was because, first, most users were responsible for a small number of services and were focusing on the performance of just one at a time, and second, some other observability tool had clued them to where or when a problem was occurring. Initially, we also provided an index which would enable lookup based first on host, but did not see enough interest to justify the additional cost. Tools that take similar approaches may limit use cases to those focused on a single service.

Tracing tools can also provide some assistance in building search queries *quickly*. Just as search engines suggest queries as we start typing, tracing tools can suggest relevant traces. For example, once a user has selected a service, a tool can suggest operations that that service implements as well as tags associated with that service. Thus, tracing tools also support a form of discovery about the data found in traces. For example, suggestions might help users understand which sorts of errors are occurring in their service or enumerate which operations their services depend on. This process can help guide users toward hypotheses about which factors are impacting baseline performance.

Once a user has a hypothesis, the next step is to look for evidence that supports or refutes that hypothesis. Searching through traces is the way to find that evidence. Some examples of hypotheses that can be explored using tracing:

- Long requests are often blocked on retries (look for spans tagged with `retry=true`)
- Cache misses account for the majority of latency when they occur (look for spans with `cache=miss`)
- Requests that time out waiting for RPCs (look for spans with errors that indicate timeouts or RPC cancellation)

While validating and refuting existing hypotheses are important use cases for distributed tracing, we will explore a set of analyses later where tracing tools also help users to form *new* hypotheses about application performance.

---

5 [Sig10]

Multimodal Analysis

In the rest of this chapter, we'll describe use cases that depend not on just one or two traces, but a statistically significant collection of them. This may be dozens, hundreds, or even thousands of traces, depending on the homogeneity of the requests. Histograms offer a convenient way of visualizing the behavior of many traces in a way that provides much more information than just a few statistics. Here we'll show how to use multimodal analysis to break down performance into a small set of broad categories that can be used to inform the next steps of optimization.

A *modality* (in the context of a histogram) is what's shown as a peak in a graph: each modality represents a set of traces that have approximately the same latency. A histogram is *multimodal* if it has multiple peaks. As noted earlier, a latency histogram for a single service or even a single operation rarely has a simple bell-shaped curve. This is because latency is usually determined by a number of discrete factors, including the following:

- Which network type the client is using, including mobile data (3G, 4G, 5G) or broadband internet
- Whether an existing connection or session can be reused
- Whether the request can be serviced from a cache
- Whether the request involves mutating any persistent state
- Whether an upstream request timed out and must be retried

For example, requests that may be satisfied from a cache may be 10 times faster on average than those that cannot. A service that uses a cache will usually have a multimodal latency distribution where one peak corresponds to cache hits and another to cache misses. Because a service may be affected by more than one of these factors, it's not uncommon to see histograms with five or more modalities.

Figure 8-8 shows a multimodal latency histogram. On the left side requests are presented as a single distribution; on the right side, requests are broken down into three groups. (Notice that the height of each bar on the left is the sum of the heights of the corresponding bars on the right.) This histogram shows what you might see if requests were divided by client network type: most broadband requests are faster than most 4G requests (and nearly all 3G requests); most 4G requests are faster than most 3G ones.

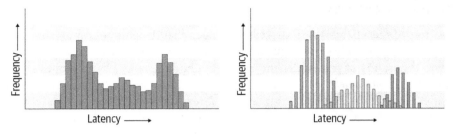

Figure 8-8. Multimodal histogram (left: combined, right: as separate components).

Understanding what distinguishes one modality from another is key to improving performance. In some cases, multimodal analysis will help to make sure you are comparing the right sets of requests (it's unlikely you'll be able to make requests that mutate persistent state faster than those that don't). In others, it will help you focus on the right set of solutions (speeding up backend processing time is less likely to improve 3G user latency than reducing the number of requests or the sizes of the results). In still others, it will help you manage performance and cost trade-offs (increasing cache size may improve latency but require additional computing resources).

Multimodal analysis offers more precision than just comparing requests based on their latency: comparing a fast and a slow request will often provide less insight than comparing traces from two different modalities. Multimodal analysis is also important in that it enables users to move from just "reducing latency" to more concrete next steps such as reducing payload size or improving cache hit rate. Once you can focus on a more specific set of requests, you can use the other techniques described earlier to find the root causes of slower requests.

Histogram Bin Width and Multimodal Analysis

While we haven't discussed many of the choices necessary in using histograms at length, one implementation detail that is especially important to multimodal analysis is bin size. The bin size is the width of the bars in the histogram. The smaller the bins, the more bins there will be, and the more detail the histogram can offer. Using larger bins can sometimes be problematic as more information about each request is lost: each bucket will represent a more diverse set of examples.

However, using too many bins can cause random noise in the original sample to appear as multiple modalities in the histogram. For example, it might be that few requests have a latency of 117 ms, even though many requests have latencies of 116 ms and 118 ms. This is probably not a result of two truly different behaviors in your application, but just a result of the fact that, even within a uniform population, measurements will still show some variation—just like you can't expect the next coin flip following a "heads" to always be a "tails."

Bin size need not be fixed, even within a given histogram. We've found using bins that are narrower at the small end of the axis and wider at the large end is a good fit for understanding request latency, especially if latency will be graphed on a logarithmic scale. This also helps users focus on behavior that will improve performance in a meaningful way since, for example, shaving off only a few milliseconds will have little impact on a request that took seconds to complete.

Aggregate Analysis

Collections of traces can also be used to draw conclusions about performance in ways that are less susceptible to small variations in individual traces. In the preceding example of comparing two traces, there was only one major difference (and so making the comparison was relatively straightforward), but often there will be many differences, some significant, and others not. By taking a larger sample of traces, we (or rather, our tracing tools) are able to better see the patterns that can lead to meaningful improvements in performance.

A simple form of aggregate analysis is just to look at the most common errors within those traces. This can be especially fruitful when looking at a sample set that contains only failed requests, as common errors are likely culprits to consider when trying to eliminate those failures (though see the following section for how this approach can be further improved).

Note that when we say "errors within those traces" we mean errors that occur within *any* span in a given trace. This is where some of the true power of tracing starts to show: while metrics would enable you to observe an increase in errors in, say, both a mobile client and a backend, tracing enables you to know that these two types of errors are both occurring within the same requests.

One of the most effective forms of aggregate analysis that we observed both at Google and elsewhere is aggregate *critical path* analysis. In this analysis, once given a sample of traces, we identify a set of classes of spans for which we want to measure the performance impact. This is usually the set of services or the operations that occur in that sample of traces (though in some cases those classes could be even more fine-grained). The result of the analysis will tell us where we should focus our optimization efforts to improve latency across the sample.

The analysis proceeds as follows. For each trace, we compute what percentage of the critical path of that trace was contributed by each class of spans. Table 8-2 shows how much of the critical path can be attributed to each span in the trace in Figure 8-2. Assuming that the labels in that trace correspond to services, in this one trace 40% of the critical path was contributed by A, 10% by B, etc. Once these percentages are calculated for each trace, they are averaged across all traces in the set.

Table 8-2. Percentages of the critical path contributed by each span in the trace in Figure 8-2

Span	Percentage of critical path
A	40%
B	10%
C	20%
D	20%
E	10%

Assuming that the other traces in the sample under analysis looked similar to this example, optimizations to services A and, to some extent, C and D offer the best opportunities to reduce the latency of traces in the population from which the sample was drawn. B and E offer less opportunity simply because they contribute less to the critical path: even reducing the duration of B to zero would only result in a 10% improvement on average to request latency.

Aggregate critical path analysis can also be performed on the *absolute durations* that each span contributes to the critical path, rather than percentages. Perhaps obviously, this will bias the result toward optimizations that have the biggest impact on the *slowest* traces in the sample. While this might be your intent, it would be better to limit the initial sample of traces to better match what you would like to optimize (for example, to those traces with 99th-percentile latency or higher) as this will reduce the impact of a few outliers in the sample.

There are a few other things to look out for when doing aggregate critical path analysis. The first really applies to any aggregate analysis: be sure that you've chosen an appropriate sample. One common mistake is to take a sample over a period of time that doesn't adequately represent the requests you'd like to optimize, perhaps by not including requests from your peak traffic periods. Requests that occur during peak traffic periods are much more likely to demonstrate where resource contention occurs.

A second warning is to look for how network time is attributed (explicitly or implicitly) to spans. In our running example in Figure 8-2, we determined that the span labeled A contributed a significant amount of time to the critical path. However, it also appears that this span makes three RPCs. If spans B, C, and E are all spans generated by the servers of those RPCs (rather than the clients) then it's likely that some of that time attributed to A was time waiting for data to be transmitted over the network. While there may be some changes that can be made to A to reduce this time (for example, by compressing or otherwise reducing the size of payloads), optimizing the code of A itself will likely have little effect.

Correlation Analysis

We finish this chapter with a final analysis—one of the most powerful that distributed tracing can offer developers looking to improve baseline performance. While many of the techniques described earlier enable you to validate or refute *existing* hypotheses about performance, correlation analysis takes things one step further by creating *new* hypotheses, along with evidence to support them. This is an entirely novel workflow for many developers: rather than having to rely on intuition and guess what could be improved, tracing tools can guide you directly to the opportunities with the highest potential to improve performance. You of course must bring your experience and expertise about the application, but rather than starting from a blank page, you are offered a "draft" to begin editing.

In the previous section, we noted that looking at common errors within a sample of failed requests can help to find which type or types of errors were the root causes of those failed requests. While this approach can be useful at times, it is prone to mistakes. In particular, while it accounts for when they occur, it fails to account for when they do *not* occur. To understand the problem, consider the following example. Suppose that there are two types of errors that appear in traces as described here. `Error 1` occurs in 90% of traces that represent failed requests; `Error 2` occurs in 100% of all traces (including both successful and failed requests).

When considering a sample of traces that exclusively represents failed requests, it may appear that `Error 2` is the more likely culprit, since it appears in *every* failed request, while `Error 1` only appears in 90% of the sample. However, since `Error 2` occurs in every request—including those that succeed—it's unlikely to be the cause of failures in our sample: this error is apparently recoverable, since it is recovered from in the successful requests.

The question we are really trying to ask is not "Which type of error is more likely to occur in failed requests?" but "Which type of error more strongly correlates with failure?" Though correlation is not causation, it is a powerful tool in discovering root causes.

To perform correlation analysis, we need not just one sample of traces but two. One sample should represent the class of traces that you want to eliminate or at least reduce, for example, failed or slow requests. The second sample should represent the complement of the first sample: usually a set of successful or fast requests. (You can think of this setup as being like a good scientific experiment, with both an experimental group and a control group.)

In addition to two sample sets, we also need a set of features with which we can look for correlations. In distributed tracing, these features will be things like the services, operations, errors, and tags associated with the spans that make up these traces. It also includes the durations of those spans as well as what percentage of the critical path they are responsible for. This analysis can consider features of *any* span in the trace: for example, even if we were investigating the top span shown in Figure 8-3, the tags of the two spans below it might be critical (pun intended!) to the analysis.

Once we have the two sample sets (let's call them A and B) and a set of features, carrying out the analysis simply means looking at each feature and asking, what's the likelihood that it occurs in sample A but *not* in sample B? This yields a "coefficient of correlation" for each feature. A coefficient of 1.0 means that a given feature appeared in every trace in sample A and never in a trace in sample B, while a coefficient of −1.0 means that a given feature appeared in every trace in sample B and never in a trace in sample A. A coefficient of 0.0 means that the feature was equally likely to appear in both samples (including all of the time, not at all, or anywhere in between). The closer to 1.0 or −1.0 the coefficient of correlation is, the more likely that feature can explain the difference between the two samples.

Going back to our example with two types of errors, we can now say that Error 1 has a coefficient of correlation of 0.9, while Error 2 has a coefficient of correlation of 0.0. This tells us that Error 1 is a much better place to start looking when trying to understand why requests have failed.

Of course, errors are only one type of feature that can help us understand what's gone wrong. As noted earlier, a span's tags and contribution to the critical path are among the important features that can be used to drive this analysis. This serves as a good reminder of the importance of good instrumentation (as covered in Chapter 4)!

Table 8-3 is an anonymized example taken from a production service and includes several tags. It shows the results of a correlation analysis when looking at traces for a single operation whose latency is in the 99th percentile or greater.

Table 8-3. Example showing coefficients of correlation for several (anonymized) tags

Feature	Coefficient of correlation
org_name: Acme	0.41
project_name: acme-prod	0.41
operation: fetching	−0.39
total_rows_read: 0	−0.37

This example shows a relatively strong correlation between latency and a single organization (in this case, a set of users). Perhaps the organization has a large amount of data or makes particularly complex queries; in either case, these queries might be quite expensive. Further investigation would be necessary to understand why. (Unsurprisingly, this also correlates with the largest project in this organization: often this analysis may yield one or two redundant tags.) In this example, latency is *negatively* correlated with queries for which no rows were read (total_rows_read: 0), indicating that these queries were usually *not* among the 1% slowest queries. This also might provide some clue as to why slow queries were slow (perhaps a new index is required?). In any case, a next step might be to look at some traces that meet these criteria.

One concern you might have when adding all of these tags is that the number of tags and the number of values of those tags (that is, their *cardinality*) might become large, leading to excessive costs in managing all of this trace data. (In particular, total_rows_read might have thousands of different values.) In Chapter 7, we identified cardinality limits as an important way of comparing observability tools. Happily, most distributed tracing tools—even those supporting correlation analysis—can easily support this sort of cardinality.

As a developer, you should add many tags to spans, including as many of the following as makes sense for your application:

- Software versions (including versions of platforms and third-party components), active experiments, and other "feature flags"
- User cohorts, segments, and other classifiers of user behavior
- Where a computation is running (for example, host, cluster, or datacenter)
- Any resources where contention may occur while servicing a request (for example, database tables, connection pools, even locks)
- Metrics of CPU, disk, or network load on a host, VM, or container

Any of these features might explain variation in performance, so including them in application telemetry is an important first step in providing the raw data for the analysis described here. It's worth calling out the last list item; while these sorts of metrics haven't historically been part of distributed tracing, associating them with spans can help explain cases where a request is slow not because of any computation performed as part of the request itself, but simply because computationally intensive requests were running nearby (for example, on the same host). This is an example of where a good observability tool will span the "three pillars" described in the previous chapter: ingesting multiple types of data (in this case metrics and spans) can support more powerful analyses.

You can also use multimodal analysis to identify the sample sets to use in correlation analysis. In the preceding example, we compared the 1% slowest requests with the remaining 99%. However, the division between fast and slow will rarely fall on such an arbitrarily defined boundary. In fact, by the nature of multimodal distributions, there will be several different kinds of "fast" or "slow" requests. The quality of a correlation analysis will be much higher if at least one of the sample sets represents a single type of behavior.

To take advantage of multimodal analysis, you should first consider a histogram of latencies and then use the traces in the slowest peak (or if that peak is too small, either several slow peaks or the largest of the slower peaks) as one of your sample sets. Use the remainder of the traces as your other sample set and continue with the analysis as described in this section.

Fully Automated Analysis

This chapter describes an analysis that can automatically enumerate hypotheses that explain slow or failed requests. Can the process of identifying performance problems and fixing them be *completely* automated? In our experience, the answer (fortunately or unfortunately, depending on your perspective) is "no."

First, there might be several tags which are all correlated with higher latency, but only one of which will be something that can be "fixed" (and is not just another side effect of the problem). Understanding how to map tags to source code, configuration, infrastructure, and user behavior requires knowledge that's not present in telemetry itself.

Second, our experience has shown that it is difficult to identify sample sets automatically, even using a form of automated multimodal analysis. Many different aspects of application performance may intersect to produce complex distributions, and it may take some trial and error as well as knowledge about the application to find the right thresholds for creating sample sets.

Finally, even when the reason that a set of requests is slow can be determined automatically, the path to making them faster frequently cannot. For example, say that slow requests are highly correlated with a particular set of accounts. Deactivating those accounts is obviously one way to improve overall latency but not a reasonable option. Instead it may require research to understand what those users are trying to accomplish and looking for workarounds or even developing new features to eliminate these slow requests.

Though some actions may be taken automatically (for example, rolling back problematic releases), human developers and operators still have an important role to play (for now, anyway).

Summary

Improving baseline performance is ultimately about defining what aspects of performance matter to you and your users, discovering the biggest factors in determining that performance, and making changes to your application to address any performance issues.

As part of discovering which factors impact performance—and especially latency— you should consider the *critical path* of each request. Being able to determine the critical path of each request is a key advantage of using distributed tracing; using it will help ensure your efforts to improve performance pay off.

Traditional uses of distributed tracing focus on analyzing *individual* requests. However, more powerful analyses use *hundreds or thousands* of requests to look for patterns in traces. They not only validate (or refute) user-defined hypotheses but also help generate new hypotheses that explain opportunities to improve performance. Whether user-defined or automatically generated, those hypotheses can leverage telemetry not just from one service, but from every service that generates spans that make up those traces.

CHAPTER 9

Restoring Baseline Performance

In the previous chapter, we discussed approaches to improving baseline performance, usually with the goal of improving user experience, reducing costs, or both. In this chapter, we'll consider how distributed tracing can help when a change—intentional or not—has caused a degradation in performance, and you need to restore performance to its previous levels quickly.

The way that your organization approaches problems like this may vary, but most organizations will follow some sort of *incident response* plan. Such a plan involves identifying when an incident occurs (either a partial or complete interruption in service or a significant performance degradation), how team members are notified, how they respond, and (once the incident is over) what sorts of follow-up are required. While there are other types of incidents besides those related to performance (for example, security breaches), we will frame many of the approaches here in terms of incident response.

In this chapter we will also focus on performance from the perspective of a single service. Most developers are responsible for at most a small number of services, and so it's natural to frame performance issues in terms of the performance of a single service. Of course, what ultimately matters is the overall application performance as perceived by your users; much of this chapter will discuss how to relate application performance to the performance of individual services.

As the focus of this chapter is on restoring baseline performance, we assume that performance has recently changed. And as software is (generally) deterministic, changes in performance are usually driven by changes to the software or to the environment in which it's running. While that might sound very broad, take comfort: changes that impact service performance typically come from one of four different areas:

Changes to the service itself
New deployments or configuration changes

Changes in user behavior
New deployments or configuration changes to downstream services that play the role of "users" of that service (including both end users and other services)

New behavior in response to new features or external events

Changes to upstream dependencies
New deployments, configuration changes, or changes to traffic from other services that share those dependencies (both direct and indirect)

Changes to underlying infrastructure
Changes to host, container, or network configuration

Colocation of services contending for the same resources

Mitigating performance problems typically means identifying which is the root cause (or causes) of the problem and then undoing that change. In the case of a new deployment, a configuration change, or possibly an infrastructure change, this often means rolling back that change. In the case of a change in user behavior, it might mean disabling a new feature or even blocking certain types of requests or queries. In both cases, it can also mean provisioning additional resources to account for slower code or more expensive queries.

To undo these changes, it will be critical to identify which team of developers was responsible for the original change. You must effectively communicate with this team, both describing the problem and providing enough evidence to convince them to stop their current work and roll back the change (or disable the feature, etc.). And in all of these steps, time is of the essence since performance regressions can have reputational, economic, and even legal repercussions.

Defining the Problem

Before we can discuss how to *restore* baseline performance, we must first *define* it. In Chapter 8, we started with the "four golden signals"—latency, failure rate, traffic rate, and saturation—but focused mostly on the first two. While traffic rate and saturation are often used by developers and operators to understand and predict system health, they have less direct impact on end users of an application: their impact often manifests in terms of latency. We will continue to focus on latency and failure rate here.

In that chapter, we also defined SLIs as a precise way of measuring performance. Defining a *baseline* for SLIs really starts with declaring our intention for what performance *should* be. This means defining an SLO. An SLO is an SLI together with a goal for what the value of that indicator should be.

For example, if one of your SLIs is 99th-percentile latency for your service as measured over the last 5 minutes, then an SLO might be that this latency is less than 1 second. Or if one of your SLIs is the error rate for your service as measured over the last 10 minutes, then an SLO might be that this rate is less than 0.1% of all requests.

When we discussed errors in the previous chapter, we covered how an error raised by one service might impact the behavior of another. However, we must also consider the case where a service fails to respond at all. To understand this case, it's important to measure error rate not just by looking at how a service reports its own error rate but by measuring it from *outside* that service. When measured this way, we can talk about how much of the time the service is available to answer requests, or its *availability*. Thus another SLO might be that a service is available 99.9% of the time as measured once per minute over the course of a calendar month.

Business Metric-Based SLOs

In this chapter, we focus on SLOs based on metrics like latency and error rate that can easily be derived from spans and are present in many distributed tracing solutions. However, you should also consider SLOs based on the metrics that are most important to your business.

For example, ecommerce applications might look at purchase rates or time-to-purchase as SLOs. Products with a mobile app component might consider key interactions with the app, including cold start, both in rate and duration.

If spans are tagged with information about user actions (whether a purchase was successful, etc.) these metrics can be derived from traces, and—importantly—regressions can be tied to specific (sets of) requests. This will ensure that you are investigating the right sorts of regressions effectively.

Choose an SLO with an eye toward historic values: there's no sense in setting an objective that you will immediately fail to meet. But SLOs should also account for the expectations of your users. In some domains (for example, for some financial applications), users are happy to sacrifice availability if they are given higher assurances that an application will perform correctly. In other domains (for example, observability platforms), users may tolerate some loss of precision if the application is highly available.

The final part of defining service levels is to describe what happens when you fail to meet your SLOs. This usually takes the form of a *service level agreement* (SLA). An SLA is an SLO—an objective—together with some consequence for failing to meet that objective. SLAs often involve some sort of monetary compensation. For example, if you fail to meet your SLO, you may be required to refund part of your customers' fees. In other cases, it may give your customers the option to terminate their contract with you before the end of its term. Unlike SLIs and SLOs, which purely relate to your application's performance, SLAs put this performance into the context of real-world consequences.

Setting SLOs and SLAs helps you to establish baseline performance and to understand when you should take action. If your goal is to keep 99th-percentile latency below 1 second, and it's increased from 200 ms to 250 ms, it's probably not worth waking up in the middle of the night for (though it might be a good place to start the next time you have some free time to spend improving performance).

While it may be tempting to define baseline performance simply as "however it's working today," using a more rigorous definition will enable you to be more confident in determining when you need to take action to restore that performance. Perhaps more importantly, it will help you determine when you *don't* need to take action: after all, making changes to production systems always involves risk, and you probably have better things to do with your time.

Human Factors

Before we dive into the details of how to use distributed tracing to determine which changes are causing a performance regression, it's useful to consider how tracing can support people and processes in incident response. Unlike improving baseline performance, responding to an incident is *unplanned* work. Since time is usually of the essence, facilitating communication and human interaction will play a much larger role in incident response than in typical engineering work.

Determining who has the knowledge to understand a problem and who will do the work is often just as difficult as debugging the code itself. Moreover, once those decisions have been made, they must be communicated effectively in the moment and recorded so that they can be understood after the fact.

(Avoiding) Finger-Pointing

No one likes to be at fault for a regression. In fact, teams are incentivized to measure performance in a way that can quickly show that they are *not* responsible for regressions. As a result, when a regression occurs, many teams will produce evidence that they are not at fault. This leads to many teams blaming others…but without evidence.

For example, suppose that service A provides a shared storage solution that is used by service B (among others). Service B's latency is degrading, and the team that owns service B is blaming service A. Service A's metrics show that it is still meeting its SLO, and the team that owns service A is claiming that service B is probably misusing the API. Perhaps this reminds you of a meeting you have attended?

Traces can help resolve this sort of conflict. In this example, they would provide a way of measuring the performance of service A from the perspectives of both service A *and* service B. It might be that service A is meeting its SLO in general but not for service B. Or we might see evidence that, in fact, requests from service B to service A could be optimized. Or it might be that the real culprit is neither service but a third party, like the network or another client of service A that is abusing a shared resource. Using distributed traces helps bring the conversation back to facts and, importantly, ensures that everyone involved is talking about the same requests.

"Suppressing" the Messenger

In many cases, there may be many services between the point at which the offending change was made and where that change is adversely affecting an SLI. For example, many services may pass through an error that occurred further down the stack. It may look as if the error rate of these services has increased during an incident (and in fact, it has), but these errors don't indicate a problem with that service, only that an error has occurred elsewhere.

When no changes were made to these intermediary services leading up to the incident, then no changes to those services can likely resolve it. However, the teams responsible for these intermediary services may still be interrupted from their day-to-day work (including being paged); they may be called into meetings to discuss the incident; or their time may be wasted in other ways.

MTTR describes how long it takes to address a regression. However, you might less frequently hear *mean time to innocence* (MTTI). This term is used to describe how long it takes to exonerate teams whose services were potentially—but ultimately not —at fault in an incident. You can think of MTTI as the cost paid across your organization for a lack of understanding about which service was responsible for a given incident.

The solution to these issues is to "suppress" the messenger. That is, rather than shooting the messenger, we should look for ways to limit the participation of teams whose services are merely conduits for errors or other problematic requests. We use "suppress" in this context in the same way that we might direct a compiler to suppress certain kinds of errors or warnings: while they might be valuable at times, in these cases they are just another source of noise.

Traces can help to exonerate these teams quickly: when looking at a trace, it's easy to see the first point at which an error occurred and where that error was simply passed through.

Incident Hand-off

Unfortunately, some incidents will last for hours or even days. In these cases, one person cannot reasonably lead—or even participate in—the response for its full duration. In those cases, it's necessary to hand off responsibility for leading, investigating, or communicating about an incident. One major challenge in incident hand-off is making sure information about the incident is transferred from one set of humans to another.

What makes that information transfer particularly challenging is that often that information is incomplete. (After all, if you understood everything about what was happening, you could make short work of the incident and probably avoid the hand-off altogether.) Traces can help in this case as well. If you can identify a class of requests that seem to be problematic and then capture a set of traces for those requests, you need not understand every detail of what's happening with those requests for them to be useful. Because traces capture not only a lot of detail about what's happening but also the causal relationships between your and other services, subsequent responders can mine them to ask questions that you didn't even consider. That is, traces offer a way to capture a dataset that is both narrow and broad: narrow because it represents only the problematic requests, and broad because it's not limited to the avenues of inquiry that you had time to pursue.

Good Postmortems

If you are an adherent of DevOps culture (and you should be!), you probably write and discuss postmortems for each incident in which your team participates. A postmortem is an opportunity to document events leading up to the incident, how it was handled, what was good about the response, and what could have been better. A good postmortem will focus on the facts: to avoid repeating either the incident itself or the mistake made in response to it, it's important to understand precisely what happened.

As is sometimes repeated in SRE circles (and playing off of a British motivational poster from World War II), "keep calm and gather data for the postmortem." It can be difficult in the heat of incident response to keep good records of exactly what you discover. For example, if an upstream service is discovered to have deployed a new release coincidently with the performance regression, that team may be pressured into quickly rolling back that release. When the performance regression disappears minutes later, we might assume that the new release was responsible for that regression. In fact, that release *might* have been responsible, but ideally we would capture some evidence of that. However, we might not have adequate staff to both respond to the incident and build meticulous records of what was happening. Instead, we should consider tools that let us quickly capture evidence—or even potential evidence—of what was going wrong during the incident.

Distributed tracing can provide an easy way to collect that evidence. Due to the very detailed nature of each trace, even just a handful of traces can provide ample information. For example, if spans are tagged with a software release version, the traces of even a few slow requests can provide evidence that that release was responsible for the regression.

Whether you record information for your postmortems in shared docs, in chat rooms, or using other tools, dropping in links to potentially useful traces is well worth your time, even while in the heat of the moment of incident response. They can be used to validate theories of what was happening during the incident. These traces can serve as powerful visual aids during postmortems and operational reviews.

Approaches to Restoring Performance

With the right SLOs in place, you can be confident that you have made a good start at understanding what baseline performance looks like and when your service has deviated from it. As much as it might feel like a solo endeavor at times, incident response is always a group effort.

We continue with several approaches that show how distributed tracing can help determine and mitigate the root cause of performance regressions. In most cases, each approach will apply to a wide range of types of changes. For example, whether you've just deployed a new version of your service, one of your upstream dependencies has, or one of your downstream users has, tracing can help you identify if and when those changes are affecting your service's performance.

Tracing can also serve as a communication tool, and each of the following approaches provides ways of facilitating communication during or after incident response.

Integration with Alerting Workflows

Incident response is often triggered by an automated alert. That is, some SLI has crossed a predetermined threshold, escalation policies and on-call schedules have been consulted, and someone's phone starts ringing or buzzing (or both). If this is your phone, you stumble out of bed, open your laptop, and begin investigating. At a minimum, this alert includes the SLI and the threshold. From there, it's up to you to begin building theories about what's going wrong and how you might mitigate that problem. Typically this involves opening one or more observability tools and looking for signs of the problem.

In rest of the chapter, we'll consider a number of different ways that distributed tracing can help identify the root causes of regressions and restore baseline performance. These techniques are particularly effective if some preliminary results are included as part of alerts. In that case, you can simply click on a link to begin investigation.

This should be relatively straightforward for all of the approaches we describe, from the simplest to the most sophisticated. For example, if an alert is triggered because an error rate has spiked, there must be at least one failed request. Or if an SLI like latency has crossed some threshold, then there will be a number of requests slower than that threshold that can form the basis of an analysis. Including traces of those requests (as well as the results of other analysis) as part of an alert can save you valuable time. While raw metrics and logs can also be included as part of an alert, neither offers the context that distributed traces can provide.

It's beyond the scope of this book to give a complete accounting of best practices around alerting. However, it's still worth a few words to remind you to *alert on symptoms*, not causes. This means that alerts should be triggered based on things that your users can observe, likely the same metrics that you choose to be part of your SLOs and SLAs. Conveniently, there are typically only a handful of symptoms that matter for most services (meaning that you have only a small set of alerts to maintain and document). On the other hand, the number of possible causes of a performance regression is orders of magnitude larger. It's the role of tracing—and for that matter, any observability tool—to reduce the number of possibilities that you must consider when looking for a root cause. If information that helps expedite this process can be included in the alert itself, all the better!

This can be taken one step further to help make sure the right people are alerted when there is a regression. For example, if an SLO is about to be violated, then *someone* should probably be alerted. But should it the owner of the API gateway (which lies closest to the user and the definition of the SLO) or of the backend service that ultimately served the requests (and returned the errors)? Probably better to start with the backend service owner, since that's where the errors originated. They can always bring a member of the API gateway team into the investigation if necessary. Using information in the trace, alerting systems can route alerts to those developers and operators most likely to be able to address the root cause. This is a way of automating the technique described earlier as "suppressing" the messenger: it can shave valuable minutes off of your MTTR and also significantly reduce the number of interruptions to others' work (and sleep) across your organization.

Individual Traces

Looking at individual traces is one of the simplest ways of leveraging tracing as part of incident response and root cause analysis. Individual traces are particularly useful when failures are black and white: for example, when a breaking change is deployed to your service or to another. This means that all requests (or at least a significant number of them) are failing, so it's easy for you to identify one such request.

Figure 9-1 shows an example of a failed request. An error is propagated from the span labeled D up through B up to the top of the trace. (Spans which resulted in an error are loosely outlined.) Looking at the logs associated with span D, we see that the error is related to the response that it got from span E (that is, some invariant that it expected was not met). This could mean one of a couple of things: either D represents a recent deployment or E represents a recent deployment. Once you've determined which service has recently deployed a new release, mitigating the issue is just a matter of finding the appropriate service owner and getting them to roll back that deployment. And as noted earlier, sending along the trace shown in the figure will be a great way to motivate them to do so! This example uses a combination of traces and logs: the trace helps identify the impact of an error, and logs provide additional information to help pinpoint the problem. In isolation, neither would be as powerful.

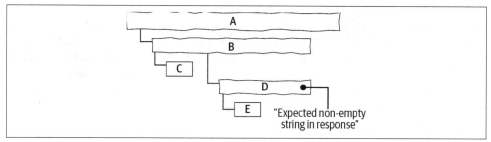

Figure 9-1. Trace showing an error propagating up the stack.

The risk of using individual traces during incident response is that, because you are moving fast, it can be easy to overgeneralize from a single trace and draw an incorrect conclusion about the cause of the incident. For example, perhaps the error shown in Figure 9-1 has been occurring for a long time and what's changed recently is how that error is handled. Or perhaps a change in user behavior is triggering that error. (In either case, it would still be a good idea to eventually fix the error, but your focus in responding to an incident should be to find the *safest* way to mitigate the problem, not necessarily the cleanest way of fixing a bug.) Some of the approaches later in this chapter will show how to leverage more than one trace—even hundreds or thousands —to avoid this sort of "premature generalization."

Biased Sampling

As described in the previous chapter, biasing trace sampling based on the SLIs that are important to your business or organization is an effective way to derive value from distributed tracing. As in that chapter, biasing toward slower or failed requests can help make sure outliers are available for analysis. However, in the context of restoring baseline performance, there are a few other kinds of bias that can also be valuable.

Most regressions in performance are caused by changes to the application or its environment, so biasing sampling with an eye toward those changes can be useful. For example:

- If you are about to make an infrastructure configuration change, make sure you have adequate traces from before and after the change.

- As you deploy a new version of your service, make sure you have traces from both the old and the new versions.

- If you are starting an experiment or slowly rolling out a new and significant feature, make sure you have traces from before, during, and after the change.

To bias sampling during these sorts of events, there are a couple of possible approaches to consider. First, your tracing tool may allow you to dynamically trigger adjustments to the sampling algorithm using an API call or a configuration change. For example, you may be able to temporarily increase the number of traces collected from certain hosts. If you do so for hosts running a new version of your service, you will bias sampling toward that new version.

A second approach is to add tags to spans to make these changes apparent in the telemetry data itself. For example, adding tags that describe infrastructure or software versions means that you can easily see when a given request hit a new version or an old one (or in some cases, both). What's especially powerful about this approach is that it also means that the tracing tool can detect these changes and automatically change the sampling algorithm to account for this. For example, if a new version of a service is being incrementally deployed, spans from the new version will have a tag that's never been seen before. This can be used to increase the sampling rate for traces from the new version and also to increase the sampling rate for traces from the *old* version (relative to services not undergoing any changes at the moment). Having both facilitates better comparisons between the two versions.

Integration with your infrastructure, deployment, and experiment management tools can help make this sort of biased sampling easier to achieve. Infrastructure and deployment tools can set environment variables that can be used to include infrastructure configuration and software versions as part of spans. Experiment management tools (including feature flagging systems) can be configured or extended to annotate spans with the current active experiments and feature configuration. In any case, when there are planned changes to your software or infrastructure, making sure your distributed tracing solution is aware (one way or another) of those changes will help ensure that you have the data necessary to understand their impact.

Leveraging Tracing with Chaos Engineering

One additional opportunity for integrating tracing with other production tools is in chaos engineering: the practice of deliberately injecting failures into your distributed system to understand how your software—and your team—will respond to them. While not technically part of incident response or restoring baseline performance, this practice can help you prepare for when real issues do occur. Distributed tracing can help provide the data necessary to address any issues that are discovered through this technique.

Of course, the failures introduced as part of chaos engineering should be rare enough that they don't affect user-visible performance. Unfortunately, this also means that requests with injected failures are unlikely to be collected using uniform sampling techniques. As in the case of new releases and other planned changes, adding tags to spans to indicate when failures are deliberate can help address this issue and make sure that traces are collected for analysis.

Tracing can also help recognize cases when injected faults *are* affecting users. Injected failures that are propagated all the way to the top of the stack can be discovered by looking for traces that contain both a span with an injected failure and a root span with an error. If these cases occur, a team member can be immediately alerted or (even better) that type of injected failure can be disabled.

Real-Time Response

Unlike planned performance improvement work, where you have plenty of time to carefully gather data to support your decisions, it's difficult to anticipate what sorts of data will be necessary when responding to an incident, nor will you have as much time as you'd like to collect it. However, distributed tracing tools can provide real-time search functionality to get you up to speed quickly on what's happening.

Figure 9-2 shows an example of trace search functionality offered by Zipkin. (Though you can see from the figure that this tool offers more than just real-time search, we'll ignore the "lookback" option in this section.) Using this functionality, you can look for traces that include a particular service, whose latency exceeds a given threshold, or that contain some particular tag or other metadata. Using this, you can find traces that are examples of slow or failed requests and—as you start to build a theory as to what's gone wrong—traces that exhibit other features that you believe might help explain the issue. For example, you might suspect a canary release is responsible for a regression, so searching for traces handled by that canary is a good place to start. By performing multiple searches, you can also compare traces to begin to understand their differences.

Figure 9-2. Screenshot of Zipkin's trace search functionality.

This functionality is similar to that provided by many log aggregation tools—both provide for ad hoc searches over a large corpus of diagnostic data. However, in most cases, logs that provide evidence of the problem will rarely provide evidence of *the cause* of the problem. Tracking down logs from service to service can be difficult, but (in contrast) distributed tracing tools can easily put those logs in the context of an end-to-end request. That is unless, of course, you've managed to add correlation IDs to all of your logs. If you have included these sorts of identifiers throughout your logs, you've essentially turned your logging system into a tracing one (though probably not a very efficient one), as discussed in Chapter 7.

Different tracing tools collect and store data in different ways, so the exact functionality offered by your tool might be different than what's shown in Figure 9-2. Despite this, we can still speculate about what's possible with distributed tracing based on the following two observations:

- Network performance (and in particular, *local* network performance) continues to rapidly improve.
- The data required for real-time response is, almost by definition, short-lived.

The first observation means that it should be possible to extract a large portion, if not all, of the tracing data from the application at a reasonable cost. This means that even rare events can be extracted and available for real-time search and analysis. The second means that—at least for real-time analysis—tracing solutions are not required to persist data for extended periods of time. This can greatly reduce the overall cost of storing traces and other telemetry.

This raises a question: what does "real-time" mean in distributed tracing, anyway? Given that most changes to a distributed application are instigated by a human and take at least a few seconds to propagate and take effect, getting results in less than a second is probably not necessary (especially since many *requests* might even take a second or two). On the other hand, waiting even one or two minutes for new data to appear in an observability tool can be excruciating if you are trying to understand if the release you just deployed has fixed a regression. Having to wait hours can make such a tool all but useless!

Ultimately, what "real-time" means will depend on other aspects of your incident response process (including how fast you can detect changes and act to address them) and on the commitments you've made to your users. If you are running a highly available application, every minute of downtime matters, and so does every minute of delay between when a change happens and when you can investigate it.

If we expect that developers will be alerted within a few minutes of when regressions occur, then most trace searches that occur as part of incident response will also occur within a few minutes of those requests. All tracing tools should capture and store some historical traces to help establish a baseline; however, tracing solutions that specialize in supporting real-time response can keep a much more detailed record of what's occurred in the last few minutes. In those cases, those responding to an incident have access to nearly arbitrary data about what's happened—precluding the need to know what queries will be run in advance or to set up filters or triggers to make sure useful traces are captured. By *temporarily* storing these traces, tracing solutions can do so at a reasonable cost.

Knowing What's Normal

While setting an SLO can help set a simple expectation for baseline performance, there will obviously be much more variation in actual performance, even under normal conditions. For example, user behavior will likely follow diurnal or weekly cycles which in turn will affect performance. Given those *expected* changes, having a more refined definition of baseline performance is key to effective incident response. One way to better understand what's normal is to compare current performance to one hour ago, one day ago, or one week ago. (If your business is a retailer, you likely need to consider other sorts of seasonality as well.)

Understanding current performance relative to what's normal will enable you to make better decisions. For example, suppose your traffic rate is steadily growing and that this increased load is (you believe) also causing increased response latency. Though it is still below your SLO, if latency were to continue to climb, you will soon cross that threshold. Should you provision more instances to account for this load? Or wait it out (and avoid unnecessary infrastructure costs)? Really the question you are asking is, are you at peak traffic or not? The answer to this question is largely based on when the peak occurred yesterday, last week, or last year.

Figure 9-3 shows two examples of how visualizations of historical data can be used to understand baseline performance and how that performance has changed. The left side is a time series graph showing periodic behavior in both latency (top) and traffic rate (bottom). Two time series are overlaid for both metrics. One graph (black) shows how the service performed last week. The other graph (which ends at the vertical line corresponding to Friday evening) shows how the service is performing so far this week. The traffic rate (bottom) shows both diurnal and weekly cycles, with the highest peaks in the evenings over the weekend. The vertical bar represents the current time. From looking at this graph at (1), you can determine that load is close to, but not quite at, peak, so provisioning a few more instances might be a good idea.

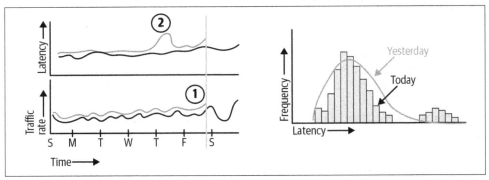

Figure 9-3. *Using historical performance to establish what's normal.*

Interestingly, there was also a spike in 95th-percentile latency (top) that occurred earlier in the week at (2). This did not correspond with an increase in traffic nor was there a spike at this point in time during the previous week. This indicates a deviation from normal and that some other event (for example, a deployment) may have caused the change in latency.

The right side of Figure 9-3 is a histogram with an overlay of past performance. The bars show the current distribution of latencies (say, for requests in the last hour). The line shows the distribution of requests for the same time period *yesterday*. In this case, there is a second peak in today's graph that did not appear in yesterday's graph. This would indicate that there is some new aspect of service performance that didn't exist yesterday or that some users' behavior has changed in a significant way.

This analysis of histograms is related to the multimodal analysis described in Chapter 8. In this case, however, rather than simply comparing two or more peaks within a single distribution, we are comparing the *number and sizes* of the peaks in two different distributions.

Note that "what's normal" need not be expressed solely in terms of software performance like latency or error rates. For example, tracking aggregate user behavior can also play a role in determining what's normal. Knowing typical conversion rates and session lengths can help to establish whether your users are deviating from their usual behavior. Any deviation might be a key symptom of a regression in software performance—or it might even be the cause of a change in software performance. In either case, understanding user behavior helps put application performance into the larger context of how it matters to your business or organization.

Automated analysis of traces in can also help establish if performance has deviated from normal. Up until now we've considered changes in performance mostly as measured by metrics like high-percentile latency. However, while looking at percentiles is often better than looking at just medium latency, focusing only on percentiles can still cause you to miss significant changes in performance. Here, we consider how an automated analysis can look at the *shape* of a latency distribution and determine whether there's likely to have been a change.

Earlier we considered how current performance could be compared with past performance by overlaying two latency histograms. While this can be a useful way to identify many kinds of changes, it still has its limits. For example, Figure 9-4 shows latency histograms for two samples. Suppose we were trying to decide if the second sample represents a change in performance from the first or just more of the same. There is less than a 5% difference in 99th-percentile latency and less than a 1% difference in 99.9th-percentile latency between the two samples. From these measurements and looking at the two histograms, you might think that the two samples represent the same underlying service behavior.

However, a huge portion of the requests on the right side (nearly half!) are significantly faster than those on the left side. Most of these fast requests fall into the first bucket in the histogram (as indicated by the arrow) and were only tens of milliseconds in duration. (Remember that, like many of the histograms shown in the book, the vertical axis is plotted on a logarithmic scale.) This could be due to the introduction of a cache or some similar optimization. Regardless of what caused it, if neither metrics like high-percentile latency nor visual inspection are sufficient to tell *when* something has changed, we must consider other tools.

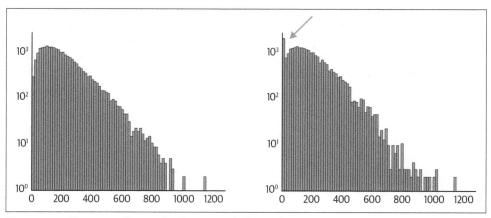

Figure 9-4. Two visually similar but very different histograms.

Fortunately, there are a number of robust statistical techniques for determining whether two sample sets are likely to be taken from the same distribution. While a thorough description of these techniques (and how you might choose among them) is beyond the scope of this book, we'll consider one technique and describe how you might use it to address this problem. What you should take away is that, first, these techniques exist; and second, they have powerful applications to measuring performance changes.

The technique that we will consider here uses the Kolmogorov-Smirnov (K-S) statistic. The K-S statistic measures the difference between two distributions as a single scalar number. To describe this technique we first need to define one other concept from the study of statistics. So far we have showed a number of histograms as a way of visualizing a distribution; here, we will show a *cumulative distribution function* (CDF). This differs from histograms in two ways. First, as the name suggests, we *accumulate* counts, so each point on a CDF is the sum of all of the corresponding histogram points to its left. Second, the vertical axis is normalized, so it ranges from zero to one. Framing sample sets as CDFs will enable us to more easily compare them.

Figure 9-5 shows two cumulative distribution functions. While the upper line grows more slowly initially than the lower one, it quickly overtakes it. If rendered in a histogram, this would be shown as a steeper peak that appeared farther to the left. The K-S statistic is generated from the largest vertical distance between the two CDFs, as shown by the arrow. The larger that distance, the more likely that the two CDFs were drawn from different distributions; that is, that there was an actual change in performance. As you can imagine, such a measure can be quickly and automatically computed for a large number of histograms.

How is such a statistic used? Is there a threshold for the K-S statistic (or any similar statistic) that, when crossed, would mean that a regression has occurred? In general, no, as the performance of many services will change over time. Even if a service has experienced the largest change in performance across your application, that doesn't necessarily mean that anything is wrong or, even if something is wrong, that that service is the root cause of the issue. However, techniques like the K-S statistic are useful for organizing information. For example, sorting services (or operations, etc.) according to the K-S statistic or other measures of change can help human responders identify root causes.

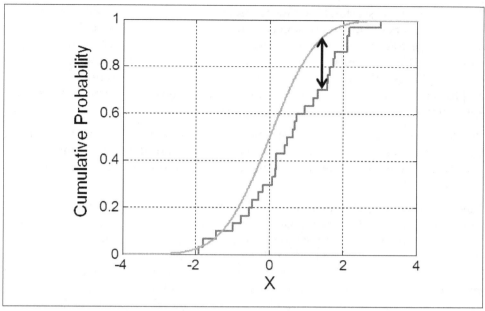

Figure 9-5. Cumulative distribution functions of two sample sets; the arrow shows the Kolmogorov–Smirnov statistic[1].

Aggregate and Correlation Root Cause Analysis

The technique described in the previous section is one example of an *aggregate* analysis: it used not just one or two traces but a statistically significant sample to determine *if* a change in performance has occurred. Once you've determined that there *has* been a change in performance, restoring baseline performance usually comes down to finding the root cause or causes of that change. (Sound simple enough?) In Chapter 8, we showed how aggregate analyses can be used to improve baseline performance; these approaches also have powerful applications in understanding changes to your application and its environment and, ultimately, in addressing performance regressions.

The first step in any of these approaches is to divide traces into two sample sets; these will form the basis of any comparison. In the context of restoring baseline performance, the first sample set should come from the regression itself. This is usually easy if the regression is happening right now. If you know that the regression is present in only a portion of requests (for example, if you know there is a problem with a canary release) then sampling from that portion is also important.

---

1 Source: Wikipedia (*https://oreil.ly/Sc0wk*).

The second sample set should represent baseline performance. This will likely be a set of traces from before the regression started, perhaps from an hour, a day, or a week ago: leverage your understanding of what's normal for your application and choose a baseline set from a similar point in whatever cyclic behavior your application and users exhibit. As in the preceding section, using overlaid time series or histogram graphs can help to understand how performance varies over time, and therefore help you identify a sample set to represent baseline performance.

Recall that correlation analysis means taking these two sample sets and then finding features of traces that appear in one of those sets but not the other. Although such correlation is not a guarantee of causation, it is often a strong clue that can lead you to the cause of a regression.

Latency, errors, tags, and other metadata can all be valuable features of traces that you can use to understand what's changed. It's worth a reminder that part of the power of distributed tracing is that it puts performance changes in the context of what's happening *throughout* your application. When determining which attributes of traces should be used as part of correlation analysis, remember that these should come from *every* span in these traces, not just the ones corresponding to your service. Even the *existence* of certain spans within a trace can be a powerful signal in understanding what's changed.

As an example, suppose that you believe that request latency has increased for your service, and you compare a sample of traces that have occurred in the last five minutes to those that occurred an hour ago. Table 9-1 shows a small set of features that might be identified by this analysis.

Table 9-1. Example of correlation analysis used to determine what has changed

Feature	Coefficient of correlation
service: inventory, service.version: 1.14.2	0.65
runinfo.host: vm73	0.41
service: inventory,service.version: 1.14.1	−0.65

The table shows that there is a strong correlation with a new version of the inventory service and the latest traces; it also shows a strong correlation between the previous version of that service and traces from an hour ago. This provides enough evidence to take steps to mitigate the problem—by rolling back the most recent release of the inventory service—and that should be sufficient to let you defer further work until after business hours and to assign it to the appropriate team. (This analysis also shows a correlation between the latest traces and one of the hosts provided as part of the infrastructure. This could be because the new instance of the inventory service was deployed on that host.)

Someone eventually needs to understand the root cause of this issue, and correlation analysis can be used to further refine your understanding of what was happening. Similar to the analysis described in the previous chapter, you might compare slow requests from the last few minutes to faster requests from before the regression. This can identify specific operations that led to higher latency in the new version and help the team responsible for the `inventory` service understand how to address them.

Aggregate analysis can also help to identify more subtle changes in service performance. When comparing two sets of traces, we can look at the latency contributions related to arbitrary tags, operations, and services and how those contributions changed over time.

One method for doing so is to consider how the critical path changes between the baseline and regression sets. In this method, the critical path is computed for each trace. (The definition of the "critical path" is covered in Chapter 8.) The average contribution for each service and operation is then determined for each of the two sets. Services and operations are ranked by the differences between these two averages.

Table 9-2 shows an example of this method. In this example, the `inventory` service continues to have a big impact on the changes in performance. Here the `write-cache` operation contributes more than five times more to the critical path in the regression set than in the baseline set. This is strong evidence that this operation is the cause of the performance regression.

Table 9-2. Critical path contributions in baseline and regression traces

Service/Operation	Baseline	Regression	Change
inventory/write-cache	63.1 ms	368 ms	+305 ms
inventory-db/update	1.75 ms	2.26 ms	+516 ms
memcached/set	4.94 ms	4.71 ms	−230 ms
inventory/update-inventory	15.2 ms	14.8 ms	−470 ms
inventory/database-update	32 ms	30.6 ms	−1.4 ms

Another method for understanding performance changes is to consider every tag found in either set of traces. For each tag, all spans in each set on which that tag appears are enumerated and the average duration of those spans is computed for each set. Tags are then ranked based on the difference between those two averages.

Table 9-3 shows an example of what this might look like. Four tags are shown with changes in average duration between a few hundred milliseconds and more than a second. The tag `item-time: new` undergoes the biggest change between the baseline set and the regression, moving from 114 ms to 1.24 seconds. This would be a great place to start looking for what code changed between releases. In other cases, these results might indicate a change not in the application itself but in the behavior of some clients (`client.browser`) or in contention for a resource (`db.instance` or `runinfo.host`).

Table 9-3. Average duration for spans in baseline and regression traces

Tag	Baseline (ms)	Regression (ms)	Change (ms)
item-type: new	114	1240	+1130
client.browser: mozilla68	111	548	+437
db.instance: cassandra.4	117	464	+348
runinfo.host: vm123	116	453	+337

Both the contribution to the critical path and total duration can play roles in finding the root cause—or causes—of a performance problem. The critical path is often better in isolating what code is consuming more resources as part of the regression; total duration can detect changes that occurred outside a single piece of code. Sometimes a change is solely a result of new code or configuration being deployed but sometimes it is also a result of the interaction between old code and new code. For example, a new version of your mobile app may make API calls using a different set of parameters. This change may show up as a tag on the span emitted from the mobile app or from the API gateway, but that span may not contribute much time to the critical path. Using both methods will help you to mitigate the problem (perhaps by provisioning additional resources) as well as put a longer-term fix into place (perhaps by optimizing the old code).

Aggregate root cause analysis overcomes many of the problems with analyses based on just a few traces: when using a small number of examples, it's easy to build—and justify—false theories that "explain" performance regressions. Moreover, automating this process can eliminate many of the problems with doing this sort of analysis manually: it can take a long time for developers to consider a significant number of traces.

With approaches like aggregate root cause analysis, distributed tracing not only enables developers to validate or refute hypotheses that they may have created through intuition or previous experience but can also help developers to *form those hypotheses* in the first place. This is especially important in a distributed system, as there may be thousands (or even millions) of different signals that can potentially point to the root cause, but even more so during an incident, when intuition and previous experience aren't always enough.

Summary

Some readers may be surprised at the approaches described in this and the previous chapters, since they might not be considered traditional applications of distributed tracing. Many developers think of tracing only as an option of last resort, to be used when other tools (including metric and log aggregation tools) fail. This could be because tracing is still unfamiliar to many developers, as tracing is the newest of the three so-called "pillars" of observability and has only become an important tool since the adoption of microservices and other distributed architectures.

This is unfortunate because tracing has a lot to offer to developers. When we considered a scorecard for observability tools in Chapter 7, we noted the importance of providing context, prioritizing by impact, and automating correlation. Observability tools must be able to:

- Show how performance problems in one service are related to the behavior of other services
- Show how a service's performance impacts *user-visible* performance (or not)
- Automatically identify which changes in a distributed application might be the root causes of performance issues

All three of these are important in prioritizing work on improving performance and in responding to incidents quickly; in the latter case, they're especially so since these capabilities mean that developers can more effectively and efficiently communicate with each other and across teams.

Unfortunately, it's not sufficient to simply layer distributed tracing on top of existing observability tools. This might be enough to enable developers to look at individual traces, but as we've shown, the real power of tracing comes through approaches like aggregate analysis that use hundreds or thousands of traces to draw conclusions. As many of our examples demonstrate, for distributed tracing to really deliver on all of the aspects of our scorecard, it must be used in a way where trace data is used alongside metrics and logs.

Put another way, while looking at *traces* can offer some insight to developers, the real value of *tracing* ultimately comes from using trace data—along with metrics and logs —to quickly understand when performance problems are occurring and to identify the root causes of those problems. It does so by explaining variation in performance: both offering hypotheses that succinctly describe the cause and providing evidence to support those hypotheses.

Tracing makes this possible by making the relationships between causes and effects explicit. It ties different kinds of telemetry together using end-to-end requests to reveal the structure of your application. Without tracing, you will often see a (potentially large) set of metrics that are all changing at the same time, and you won't be able to figure out which are the root causes. With tracing, you can identify which metrics are relevant to the issue you are trying to address *and* have the context to understand why. While tracing by itself isn't a complete observability solution, it is a necessary part of observability for any distributed system.

CHAPTER 10

Are We There Yet? The Past and Present

If you've read this book, then let us offer our congratulations! We have officially covered the full range of technical topics, and you are ready to put distributed tracing to good use in your own applications.

We're now going to turn our gaze toward the future, and discuss some new challenges that distributed tracing might be able to solve in the future (possibly with some tweaks to the way things work under the hood).

We'll also look back at how some of the concepts described in this book came to be. They certainly didn't materialize out of thin air! Rather, distributed tracing as we know it is the result of a gradual evolution—a process that is not yet over. What lessons can we learn from the journey so far? And in what ways might distributed tracing continue to evolve?

Of course, we cannot predict the future with total certainty. We can, however, point out places where careful decision-making today might make your life substantially easier down the line. We've already emphasized this sort of judicious decision-making throughout the book, such as keeping instrumentation implementation-agnostic, and pushing instrumentation to the framework level where possible. For the future, it's all about making ourselves robust to what *might* happen. What kinds of new use cases might distributed tracing solve? How might we use or repurpose the constituent pieces of distributed tracing?

For many of these questions, we can find possible answers by looking to the world of distributed systems research. Researchers are often proposing new designs and optimizations, identifying new classes of problems, and presenting new perspectives on old problems. In the rest of this book, we will discuss some of this research.

Distributed Tracing: A History of Pragmatism

There's a surprising contrast between how long distributed tracing has been around and how long distributed systems have been around.

Distributed systems have been around for more than half a century. So too have problems related to understanding their behavior and their performance.

By comparison, distributed tracing tools only started to emerge a little over a decade ago! What's more, only within the past few years have we started to see standards for distributed tracing, open source frameworks, and the growth of a community.

Request-Based Systems

To understand why this is, we have to look back at where today's microservice architectures came from. Although the history of distributed systems stretches back decades, many of the systems that we have today can trace their origins back to the late 1990s, when the explosive growth of the internet was in full swing. This growth led to a huge proliferation of *request-response systems*, such as two-tier websites, with a web server frontend and a database backend. While request-response systems as a concept were certainly not new, the web put this type of system front and center.

Response Time Matters

A subtler change occurred with the growing prominence of request-response systems. Previously, the most common approach to evaluating systems' performance was to measure system health in aggregate, by considering system-wide metrics such as throughput and relating them to system-wide measures such as performance counters over time.

For internet systems, though, throughput wasn't the most important metric. Instead, it was response latency. First and foremost, it was important for the system to respond promptly to requests, because there's usually a human with a limited attention span sitting at the other end. Some of the major internet companies even quantified this: in 2006, Google found that increasing page load time from 400 ms to 900 ms caused a 20% drop in traffic.[1] Other studies in recent years have measured similar effects.[2]

---

1 [Lin06]

2 [Sou09]

Request-Oriented Information

This shift in focus also changed which information was most useful for system analysis and troubleshooting. Understanding the factors contributing to response latency required being able to drill down into slow requests to see where the slowdown came from and why. Requests were a new dimension for reasoning about systems, orthogonal to any one machine or process in aggregate.

However, this new request-oriented perspective also presented new challenges. Teasing out request-oriented information wasn't easy, because request-response systems execute (and interleave) many requests concurrently. Many of the existing approaches to performance analysis at the time weren't quite the right fit, often because they focused on aggregate system measures and throughput.

Distributed tracing grew out of this need. Researchers and practitioners were interested in analyzing performance and troubleshooting problems in request-response systems. Some pieces of distributed tracing came from these early explorations. Eventually, simple request-response systems evolved into the complex microservice architectures we have today. Likewise, some of the early request-oriented approaches to analysis and troubleshooting were adapted and generalized so that they could extend to these new scenarios.

This is the origin of distributed tracing. Instead of thinking of distributed tracing as a standalone entity, we should regard it as a pragmatic combination of different design pieces, chosen because they make the most sense for the systems and environments that we have *today*. Although distributed tracing is not the only approach we could have taken, it is probably the best approach for the kind of analysis we want to do today.

Notable Work

Many people have contributed to distributed tracing over the years. From this large body of work, there are four pieces that have been especially influential, because they embody key ideas that have shaped today's distributed tracing frameworks.

The first is a research prototype called Pinpoint. The second is an industry research prototype called Magpie. The third is a research prototype called X-Trace. The fourth is a production system from Google called Dapper.

Pinpoint

Pinpoint was a research prototype developed in 2002 by researchers at the University of California at Berkeley and Stanford University.[3] Its goal was to identify the root causes of problems in internet services.

Pinpoint represented a shift in approaches to problem-solving. The authors recognized the growing mismatch between the problem-solving techniques of the time, and the new class of dynamic, always-on, constantly evolving internet services. Before Pinpoint, a common approach to root cause analysis was to statically model systems. But in a constantly evolving internet service, keeping models both up to date and correct became a gargantuan task.

Today, these challenges might seem obvious. Imagine trying to statically model your microservice architecture, along with all of its dependencies! Imagine the logistical nightmare of keeping this model up to date with every change committed!

Pinpoint was one of the first to argue for a request-oriented and data-driven approach. Rather than proactively modeling the system, the authors thought it better to measure the system and use the recorded data to troubleshoot problems after the fact. Sound familiar?

Key to Pinpoint was being able to group information on a per-request basis. To do this, Pinpoint assigned each request a unique request ID, which it maintained in thread-local storage—an idea that eventually became the trace contexts that we propagate today. Pinpoint didn't fully explore these ideas, though; it was only intended for a single-machine Java Enterprise environment, so maintaining request IDs could be done easily within the middleware. Pinpoint did not yet deal with context propagation between machines or user-created threads.

Magpie

Magpie was an industrial research prototype developed in 2004 by researchers at Microsoft Research Cambridge.[4] Its goal was to record detailed end-to-end traces (much like the traces we get today with Jaeger or Zipkin) and annotate those traces with fine-grained information about the resources consumed during execution (such as I/O and CPU measurements). Much of its technical focus was on disentangling concurrent requests that execute *within* the same software components.

Magpie was a more broadly applicable tool than Pinpoint, because the authors designed it for arbitrary, heterogeneous .NET applications. Like Pinpoint, Magpie needed request-oriented information. However, it ran headfirst into a problem that

---

3 [Che02]

4 [Bar04]

Pinpoint had carefully sidestepped: in Magpie's heterogeneous environment, there was no ubiquitous middleware and no easy way to propagate request IDs; the only option was exhaustive source code instrumentation. The authors faced a tough decision, and ultimately decided *not* to propagate request IDs. Instead, Magpie inferred correlations mostly from existing outputs.

Specifically, Magpie integrated with Windows XP's Event Tracing for Windows (ETW), a lightweight event logging framework which already recorded many thread-, networking-, and resource-related events. Relationships between events could often be inferred already from the events, including events occurring in the same threads, and between some concurrent activities (such as kicking off a new thread). The authors only had to add additional events in a few choice locations to complete the end-to-end picture of a request (e.g., if there was network communication, the sender and receiver would need to explicitly log a connection ID on both ends). From these events, all that remained was a postprocessing step to construct traces from the recorded events. Magpie relied on a developer-supplied scheme to describe how to parse events and extract correlation IDs.

Magpie is an interesting system because it grappled with the difficulty of making a general-purpose tool. Pinpoint could take shortcuts because it only dealt with J2EE applications; Magpie could not. Since Magpie, other research has explored inference-based approaches; for example in 2014 Facebook presented a similar system called "The Mystery Machine."[5]

However, while inferring request structure is an appealing alternative to doing exhaustive instrumentation, the downside is that it's a less scalable and more brittle approach, since it depends on event parsing and correct developer-supplied schemas.

Ultimately, distributed tracing *does* use context propagation, and practitioners have collectively decided that it *is* worth the instrumentation effort.

Although request traces alone are a useful starting point, Magpie also demonstrated the value in incorporating fine-grained information like resource usage into traces. This is something we can think about doing today, because we often have other sources of information outside of distributed tracing (such as ETW events), and we can enhance their value using that information to augment traces.

---

5 [Cho14]

X-Trace

X-Trace was a tracing framework developed in 2007 by researchers at the University of California at Berkeley.[6] Its main goal was troubleshooting requests whose executions spanned many different machines, layers, and administrative domains. X-Trace began to crystalize some key pieces of distributed tracing that are used today, and its open source implementation is still in use.

In the time between Pinpoint (2002) and X-Trace (2007), internet services continued to evolve, growing more complex, more heterogeneous, and more distributed. The need for request-oriented tracing grew in importance, but the approaches taken by tools like Pinpoint and Magpie were starting to show cracks. The main issue was their tight integration with the environments they operated in. It was difficult or impossible to incorporate information spanning different operating systems, programming languages, or layers (such as the network). Today this is something we have grown to expect—there is very little we can assume in common across our microservices!

X-Trace therefore focused on generality: how can we get request traces in such a heterogeneous environment? Its guiding design philosophy was to demand as little from the people using the tool as possible, by imposing minimal assumptions and requirements. To achieve this, X-Trace made two important design choices: first, a standard for context propagation, so that information recorded in different components could be combined coherently; and second, out-of-band report collection, to separate the *recording* of information from its usage.

To avoid having to infer any relationships between events, X-Trace proposed including a *parent ID* as well as a request ID. The parent ID was dynamic, and would be updated every time a new event was recorded. Each event would explicitly record the ID of its causal predecessor.

By including a parent ID, X-Trace's backend components could deterministically reconstruct the order and concurrency of events happening during the request. The backends did not have to rely on post-processing to infer relationships using timing or knowledge of the system's internals. It meant that developers of different system components could make different choices about how to log events, in terms of level of detail as well as the information contained in events. The only requirement was to incorporate and propagate the X-Trace metadata.

X-Trace also separated the recording of information from its usage. This meant developers using it would not have to commit up front to a particular diagnosis technique or use case. The authors foresaw how administrators of different components would also want control over their portion of the trace data (thus not exposing

---

6 [Fon07]

detailed internal information about their systems). Out-of-band data collection achieved this by imposing an abstraction boundary between data generation and the backend concerns of data collection and storage.

Distributed tracing frameworks today follow the same philosophy as X-Trace did: only include the minimal pieces necessary to capture traces. That way, frameworks can still be used even by extremely heterogeneous systems. X-Trace's parent ID is analogous to the parent span IDs used in today's distributed tracing frameworks.

Dapper

Dapper is a tracing framework developed for internal use at Google. It was described in a 2010 whitepaper and is still in use today.[7] You might already be familiar with Dapper, as its design forms the basis of today's most popular distributed tracing frameworks.

Even back before 2010, Google's internal systems were a lot like today's microservice architectures: heavily RPC-based, with a single request invoking many different services, often in parallel. Google faced the same challenges that had motivated prior work, and set about building a distributed tracing framework that would give them request-oriented visibility into large, heterogeneous production systems.

Dapper was the name of this distributed tracing framework. It elaborated on some of the concepts presented by Pinpoint, Magpie, and X-Trace, while simultaneously dealing with new operational challenges that arose from practical experience.

A key concept introduced by Dapper was the *span model* of tracing. By now you'll be familiar with the concept of spans, as a key building block of distributed tracing. However, prior to Dapper, distributed traces were based on the notion of *events*— instantaneous points in time that are very similar to individual logging statements. Events are useful for describing what happened, but they don't directly lead to actionable data, which was important for Dapper. Instead, its authors observed that well-defined segments of request execution (such as individual RPCs) aligned *very* well with their goal of diagnosing performance problems, especially those relating to request latency. Treating spans as a first-class primitive at the *instrumentation* level meant that traces would immediately expose timing information about the most important and meaningful parts of a request.

Before Dapper, the authors of X-Trace had argued that distributed tracing should impose a minimal set of requirements. Dapper, however, imposed an additional requirement on its users, by incorporating spans as a first-class concept. With this careful design change, it substantially improved the *utility* of the resulting traces.

---

7 [Sig10]

Dapper was the first publicly described distributed tracing framework used in production by a large company. In addition to refining the tracing models of prior works, the paper also brought to light operational challenges that hadn't been previously considered, including the need for trace sampling, trade-offs surrounding runtime overheads, security concerns, and how to make trace data accessible to users.

Where to Next?

As the nature of distributed systems changed over the years, so too did the requirements of distributed tracing frameworks. The initial work primarily focused on technical requirements around *how* to get request-oriented information. Gradually, they grew to also incorporate practical requirements, such as how to ease adoption and how to increase trace data utility. As distributed tracing frameworks saw more widespread production use, operational requirements came to light involving scalability and tracing backends.

Although these requirements have shaped the design of distributed tracing frameworks, they aren't set in stone. In particular, new system designs and architectures continue to surface, such as serverless computing, and the increasing representation of streaming systems. As our computing systems change, they may influence or necessitate changes to our distributed tracing frameworks.

Likewise, we do not have all the answers when it comes to troubleshooting distributed systems. Distributed tracing gives us valuable visibility, and requests have proven to be a useful dimension along which to capture information. However, methods to extract value from distributed tracing data are still in flux and less established than the techniques for getting the data. New advances in trace analysis may provoke changes to what data is captured by systems.

In the remaining chapters, we'll take a look at recent research which examines some of these questions. These works bring to light new requirements and new approaches to address existing requirements. Whether these new ideas will ultimately prevail still remains to be seen.

CHAPTER 11
Beyond Individual Requests

You've already seen how traces capture useful information about the end-to-end behavior of individual requests. This includes the time taken by each individual RPC, how much data was transferred at each hop, timeouts, and error responses. By inspecting a single trace carefully, you can often explain why the request took the time that it did. For example, you might see that a particular request missed in the cache. Perhaps a service returned an exceptionally large response record that took a long time to serialize and deserialize. Maybe there's a straggler in a large RPC fanout that responds many milliseconds after its peers. Perhaps the trace reveals the dreaded staircase pattern, where RPC calls that should be parallel are in fact executing serially.

Any one of these situations would reveal something important about that particular trace, but as the span timing diagram in Figure 11-1 illustrates, it's hard to interpret these behaviors in isolation. What you can't tell from individual traces is how often the situation occurs, and in response to which types of requests. Therefore, should you—the service operator or owner—take some action to fix the problem, or is it a one-off that is unlikely to happen again in your lifetime? Which of the suspicious-looking parts of a trace are actually unusual? By comparing a single trace to an aggregate, or one aggregate set to another, you can learn *contextual* information that helps answer such questions.

The benefits of aggregate traces don't stop there. In addition to giving context for interpreting an individual trace, groups of traces can enlighten us about the system as a whole, even when everything is working normally. One of the most common applications for trace aggregations is to extract the dependencies between services in a production system (see Figure 11-2), while others include capacity planning, A/B testing, and detecting workload trends. In "Aggregate Analysis" on page 171, we talked about using aggregate critical path analysis to discover where to focus optimization efforts, and in "Correlation Analysis" on page 173, we showed how correlation analysis can help with root cause diagnosis.

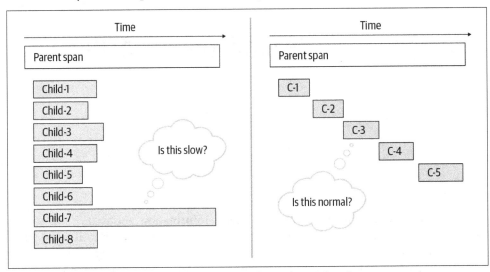

Figure 11-1. Interpreting individual traces without data is hard.

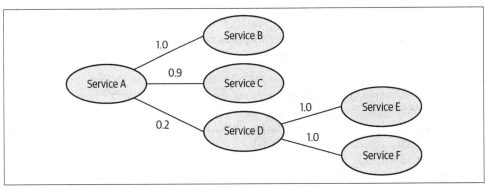

Figure 11-2. A service dependency graph; the edge weights indicate the fraction of traces containing that dependency.

To recap, trace aggregations provide context in two complementary ways. First, they show whether a particular measurement or behavior is anomalous compared to the typical trace as well as the prevalence of that characteristic. Second, aggregations capture what is normal in the system, defining a reference point for typical behavior and generating data for tasks such as provisioning, alerts, and tracking trends over time.

In the rest of this chapter we will dig a little deeper into how to use the context provided by aggregate traces to focus debugging efforts and extract insights about system behavior.

The Value of Traces in Aggregate

Let's look at some concrete examples to illustrate how trace aggregations are useful in practice.

Example 1: Is Network Congestion Affecting My Application?

You have a congested link in your datacenter network, indicated by some metric such as counters from the network switch. You want to find out what impact, if any, the congestion is having on your application traffic. Specifically, given a trace of a request that is potentially affected, you would pose the question: "Is this latency high?" To answer, you first need to decide what "high" means, and typically the 95th or 99th percentile would be a good choice of definition (see "High-Percentile Latency" on page 150). Then, take a control group of traces (say, a similar population over a period when the link was not congested), and compare the 99th-percentile latency with that of traces captured during the congestion.

Conversely, you may use the same information about what defines high latency to pick example traces for closer inspection. In this example, you could examine communication patterns in traces exhibiting high latency to decide whether the slowness is correlated with the problematic network link.

Example 2: What Services Are Required to Serve an API Endpoint?

You've decided to serve some of your API endpoints out of a different datacenter and you wish to avoid cross-datacenter traffic by keeping together the microservices used to serve the same endpoint. To help in planning, you want to identify how many microservices participate in serving each endpoint. "What is the average number of services involved in requests to a particular API endpoint?"

To answer this question using aggregated traces, you would group by endpoint requests and then count the number of unique services that were present before taking the average of each group of traces. Because you're looking at the aggregate, you're not misled by natural variations in the number of services involved. Dynamic dependencies, such as when a cache miss causes a backend storage service to be invoked, are common in microservice architectures, and a single trace may not contain the entire set of dependent services.

In addition to system-wide insights, you can use contextual knowledge derived from the aggregate set of traces to be more effective when debugging with traces. Focusing attention on traces in the tail of the relevant distribution is often a good start.

For instance, if you observe that the RPC send and receive times in a slow trace are in the 99th percentile of the distribution for that value across all traces, then that's a strong clue that the problem might lie in the network. On the other hand, if you see a slow RPC but note that it is orders of magnitude larger than the average size across all traces, you may reasonably conclude that the propagation delay in this case is as expected and not (necessarily) relevant to the problem you are debugging. Notice that both cases have involved using an aggregation function over some property of the traces (99th percentile of transmission time and average message size, respectively) to provide context for debugging.

Being able to check whether the characteristics of a specific trace are abnormal means that you can focus your debugging in the most promising places. Being able to check whether the suspicious stuff occurs in *enough* traces to matter directs debugging efforts to the most impactful problems.

Organizing the Data

The examples we described in the previous section rely on applying aggregation to different components of the traces. You answered the first question ("Is this latency high?") by looking at the distribution of a single value—the duration—that is a basic property of each trace. By contrast, the question "What is the average number of services for requests to a particular API endpoint?" requires applying an aggregate function to a value derived from counting the number of services contained within each trace.

What this means in practice is that the best way to organize aggregate trace data to be able to answer such a range of questions is not obvious. If you only want to answer the first type of question, then you can store trace attributes in flat tables, for example in a relational database. If the second type is more important, you might consider using a graph store (recall that traces are really graphs). In either case, it may also be useful to run user-defined queries that apply to arbitrary tags, and so you will probably want a way to support them too.

Clearly, how best to make traces available for aggregate analysis depends on the particular requirements of the operating environment. For this reason, we are not going to say that one way is better than another, but instead we will use a strawperson solution—taking the "flat tables" approach—to illustrate the trade-offs involved more concretely.

A Strawperson Solution

We'll start by picking SQL as our query language, leaving the specific storage backend unspecified—for example, it could be a relational database or a Hive data warehouse. In the following examples, we'll use nonstandard, SQL-like pseudocode.

Let's begin by considering how you would use SQL to answer the question from Example 1. This is actually straightforward. As described earlier, you choose 99th-percentile duration as the aggregation function, which you then apply to your collection of traces. Thus the query to learn the exact value of "high" will look something like this:

```
SELECT PERCENTILE(duration, 0.99)
FROM traces
```

More realistically, you will likely want to filter the traces according to attributes like the date or the type of request, and this extends the query to:

```
SELECT PERCENTILE(duration, 0.99)
FROM traces
WHERE date = `today` AND type = 'http'
```

Notice that we have assumed a table called traces, with one row per trace and columns for duration, date, and type. You can imagine also surfacing other properties of traces in this same table, such as the trace identifier, timestamp, and other common attributes.

Let's move to the second example question: "What is the average number of services involved in requests to a particular API endpoint?"

Here you're interested in a derived attribute of the trace, specifically the number of services. We mentioned previously that a graph store might be a good choice here. However, for our strawperson we're going to stick with the flat tables and explore their pros and cons for different types of queries.

Let's assume we have a second table called spans, with one row per span and, at a minimum, the fields TraceID, SpanID, and service. This time, as shown in Example 11-1, you're going to filter on traces with the API endpoint of interest, and then take the average of the count of unique services:

Example 11-1. Spans table

```
SELECT AVG(num_services) FROM (
  SELECT COUNT(DISTINCT spans.service) AS num_services
  FROM spans JOIN traces
    ON traces.TraceID = spans.TraceID          —tables joined on TraceID
  WHERE traces.api_endpoint = '/get/something'
  GROUP BY spans.TraceID )                      —service count per trace
```

If you aren't familiar with SQL, this query might seem complicated. Let's step back and consider what's going on: We have flattened the constituent spans of each trace into a set of rows in the spans table. After filtering in the traces table to just the rows with the api_endpoint of interest, we choose only spans with a matching TraceID and then count the number of unique services in each group of spans. Finally we take the average of those counts to get our answer. That's it!

This basic idea of squishing trace graphs into flat tables is very powerful. The general approach is to have different tables for the different kinds of objects that comprise a trace. Thus in this example we have the top level `traces` table, holding information about traces, and a second `spans` table holding information just about spans. In practice, we might also consider tables for certain common tags, or even derived properties of traces like the critical path. The key to it all (pun intended) is in using `TraceID` and `spanid` as join keys, which then allows us to compute aggregate functions across traces, spans, or their attributes.

What About the Trade-offs?

The astute reader may be wondering why we went to the trouble of using a join in the previous query. We could have avoided it simply by making the number of services a field in the `traces` table, as in Example 11-2:

Example 11-2. Traces table

```
SELECT AVG(num_services)
FROM traces
WHERE api_endpoint = '/get/something'
```

However, the `num_services` column is not a base property of a raw trace, so this implies a precomputation that walks over every trace in the dataset to count the number of services. Indeed, the data in these tables has to come from somewhere, typically a regularly scheduled batch-processing job, or perhaps a real-time streaming computation. The trade-off that we're making in this example is between adding complexity to the preprocessing and adding complexity to the query. We'll say more about preprocessing traces for aggregate analysis later, but first let's think about sampling and how it relates to trace aggregation.

Sampling for Aggregate Analysis

In an ideal world, when we apply an aggregation function to a population of traces, we get an answer that is true not only for the traces, but also for the real-world system. In other words, if the traces indicate that the 95th percentile for RPC server processing time is one second, then that's also the case in your actual system. Unfortunately, there are good reasons why it may not be the case that the aggregate set of traces precisely reflects reality. In particular, as we explained in "Biased Sampling and Trace Comparison" on page 165, it's not always desirable to sample in a completely representative manner. This is not to say that aggregate analysis of sampled traces isn't useful—it is—but use caution when interpreting the results.

One way to avoid the problem of sampling bias is simply not to sample! Just apply aggregate functions as soon as possible to *all* traces, which guarantees the integrity of the result. If you already know which aggregation functions you're going to be running, you can even throw away the raw traces and just keep the result, saving on storage costs and making future queries very fast and cheap. The downside with this approach is that you can't change your mind later and apply a different aggregation function. In the first example we used earlier ("Is this latency high?"), this means you would store the precomputed 99th-percentile latency, so the lookup would be fast and cheap, but it also means you couldn't decide to check the 75th-percentile latency instead (unless you decided in advance to store that too).

In summary, there's a three-way trade-off between *accuracy*, *flexibility*, and *cost*, which you can control by setting the sampling rate and choosing when to apply aggregation functions. The following questions guide this choice:

- How much error in the aggregation results is acceptable? This sounds like a scary question, but in practice, every observability system provides imperfect data and thus has inherent error. Here we encourage you to choose the trace sampling rate intentionally in order to find the right balance between accuracy and cost.

- Do you know in advance what questions you will want to ask of your set of traces? Applying aggregation early and keeping just the answer will be much cheaper, but at the expense of flexibility of future queries.

Let's turn now to the processing pipeline itself.

The Processing Pipeline

By now you know that a trace is made up of records produced by multiple machines in a distributed system. The first step in making that data meaningful for inspection is to stitch together related records into a single trace object. This has to be done whether we make traces available for aggregate analysis or simply provide a way to look at them one at a time.

In addition, tracing data is often imperfect: we see incomplete and buggy instrumentation generating invalid records, or loss in the collection system itself resulting in broken traces. As a result, processing to clean up the trace data is often performed at this stage also.

Assuming these two necessary steps happen somewhere, our concern now is how and when to prepare the data for on-demand aggregation, as well as which, if any, aggregation functions to precompute. Referring to Example 2: precomputing the number of services in each trace is a function performed in the pipeline, while calculating the average number of services per trace using a SQL query is an aggregation you perform later and on-demand.

In Figure 11-3 we illustrate two possible architectures for the processing pipeline. In both diagrams the trace data flows from the top (the production services) to the bottom, where we depict the output as flat tables, as in the strawperson data representation described earlier (of course, other representations are feasible as well). The diagram doesn't show how the tables are eventually used, but we would typically use them for interactive queries, batch processing, and even visualizations and dashboards.

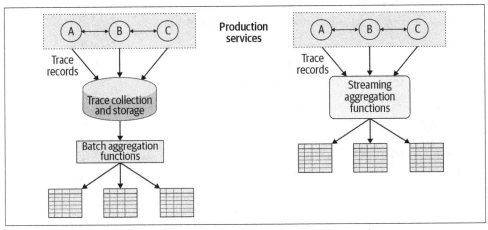

Figure 11-3. Two possible architectures for the trace processing pipeline.

The left side of Figure 11-3 shows a pipeline in which we store the cleaned-up traces before applying batch processing to produce the tables. If you don't already have a processing pipeline in place but wish to apply aggregate analysis to your traces, then this arrangement is a good way to get started. You can use your existing store for individual traces, or copy them to a different one, and then run a regularly scheduled batch job over the data without changing anything about your current tracing infrastructure. The outputs may be somewhat delayed, but you can start learning insights from trace aggregations without a big investment in additional infrastructure.

On the right side of the diagram, we depict a streaming system that processes traces as they arrive and continuously updates the output tables. A semi-real-time system like this gives access to trace aggregations much sooner, and holds the exciting possibility of being able to perform tasks like live debugging using the outputs and tying alerts to trace aggregates. These benefits come with a price: the operational burden of such a system is higher, particularly because tracing data is inherently unpredictable, often arriving in large bursts of data, and you have to ensure the system can keep up with the rate of incoming records.

Regardless of how traces are stored, being able to quickly find traces that match specified criteria is extremely useful. One way to achieve this is to build an index as part of the processing pipeline. Because users may want to look for traces that match *any* of a large number of attributes, we recommend indexing on as many properties as possible. Even when aggregate analysis is not feasible in real time, the ability to discover and inspect individual traces with specific characteristics is valuable for debugging.

In fact, building a wide index is just one example of functionality you can build into your processing pipeline. Another is to precompute aggregations, such as the number of services in a trace, as we discussed in "What About the Trade-offs?" on page 214. A third important kind of processing is to extract information from heterogeneous data in traces, which we discuss next.

Incorporating Heterogeneous Data

The processing pipeline extracts properties of, and computes aggregations over, general attributes of traces like the number of services. It is also a place where you can introduce domain-specific processing of tags. We talked about effective tagging in Chapter 4, where we noted that tags enrich a span with more information and let you apply powerful, custom aggregate analysis.

Custom Functions

Let's consider a simple example that builds on our strawperson scenario. If you instrument services so that RPC spans contain tags for the client and the server's datacenter, then you could extract this information (by parsing tags to find the ones referring to the datacenter) into your spans table as two extra columns. Now when you ask "Is this latency high?" you can take into account whether the traces of interest contain inter- or intra-datacenter traffic, with the former likely being across wide-area network links and thus expected to be significantly slower.

Taking this idea further, when different teams own different microservices, each team can write its own service-specific tags and then perform custom processing on those tags in the aggregate traces. This is a great way to get more visibility into service behavior. For example, if a service makes outgoing calls to different services depending on the arguments of the incoming RPC, the team owning the service might write custom tags into the trace recording the arguments and so have an "explanation" for the outgoing RPCs.

Supporting custom functions in your processing pipeline is a bit like user-defined functions (UDFs) for a SQL query tool—they are powerful and flexible, but there are some tricky questions that you need to address:

- How do users express UDFs? How do you make them safe (not crash the system, or get stuck in an infinite loop)?
- How do you prevent UDFs from using too much resources, like CPU or memory, or taking too long?
- How do you ensure that UDFs stay in sync with changes to instrumentation in the source code? If a tag is changed, or removed, whose responsibility is it to update the code in the processing pipeline?

As software engineers, we ask these types of questions in other domains also, especially when thinking about best practices. Like any important piece of infrastructure, you need to consider how the processing pipeline fits into the larger software ecosystem and plan for its robustness and longevity.

Joining with Other Data Sources

Most microservices operators collect vast amounts of metric data at many levels of the software stack. Combining this data with traces extends the reach of our understanding and insights significantly. For instance, you might ask "Is this RPC latency high, given the kernel version installed on the server machine?" In other words, you want to break down the 99th-percentile latencies by kernel versions, because after all, the Linux TCP stack in the kernel is being constantly tweaked and may well play a part in the tail latencies that you observe in production.

How do you achieve the ability to answer questions about traces that involve other types of data? In this case you could arrange for a tag to be added to every RPC that records the kernel version at the server, but that would be inefficient and not a general solution. There may be many other pieces of data from external sources that you will want to join against, some of which may be infeasible to generate tags for.

A more flexible approach is to ensure that suitable join keys are present in both data sources in a form amenable to querying. Thus, with our strawperson solution, we might maintain a table, populated by a different process, called `kernel_versions` with fields `hostname`, `version`, `start_time`, and `stop_time`. Now you can write the query, shown in Example 11-3, to extract 99th-percentile RPC latencies by kernel version by joining `hostname` from each row in your `spans` table with `hostname` in the table that tracks the current kernel versions:

Example 11-3. Extracting 99th-percentile RPC latencies

```
SELECT kernel_version, PERCENTILE(duration, 0.99)
FROM spans JOIN kernel_versions
  ON spans.server_hostname = kernel_versions.hostname
WHERE
  spans.timestamp > kernel_versions.start_time
    AND (spans.timestamp < kernel_versions.stop_time
      OR kernel_versions.stop_time IS NULL)
    AND spans.date = `today` AND spans.type = 'http'
GROUP BY
  kernel_version
```

The presence of hostname in both tables makes the query simple. In general, designing data query systems with the expectation that different sources may be combined in the same query unlocks a great deal of information, and tracing data is no exception.

This concludes a lightning tour of the benefits of aggregation. For readers thinking about building and/or deploying a processing pipeline for aggregate analysis of traces, we highlighted some of the trade-offs and implementation issues. To conclude the chapter, we'll recap the key points by describing how they appear in a case study of a real-world tracing system.

Recap and Case Study

Canopy is a distributed tracing infrastructure in use at Facebook, described in a paper published in 2017,[1] whose authors include Jonathan Mace, a coauthor of this book. In contrast to conventional tracing systems like Zipkin or Dapper, Facebook engineers designed Canopy from the start to support aggregate analysis and to incorporate heterogeneous data, such as logging statements, performance counters, and stack traces.

The Value of Traces in Aggregate

The number of traces at Facebook is immense, with over a billion captured per day, and so in Canopy aggregation is the norm, rather than the exception. Similar to the basic design of our strawperson tables, Canopy aggregates traces into *datasets*, in which each column is a *feature*, the term it uses for a value derived from aggregated traces. When analyzing performance data, Facebook engineers query datasets directly, as well as access them via visualization tools and in dashboards.

---

1 [Kal17]

Organizing the Data

Canopy supports multiple APIs for instrumentation, which means that the raw trace data it consumes has a variety of forms, from records representing the RPCs we are familiar with in other tracing systems, to events capturing the causal relationships between asynchronous function calls, and many others. In Canopy's processing pipeline all of these lower-level data models are mapped to a standard intermediate representation called a *modeled trace*, from which the pipeline extracts features and outputs the final datasets.

In terms of the trade-off between precomputation and query complexity, the designers of Canopy have come down firmly on the side of eager precomputation of features in the processing pipeline. This has the advantage of supporting almost real-time interactive analysis on trace aggregates, but it is possible that some of that precomputation is redundant.

As well as producing aggregated datasets, Canopy stores individual traces on disk for deeper analysis when required. This is the ideal situation for the engineer debugging a performance problem: The datasets, and higher-level tools written against them, let them quickly identify where to look more closely, and then they can retrieve exactly the right traces for detailed examination.

Sampling for Aggregate Analysis

Canopy doesn't attempt to obtain a representative (accurate) set of traces; rather it focuses on providing value for specific use cases, while keeping the volume of tracing manageable. Individual users or teams define policies that set sampling rates on a case-by-case basis according to request characteristics like the endpoint or datacenter. The rates are further constrained by fixed limits set per user and globally.

The Canopy paper strongly implies that the main priority for the system is flexibility, rather than accuracy (which is not possible with per-user sampling policies) or cost (the paper does not discuss cost directly). Within this choice there is some nuance: by placing aggregation into the processing pipeline, Canopy designers have potentially limited *flexibility*. However, this is mitigated by also storing the original traces on disk at some *cost*, leaving open the option to compute additional aggregations offline at a later time.

The paper discusses characteristics of the Canopy system itself. For example, it reports how often individual columns across many datasets were accessed by user queries over six months (it notes that one column—page load latency—is by far the most popular). A potential use of such information that is not mentioned in the paper would be to refine the set of aggregate analysis functions run in the pipeline, thus reducing complexity and the cognitive burden on engineers for commonplace queries.

The Processing Pipeline

The heart of Canopy is its processing pipeline, which looks somewhat like the streaming system we showed on the right side of Figure 11-3. The pipeline, which runs continuously online, takes incoming events and builds modeled traces, which includes cleaning up the traces by detecting and correcting buggy and incomplete instrumentation, aligning timestamps, inferring missing information, and so on. The pipeline then applies aggregation functions to traces, and finally outputs multiple datasets.

The Canopy designers have taken a great deal of care to ensure that the processing pipeline can keep up with the rate of arriving data records (reported as 1.16 GB/s). The system contains mechanisms like isolation queues, offloading work to be processed asynchronously, and ways to shed load when necessary.

To deal with the diversity of input data and custom aggregations required by different engineering teams, Canopy has extensive support for user-defined aggregation functions in the processing pipeline. An interesting discussion in the paper describes how the original system design included a domain-specific language (DSL) for expressing UDFs as simple pipelines of filters and transformations. It turned out that users needed more complex computations than expected and the DSL had to evolve to include more general-purpose features. Moreover, interactive exploration of the analysis functions proved to be a requirement, leading to integration with iPython notebooks.

Incorporating Heterogeneous Data

There are two characteristics of Canopy that make it particularly well suited to handling heterogeneous data. First, translating all events into a common trace model means that different types of data (say, traces of browser page loads versus the backend RPC call graph) can be fed directly into Canopy's processing pipeline and unified in traces as appropriate. Similarly, on the output side of the pipeline, the capability to introduce or adapt user-defined aggregation functions supports the customized extraction of information from these various data sources.

In contrast to the approach we suggested earlier of keeping the other data sources separate but *joinable*, Canopy is designed to integrate heterogeneous data tightly. This adds complexity to the processing pipeline, but simplifies access to relevant features of a trace. Data that is not trace-related, such as the kernel version on each server, will still need some kind of join key with trace datasets to be accessed programmatically.

In conclusion, Canopy provides a powerful real-time tracing system that supports customized aggregate analysis, while also keeping individual traces for detailed inspection. In practice, companies without the resources of Facebook are unlikely to choose to build and maintain such a costly system, but the design offers many good lessons that also apply to simpler systems for aggregate analysis of traces.

CHAPTER 12

Beyond Spans

Most distributed tracing systems that run in production today represent requests as a tree of spans. This representation is simple to understand and well-suited to a large number of common workloads, but it isn't a good fit for all of them. In this chapter we'll look at how the span came to be the first-class citizen of tracing, and then explore its shortcomings for systems like machine learning models, streaming, pub-sub, and distributed dataflow. Devising new abstractions for tracing is an exciting area of active research and development and we'll try to give you a flavor of what's coming in the near future.

Why Spans Have Prevailed

In Chapter 10, we described how early tracing systems influenced the design, and even the terminology, of present-day systems. As distributed systems evolved and became more complicated, users had a pressing need to understand request-response slowdowns, especially when requests were interleaved and executed concurrently. This led to a remote procedure call (RPC)-centric approach, tightly integrated with the way that the systems being traced were implemented. These days, distributed systems have more diverse execution and communication patterns, and for many popular systems the "traditional" request-oriented tracing design is not a good fit. Nevertheless, having the RPC—represented by a span—as the core datatype in distributed tracing has served us well over many years. Let's start by looking at the reasons.

Visibility

It is self-evident that tracing RPCs shows you which components of your system communicate using RPCs. In microservice applications, RPCs enable the loose coupling of independent services, a key feature of the modularity, scalablity, and maintainability of those applications. At the same time, this decoupling makes the end-to-end picture of how the microservices communicate to serve an individual request murky, to say the least. We already talked a great deal about how important tracing is for understanding the behavior of your microservice architecture—here we want to emphasize that a trace comprising a tree of spans is the perfect abstraction for visibility into this style of distributed system.

Similarly, we use RPCs in many distributed systems that are not microservice architectures. RPCs are so pervasive that tracing them invariably tells us something about what's going on, even when they aren't the primary mechanism for communication. The upshot is that while we continue to use RPCs in our distributed systems (which is probably forever), we will continue to use spans in our distributed traces!

Pragmatism

It is hugely convenient for users if the low-level tracing mechanisms, such as context propagation and emitting the trace records themselves, are built into the RPC subsystem. Integration at this level typically provides a simple API for users to create instrumentation, and takes care of all the messy and sometimes complex implementation details (see Chapter 2). The ubiquity of RPCs means that once tracing support has been added to an RPC subsystem, you get tracing—and spans—for very little extra effort.

However, there is a price for this convenience, paid in the form of spans as the one-size-fits-all abstraction. Because RPC systems are the common base layer of many different applications, adding support for specialized tracing abstractions that might only apply to a handful of applications is not generally practical. Alternatively, you could have a completely separate tracing system, not tied to RPCs and thus more flexible, but then you'd have to deploy and maintain it separately, adding operational burden. As a result, to make use of the convenience of the RPC layer to record stuff that doesn't look like a span, you have to shoehorn your information into something that does. We will describe a few examples of this later.

In practice, the operators of distributed tracing systems tend to favor convenience over flexibility, but it's possible that the scales are tipping—perhaps after reading this chapter you will come to your own conclusions.

Portability

The RPC layer of a distributed system occupies a unique place in the software stack, existing *below* applications and *above* the operating system and system-level services. This means that spans are agnostic to both the application and the system and thus inherently portable to different applications and different platforms.

It's interesting to note that when spans incorporate information from both layers they can provide a unique window onto how application-level actions map onto the physical world. A good example of this is when a span reports the IP addresses of the hosts involved in the RPC—a performance engineer might use that information to diagnose why the RPC is slow. Without the information that identifies the servers, the engineer can detect the slowness, but has less data to help find the root cause.

Compatibility

Spans represent a fairly low-level abstraction, capturing the bare minimum of details of a request-response communication style. With just a handful of conventions for representing spans in common use, compatibility between software systems from multiple sources is straightforward, making it feasible to collect end-to-end traces across diverse components and to reuse existing visualization and analysis tools. The fact that spans have become such a basic building block of tracing is also to our advantage when converting spans from one format (say, OpenTracing) to another (say, Zipkin), because both forms broadly capture the same information.

Flexibility

Finally, the "killer feature" of spans is that in most popular tracing systems they are defined with a minimum of structure. You may argue that this is a drawback, leading to ambiguity and imprecision, but it also results in tremendous adaptability. If you want to reuse the span data structure to represent some activity that is not an RPC, it may be possible to do so simply by defining custom tags.

The case for spans is strong, but let's take a look at the other side of the argument.

Why Spans Aren't Enough

With all these good reasons for the continuing prevalence of spans, what then is the problem? What do we mean when we say that spans aren't a good fit for all distributed systems, and why does this matter? Spans have prevailed because they are well suited to the dominant request-response style of distributed computation, but other communication paradigms are becoming more popular. These new systems are a lot like the old ones in that they can have complex interdependencies between components, and performance debugging is challenging. Distributed tracing seems like it ought to be just as valuable for the new systems, but trying to capture their behavior using spans can be awkward, as we'll now describe.

As a running example, we'll use a hypothetical social media platform that operates out of several datacenters. It runs a microservice architecture and serves each individual request entirely out of one datacenter, with a frontend load balancer that spreads requests evenly across the datacenters. Each request corresponds to an HTTP-based

API endpoint, so there are requests for fetching the user's feed, personalized recommendations and ads, and so on. On the face of it, this *sounds* like a perfect fit for the tree-of-spans tracing approach, so let's look at where it falls short.

Graphs, Not Trees

The first problem is when an end-to-end trace is a *graph* rather than a *tree*. In other words, the flow of control contains *joins* (where a child span has multiple parents) as well as *forks* (where a parent has multiple children). As we mentioned earlier, spans don't have a great deal of predefined structure, but one thing they do require is for each span to have no more than one parent (and a span with no parents is the root of the trace).

One common cause of this behavior is when multiple RPCs are *batched* into a single onward RPC. Batching is often used to improve the efficiency of repeated requests to the same server—instead of sending many small messages, send a single large one. In the social media example there are many places where batching will likely be happening in the backend. For instance, a single timeline request might fetch multiple items for the timeline in parallel. If some of those items involve retrieving data from the *same* servers, then the system might batch those requests into a single RPC.

Figure 12-1 shows how batching produces graphs of spans, rather than trees. In the diagram, multiple incoming requests to service A are combined into a batch that results in a single outgoing request to service B. Now, what is the parent of the span representing the call from A to B? In reality, the outgoing RPC depends on all of the incoming RPCs, but we can't represent this directly in current tracing systems. Instead, we have to find a workaround.

One reasonable approach is to pick the first or the last request added to the batch to be the parent. The right side of Figure 12-1 shows the actual trace graph together with the compromise tree resulting from the workaround (the paths from X/Y/Z back to the root are elided in the diagram). Clearly, the compromise tree doesn't correctly represent the true dependencies. For instance, the RPCs from X and Y that contributed to the batch will appear to terminate at A, becoming leaf nodes in the trace tree. Moreover, from the point of view of the performance engineer, the latency introduced by batching may be a significant contribution to overall latency, and so the time spent waiting by each parent request should also be recorded. Once again, you can work around the lack of expressivity by adding timestamped annotations that record when items are inserted into the batch, but you will need custom processing to subsequently extract and process the information.

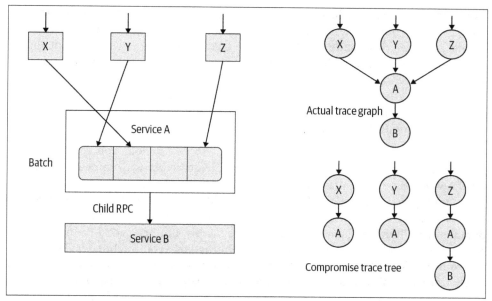

Figure 12-1. RPC batching leads to spans with multiple parents.

Inter-Request Dependencies

A generalization of the previous problem is when multiple *traces* (rather than spans within a single trace) are interdependent, as if Service A in Figure 12-1 batched incoming requests that belonged to multiple different traces into the outgoing request to Service B. In our example social media platform, we can image a "RemoteReplicaUpdaterService" that batches unrelated updates in one datacenter in order to send fewer, larger RPCs across the wide area network to the other datacenters.

Fortunately, with this batching style of inter-request dependencies, you can take advantage of the flexibility of spans to use existing tracing systems without much disruption. Simply add a tag to the nonterminating trace that records the other TraceIDs (and perhaps also information about nontraced requests) that went into the batch. Indeed, FollowsFrom references in OpenTracing are intended to handle this use case.

Another, more significant challenge for inter-request dependencies with conventional tree-of-spans tracing arises when the definition of a trace is too restrictive for the type of end-to-end type request that you are interested in. Let's explore this scenario by assuming that our example social media platform operates a conventional tracing system. Its frontend server makes the decision to sample a request (i.e., to trace it) at the ingress to the set of microservices that comprise the backend serving system. This means that a trace is implicitly defined as the set of actions involved in serving a single HTTP request. So far, so good.

However, if the social media company decides in the future that it wants to extend its tracing system out to clients, for example by adding tracing logic into its bespoke mobile app, then this notion of a trace suddenly doesn't work as well. In client apps, a single user action typically involves *many* requests to the backend, each of which is sampled independently by the frontend server. Thus, although inside the datacenter each trace corresponds to a single HTTP-based API endpoint, from the perspective of the user, an action like navigating to the home page might involve RPCs to several different endpoints, to fetch content, ads, and profile information.

To make a single trace that represents one of these user actions you could combine multiple traces after the fact, provided they are tied together with some common tag. But how do you ensure that your frontend sampler will choose all (or none) of the traces for a given user action? Perhaps you could sample on the client, but now you have devolved the sampling decision from a handful of servers in your datacenter to potentially millions of clients that may fail frequently, not have good connectivity, or be running an old version of the software. Alternatively you might consider extending your external API to indicate to the backend that some set of RPCs belongs to a single trace, but this could leave you vulnerable to denial-of-service attacks.

There are many other subtle issues at play here, but the takeaway point is that additional complexity is inevitable when the conventional notion of a trace is insufficiently expressive.

Decoupled Dependencies

Publish-subscribe (pub-sub) systems play an important role in many microservices architectures. By decoupling the writer of a message from its readers, pub-sub smooths out load spikes, allows publishers and subscribers to scale and evolve independently, and lets subscribers come and go without needing to notify the publishing service. A consequence of this decoupling is a dilemma for tracing, illustrated in Figure 12-2: should the loosely coupled communication via the pub-sub system be treated as a single trace or many?

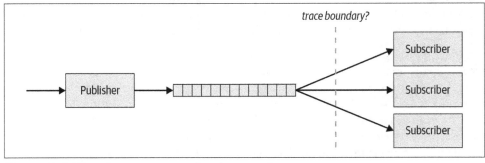

Figure 12-2. How do you trace a pub-sub system?

Let's consider the single-trace solution, which may indeed be appropriate for some microservice systems. When the writer publishes a message to the pub-sub system, you trace it as a one-way RPC (most tracing systems have support for such messages), and propagate the trace context as normal. Subscribers pick up the context along with the message and continue propagation, giving a single, unbroken end-to-end trace that includes *all* your dependent services. One of the benefits of pub-sub is its loose coupling, but this can easily have the unfortunate consequence of obscuring which services are interdependent. Tracing across the pub-sub boundary solves this problem, and also has the advantage of treating the pub-sub system like any other microservice, giving visibility into how the pub-sub system itself fits into the overall ecosystem of microservices.

However, this model isn't necessarily the right choice. Turning again to our social media platform, let's assume its "RemoteReplicaUpdaterService" uses a pub-sub system to asynchronously disseminate state updates to storage replicas in its other datacenters. Here, the single-trace approach becomes awkward: There may be a large number of subscribers for each publisher, different subscribers to the same publisher may be involved in unrelated activities that don't belong in the same trace, and there can be a delay between writing and reading a message.

You can handle these issues by starting a new trace for each message read by a subscriber, perhaps retaining a reference to the message writer's TraceID as a tag in the new trace. But now, even though the tracing mechanisms themselves are straightforward, you've made it more complicated to track end-to-end dependencies.

Returning to our example: maybe the social media platform also runs a second pub-sub system that it configures with much tighter delay bounds in order to propagate user-visible changes in a timely fashion. When a follower is blocked, it's important that the change appears as quickly as possible in every copy of the follower graph. End-to-end tracing through the pub-sub system may be an important debugging tool for these types of requests, and now someone has to choose which mode of tracing to adopt, or else configure the two pub-sub systems differently. The tracing dilemma for decoupled dependencies has become an operational burden.

Distributed Dataflow

In the last 15 years or so, data-parallel, distributed execution frameworks like Hadoop and Spark have become tremendously popular. In contrast to request-oriented systems, distributed tracing for these frameworks is almost nonexistent, with developers relying on metrics, logs, profilers, and debuggers to monitor performance and solve problems. Why is this? The answer is not clear, especially given that a framework like Spark is more homogeneous and self-contained than most microservice architectures, and thus potentially less effort to instrument for tracing.

However, there are other challenges: distributed dataflow is designed to operate at very large scales and as a result a single job could run for hours (or longer!) and may comprise millions of RPCs. The *control plane*, which includes services like the cluster scheduler and resource manager, can play a significant part in the end-to-end completion time of a job. Should you instrument the control plane for tracing also? Finally, the distributed dataflow paradigm executes programs as directed by acyclic graphs, and as discussed earlier, graphs are not well supported by existing tracing systems.

Streaming systems, often built over the top of distributed dataflow systems, offer yet another challenge to the spans-oriented tracing model. How should you define the concept of "request" for processing that runs over a continuously arriving, infinite stream of data? Perhaps you should consider a different core abstraction, like tracing how specific data items are passed between processes, read, and mutated (this is known as *data provenance* in the academic community)? Alternatively, you could forget about tracking an individual activity or piece of state, and instead just snapshot the execution of the entire system during a fixed time window. New styles of trace will require new tools for analysis and visualization, so you would have to start from scratch to extract value from your traces.

Machine Learning

Machine learning (ML) systems comprise yet another style of distributed computing, with performance analysis and debugging challenges for which existing distributed tracing systems have no out-of-the-box solutions. Because of this, ML systems tend to have their own custom tracing tools, such as the trace viewer built into the Tensor-Flow TensorBoard visualization toolkit. For service owners that run machine learning as just one part of their infrastructure (say, to predict the best ad to serve for a specific web page request), this has the drawback that the ML systems operate outside the regular observability framework, which is especially undesirable when the ML is production-critical and resource-intensive.

Although there are many types of ML models (logistic regression, support vector machines, deep neural networks, etc.), they have in common (at least) two ways that RPC-based tracing is not a good fit:

Steps, not requests
> Training a machine learning process involves repeated *steps*, in which operators —schedulable units of work like matrix multiply, or the reading of a file—compute over the current state of the training data and produce updates. At the end of each step, the operators exchange updated values. Although you can think of each operation within a step as being a span, causally related to its parents and children by its input and output, respectively, there is no conceptual equivalent of an end-to-end request. Instead, because a key metric is the time taken per step,

ML tracing tools typically provide the ability to look deeply into the concurrency and scheduling of operators within a single training step.

In contrast, ML *inference* has a more request-oriented flavor. However, to improve efficiency, inference models batch requests (similar to the situation we showed in Figure 12-1), leading to the issue of inter-request dependencies that we discussed earlier.

Multilayer performance monitoring

Hardware acceleration is often a key component of machine learning deployments. Particularly during training, the movement of data between devices over the PCI bus and/or the network can be a major bottleneck, and whether an operation is scheduled on CPU or GPU can affect its running time significantly. As a result, to debug performance problems in a distributed ML job, you need visibility into how the runtime schedules work on each server individually, as well as across the cluster.

In addition, different ML models have diverse characteristics—for example, language models often use large tables, known as *embeddings*, that can be hundreds of gigabytes and hence have to be shared across multiple devices. However, the model may only access a handful of rows in each step, leading to complicated scatter-gather communication patterns. Similarly, models that rely on AllReduce, an efficient group communication primitive for updating state across many nodes, may be highly sensitive to its implementation specifics, which in turn depend on the available device and network hardware.

As a consequence, distributed tracing for ML systems must incorporate data not only at the level of RPCs (or AllReduce operations) between computers, but also at the level of the low-level behavior and causal dependencies within each computer.

In fact, the second of these problems is more general—metrics from components *underneath* the RPC layer are critical to understanding the performance of requests, as we explain next.

Low-Level Performance Metrics

Performance debugging is often about *detecting* problems by looking across the entire system, followed by zooming in deep to *diagnose* the cause. Distributed tracing is great for the first task, especially when using aggregate analysis of traces, as we discuss in Chapter 11. On the other hand, when it comes to explaining a slow RPC that might be caused by a low-level issue like a VM hiccup, suboptimal thread scheduling, or network packet loss, span-oriented tracing is not a good fit. Low-level events are *usually* not caused by the activities on behalf of any one request, but rather the set of all things currently running on the server. So in some sense, attribution to a specific trace isn't terribly meaningful.

Another problem with incorporating fine-grained performance metrics is timescale. RPCs happen quickly—very quickly. Tracing systems use microsecond or even nanosecond timestamps for good reason. Yet, for reasons of scale and performance, observability systems typically aggregate metrics every minute, or at best every few seconds. These timescales are orders of magnitude different!

The trend to move performance-critical functionality from software into hardware is another challenge for span-oriented tracing systems. We already mentioned the prevalence of accelerators for ML. Another increasingly widespread example is the use of remote direct memory access (RDMA) for distributed applications with stringent network performance requirements. Meanwhile, the research community is advancing the state of the art exploring how to use programmable network switches for complex tasks like executing consensus protocols.[1] How to associate low-level hardware counters with the high-level concept of a trace is an open problem, as is how to surface this information in a way that is useful for performance debugging of slow requests, or for the aggregate analysis of multiple traces.

But what about metrics from *within* the application, like requests per second? If your service is experiencing high sustained load, could this be a useful indicator as to why an RPC is slow? Well, maybe! Perhaps the high load is occurring now, but won't start impacting requests until later (e.g., once the queues are full). Perhaps the high load is having an adverse effect, but the trace sampling just so happens not to select any of the suffering requests.

This is not to say that system metrics together with traces can't be useful for performance debugging. Indeed, we talked about the idea of a unified observability platform in Chapter 6 and pointed out some of its advantages. However, the alliance of spans and metrics is an uneasy one that must be handled with care.

New Abstractions

We've described a selection of the issues that arise when spans are not the right abstraction for the task at hand. In this section we'll discuss some of the changes afoot to help overcome some of the shortcomings of the tree-of-spans approach to distributed tracing.

The tracing community has been well aware of the problems with spans for years; there is a great deal of fascinating, and often quite nuanced, discussion in various online forums. Efforts are underway to address some of the more pressing problems

---

1 [Dan15]

by evolving the specifications for OpenTracing and OpenZipkin, for example supporting multiparent spans by means of the OpenTracing tag `FollowsFrom`.

OpenCensus (now part of OpenTelemetry) is one of the "new wave" of tracing paradigms. It supports the propagation of *tags* (not to be confused with the explicit tags we write into spans) between services, along with the usual trace context information like the `TraceID`. Tags act like labels, which the system associates with metrics collected at each node in the trace tree and subsequently aggregated. This is pretty neat: a tag like `originator:photo-app`, combined with a measure like `vm_cpu_cycles`, lets you see the end-to-end CPU costs for requests coming from `photo-app`, and moreover, to compare them with the CPU costs for requests coming from a different originator, say, `video-app`.

Essentially, OpenCensus gives you a way to associate metrics with traces. It doesn't fix the problem we described earlier of precise attribution of low-level metrics to a particular request, so you still need to choose your metrics carefully. Some types of measures (like counting CPU cycles on a thread while it's doing work on behalf of exactly one request) are well suited to this use, others (like network link utilization) are not. We will describe OpenCensus in more detail in "Census" on page 241.

Production tracing systems must use caution when adopting new abstractions so as not to disrupt existing infrastructure. However, the research community does not have such constraints and has explored some interesting approaches. For example, to mention an idea that is particularly well suited to systems like streaming distributed dataflow, rather than attempting to correlate related events on different machines, collect performance data from every machine in the cluster at the same time. In theory, you could do this by firing off a sampling profiler, or a kernel trace, to run for 30 seconds (say) on every server at the same time. But then you would have to backhaul all the profiles and run an expensive computation to merge them after the fact, and in a large cluster the cost of doing this could be prohibitive.

An alternative approach is to push the trace analysis into the same cluster that is being traced. This idea has been at the heart of various research systems, for example the Fay system published in 2011.[2] In Fay, the user provided a declarative query that the system parsed and turned into dynamic instrumentation, customized to just that query. It used a runtime module on each server to filter and aggregate the outputs from the instrumentation before uploading the results for further processing (such as for aggregation and visualization).

Dynamic instrumentation would be a bold undertaking in a production cluster, especially when the cluster supports multiple tenants and resource isolation is important. Perhaps inspired by the ideas in Fay, you can imagine a rolling buffer of locally

---

2 [Erl11]

collected trace data, sampled, filtered and even joined on the spot with data from other servers on demand. In Chapter 13, we'll describe another research system, Pivot Tracing, that does exactly this.

Could such distributed-tracing-plus-analysis techniques be combined with the familiar trace context propagation mechanism to enable a different form of distributed tracing? Or will some other approach be sufficiently compelling that it finds widespread adoption? It's hard to tell at this point where we are headed, but there's no doubt that exciting times are ahead for distributed tracing.

Seeing Causality

For users of distributed tracing, one of the most important questions to answer is "Why was this request slow?" The answer is hopefully contained within a trace, or in how it differs from comparable traces. But sometimes you cannot find the answer just by looking at traces: you can see there was a problem, and you may even see which service was unusually slow, but there are no obvious clues as to the cause.

One explanation is that the tracing instrumentation is insufficient to debug the particular problem. For instance, if you don't record when a timeout expires, then you may not be able to tell when that timeout causes an error response. But in other cases, your trace was slow because of external factors. If a server experiences a transient period of CPU overload, for example, and the thread processing your request simply doesn't get enough CPU time to complete the work, then you will not capture this in a trace. Another tricky scenario is if your request is blocked waiting for a lock—perhaps a lock in a third-party library that you don't even know existed—and unless you instrument the wait and hold times for synchronization primitives, which would add overhead to a performance-critical operation, then you simply don't have the visibility to diagnose such a problem.

These examples illustrate the limitations of the visibility you get from traces alone. Fortunately, you may be able to correlate the slowness in your trace with *logs* and *metrics* (see Chapter 7). Because tracing shows you where and when to look, it's feasible to use the other observability pillars to diagnose the problem. As long as the full tree of causal relationships is captured in the trace, you can take advantage of other data sources to fill in the visibility gaps when required.

But what about when causality is not tracked completely? If you rely on components in your distributed system that don't support tracing (in other words, that don't propagate the trace context and/or record spans) then you may not even be aware that you have a dependence on them. This may sound like poor operational practice, but it's surprisingly easy for this to happen with complex, distributed systems running a variety of in-house and open source software.

The research world has proposed ways to *infer* causality just from the black box behavior of a distributed system. Back in 2003, Project5 explored whether the timing of messages between components could reveal causal relationships, especially for nested RPCs.[3] More recently, the Mystery Machine takes a different tack, applying hypothesis testing about program behavior to the information in large numbers of system logs in order to deduce a causal model of system behavior.[4] These ideas are promising, and perhaps in future we will use such techniques to automatically fill in missing dependencies in traces.

Returning to the question "Why was this request slow?," we have discussed how missing instrumentation or dependencies in traces can make the question hard to answer. A different challenge for tracing, that is very common in practice, is when the root cause originates outside the scope of visibility (or perhaps even the lifetime) of the request suffering the slowdown. Traces capture direct dependencies, but sometimes the problem comes from *indirect* dependencies.

Let's look at the shared queue shown in Figure 12-3, where the expensive request A is at the front of the queue, slowing down requests B and C which are queued behind it. The queue introduces an ordering of requests that can result in head-of-line blocking. Typically you wouldn't instrument fine-grained operations like enqueue and dequeue because of the overhead, so how do you detect when the queueing delay is adversely impacting some requests?

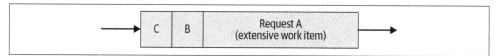

Figure 12-3. In a shared queue, request A slows down requests B and C.

Once again, the tree-of-spans tracing model doesn't easily express what's going on here. There is an implicit dependency between requests that is *temporal* rather than *functional*. Requests may interfere if one of them is slow, but if the queue never backed up, there would be no dependency between them. There is some exciting research work in this direction (including, for example, the recent Zeno project that describes this idea using the term *temporal provenance*),[5] but detecting and diagnosing such interference from sequencing remains an open problem.

In this chapter we've looked at the kinds of distributed systems for which the tracing model of a tree of spans is not well suited, along with a taste of some new abstractions on the horizon.

---

3 [Agu03]

4 [Cho14]

5 [Wu19]

CHAPTER 13

Beyond Distributed Tracing

At the very beginning of this book, in the Introduction, we argued that most applications today are distributed in some fashion, whether as simple client-server applications or more general architectures like microservices. Distributed architectures give clear benefits, especially with scalability, reliability, and maintainability. The biggest drawback, however, is that distributed architectures *break* traditional methods of profiling, debugging, and monitoring. Such methods were designed to capture information in a component- or machine-centric way (because they were designed when applications only ran on a single machine). By contrast, in distributed architectures, we care about end-to-end executions of requests across multiple components and machines. Traditional methods aren't enough for distributed architectures because they lack *visibility*: they weren't designed to be able to correlate and combine events across multiple components and machines.

This is the point of distributed tracing—to meet the profiling, debugging, and monitoring needs of modern, distributed architectures. Distributed tracing is designed for distributed architectures and addresses the key challenges of incoherence, inconsistency, and decentralization that we described in the Introduction. With distributed tracing, you gain visibility across your entire stack. Distributed tracing gives you a way to profile, debug, and monitor our distributed applications, where previously it was tremendously difficult.

Today, distributed tracing has become a de facto component in modern distributed applications. It is the most popular and most well-established tool for profiling, debugging, and monitoring requests. There are multiple open source initiatives and implementations, several of which we have discussed throughout this book. Clearly, distributed tracing has proved its worth.

With all this said, distributed tracing is not the *only* way to gain visibility of your distributed application. In fact, just as we discussed some of the core distributed tracing history in Chapter 10, there are several interesting projects that explore different (though, not entirely dissimilar) approaches to profiling, debugging, and monitoring. In Chapter 3, we touched upon one: Census (open-sourced as OpenCensus, and today forming the metrics component of OpenTelemetry). The way Census captures metrics is very similar to distributed tracing, but there are also important differences between the two.

In this chapter we will examine Census in more detail, along with two other projects: Pivot Tracing, a 2015 research project from Brown University; and Pythia, a 2019 research project from Boston University. These projects tackle similar sorts of problems to distributed tracing and they also make use of similar underlying techniques. In particular, they all use context propagation—albeit not always in the same way as distributed tracing. This is not entirely surprising, given that a *lack* of cross-component context was the main shortcoming of previous approaches. We'll also make sure to describe some of the important motivations and design choices made by these three tools, which differ from those of distributed tracing.

Limitations of Distributed Tracing

When you deploy distributed tracing, and instrument your systems, you have to make a number of practical choices. It's not always obvious what the right choices are when you're doing instrumentation. Sometimes there might not be an obvious best choice. This is why distributed tracing can be quite difficult to get right, and why we need to resort to best practices when doing instrumentation.

In Chapter 1 we introduced three fundamental problems that generally occur when you're using distributed tracing. Let's briefly recap these:

Generating trace data
Choosing where in a program useful data exists, and instrumenting the application to record it

Collecting and storing trace data
Deciding under what circumstances trace data should be emitted, and how to route it from its origin to the tracing backends

Extracting value from data
Using traces to profile, monitor, and debug your application in a meaningful way

Even if you make all the right choices, you might still encounter unavoidable limitations. In data generation, you need to be able to predict what kind of problems might occur in the future and what data should be recorded to help problem diagnosis. On the collection and storage front, you need to balance sampling only a fraction of traces, paying high computational costs, and getting enough data to be meaningful for problem diagnosis. Lastly, extracting value from traces is up to you: you are responsible for identifying and debugging problems. Distributed tracing just provides you with some data to help—and because of the first two problems, that data might be misleading, redundant, or incomplete.

Challenge 1: Anticipating Problems

When you deploy distributed tracing, it's up to you to decide what data to record—that is, what parts of the program to instrument with spans, and what additional tags and annotations to add to those spans. At first glance this doesn't seem too tricky, because for most applications it's easy to identify the most important parts of the code. For example, you would almost certainly want to wrap all of your RPCs in spans to measure response latency and status codes.

Beyond some of the obviously important high-level parts of your application, there are a wide range of instrumentation choices you can make. Should you break down the high-level RPC span into multiple child spans representing each stage of execution? Should you intricately instrument your caches and resource consumption? Should you augment your traces with additional log annotations, to provide more context about what's happening during a span? Your high-level goal is to instrument the things that are going to be the most useful. But you can't instrument everything, both because of the time-consuming nature of doing instrumentation and more fundamentally because your application needs to cope with the volume of spans being emitted. Computational costs are a driving challenge of distributed tracing, as we discuss in Chapter 6.

In the worst case, it might be impossible to predict a priori where to put your instrumentation, because nobody can perfectly predict where and how problems might arise. On the one hand, the point of distributed tracing is to be able to investigate unexpected behaviors and debug problems, so you'd hope that traces contain useful information for diagnosing problems when they do arise. On the other hand, sometimes you'll be unlucky, and the information you need to diagnose a problem just might not be present in traces, or even in other data sources like system logs.

When you don't have visibility of a problem's root causes, then diagnosing the problem becomes a tedious and time-consuming task. If you want to add new instrumentation, in the hopes of shedding more light on the matter, you'd have to go back to your code to do it. This is fundamentally slow, because deploying new instrumentation is part of the development path of applications—getting that new instrumentation into the production system might take a while. In the worst case this is a repeated process—for example, how often do you get print debugging right the very first time?

Of course, it isn't all doom and gloom. What we're describing here is an exceptional case for distributed tracing. In the grand scheme of things, the instrumentation you'll have in place will be enough to solve most problems most of the time. But what if you do want to focus on these *unanticipated* problems? Two of the tools we'll be looking at in a moment—Pivot Tracing and Pythia—target this use case in particular. Pivot Tracing and Pythia are a lot like distributed tracing, but their main goal is to home in on problems that existing instrumentation might miss.

Challenge 2: Completeness Versus Costs

Computational costs are a never-ending battle, as you saw in Chapter 6. Computational costs shape your instrumentation choices and arise from multiple places in the tracing pipeline:

- The critical path of requests to generate trace data
- Background threads and processes that receive and buffer local trace data
- Network transmission of trace data to the tracing framework's backends
- Processing and storage by the tracing backends once trace data is received

The main way distributed tracing mitigates computational costs is by sampling. Sampling is simple but effective: you only have to pay computational costs when you actually trace a request, so sampling is a configuration knob that lets you reduce computational costs by tracing fewer requests. The most common sampling method is also the simplest: uniform random sampling, decided at the very beginning of a request. If a request isn't sampled, no trace data is generated at all.

Computational costs are one of the most important factors for profiling, debugging, and monitoring—*especially* for tools that run in production systems. A central tenet of profiling, debugging, and monitoring tools is "do no harm." Distributed tracing is no exception, and neither are any of the other tools we'll talk about. Unlike distributed tracing, Census, Pivot Tracing, and Pythia take different approaches to dealing with overheads, and *don't* solve the problem using sampling.

Challenge 3: Open-Ended Use Cases

The value of distributed tracing doesn't arise from individual spans or annotations in isolation—its value is in *combining* all of a request's data coherently from start to finish. This is why distributed tracing frameworks sample traces on a per-request basis. They sample either all of the trace data for a request or none of it. This is called *coherent sampling*. Coherent sampling is necessary for distributed tracing. Think about its original goal: to help relate information from multiple points in a request's execution, especially across different machines and components. It would be no good if distributed tracing arbitrarily recorded just bits and pieces of a request!

When you instrument your systems, you instrument the spans and annotations that you think will be the most useful for the future—for example, latency and metrics of important top-level spans; annotations at critical parts of our program; and as described earlier, information to anticipate future debugging needs. Traces can end up containing a lot of data! For example, Facebook described in its Canopy paper how the volume of data in a single trace can become overwhelming, due to multiple different users and use cases all feeding data into the same traces.[1]

Fortunately, sampling gives you a convenient way to balance computational costs. For example, you can now increase the amount of detail that goes into a single trace, and simply reduce your sampling probability to average out the total cost across all requests. In their Dapper paper,[2] the authors from Google commented about how sampling was very useful, as it enabled them to capture very detailed traces.

Not all tools for profiling, debugging, and monitoring need to capture so much detailed information. Part of why distributed tracing does record detailed information is because the use case is so open-ended—record all the data now, store it somewhere, and make it available for whatever future use case you have in mind. By contrast, Census, Pivot Tracing, and Pythia have more specific use cases in mind, which enables them to record less speculative data up front.

Other Tools Like Distributed Tracing

We'll now take a look at three tools that are similar to distributed tracing. First, Census is an internal tool from Google whose primary focus is on cross-component metrics; Google released an open-source version called OpenCensus in 2018. Next, we'll look at Pivot Tracing, a research project published in 2015 by researchers from Brown University. Pivot Tracing focuses on diagnosing recurring cross-component problems quickly, by using dynamic instrumentation. Last, we'll look at Pythia, a research project from Boston University introduced in 2019. Pythia focuses on automatically finding and turning on useful instrumentation when problems arise: that is, finding and dynamically enabling the instrumentation needed to explain a problem.

Census

Census started as an internal project at Google for collecting cross-component metric data from Google services. Google never published anything about Census in detail, but in 2018 it released an open source version called OpenCensus. Soon afterward, OpenCensus was merged with OpenTracing to become OpenTelemetry. You can read a bit more about this history in Chapter 3 as well as about the relationship between OpenCensus and distributed tracing. Our focus here is specifically on the metrics part of Census.

---

1 [Kal17]

2 [Sig10]

Just like distributed tracing, the fundamental motivation for Census is to capture and relate information across multiple machines. In this case, the focus is metric data, which we'll explain with an example.

A Motivating Example

Suppose you have two frontend APIs, A and B, as well as a number of other intermediate services that A and B call. Figure 13-1 illustrates these services. Those intermediate services might themselves make calls to other intermediate services, but eventually, requests end up querying a backend database, DB. Both frontend APIs—that is, both A and B—eventually result in calls to DB, but A and B aren't the services directly making those calls.

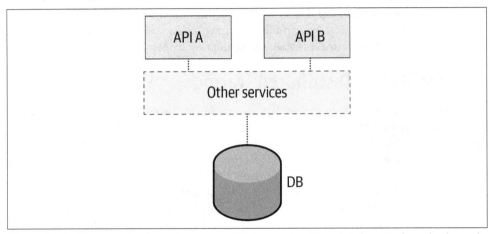

Figure 13-1. Two frontend services, A and B, interact with a database indirectly through several other services.

There are a few useful questions you might want to ask in this scenario. If you're a developer of A or B, you might want to know things like how many database calls each request makes, or how much of your request's overall latency is spent at the database. If you're a developer or operator of the database, then you might want to know which frontend APIs are using the database the most, so that you can better attribute costs or put together an SLA.

There's just one problem: since A and B don't call to the database directly, nobody has the means to answer these questions by themselves. In a standalone application, it would be straightforward to drill down into these sorts of metrics. But in a distributed application, the information is unavailable by default.

A Distributed Tracing Solution?

Distributed tracing would provide one possible solution to this problem. Figure 13-2 depicts a trace of API A in this setup. Certainly, the trace would contain all the necessary information:

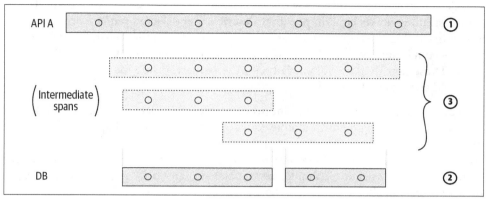

Figure 13-2. A trace of API A will record the number of database calls and the latency of each.

❶ The top-level span tells you that this request came through API A.

❷ Lurking way down in the child spans will be spans for database calls, telling you both the number of database calls and the latency of each call.

❸ Also included in the trace will be detail from every service that is invoked along the way.

Through straightforward postprocessing you can extract aggregate statistics to answer some of the questions mentioned earlier. However, there's a big drawback with using distributed tracing here. You'll inevitably be sampling distributed traces rather than tracing every request, because every service invoked adds extra detail to the trace, meaning extra overhead. You wouldn't be able to capture traces for 100% of requests because of the huge computational overheads that would introduce.

When it comes to metrics, you'll often be interested in *outliers*—how does your application behave in rare but important edge cases? Time is often spent diagnosing requests with outlier latency, in the 99th percentile and above. By sampling traces, you will miss many of the most important requests for diagnosing problems. It might give you the false impression that there are no high-latency outliers at all.

Tag Propagation and Local Metric Aggregation

Census addresses this specific use case, and it captures metrics for 100% of requests. Census doesn't record individual traces at all, so it doesn't use sampling to deal with computational costs. The key to Census is context propagation. Like distributed tracing, Census propagates contexts with requests, but those contexts don't include Trace-IDs. Instead, contexts contain *tags* that describe user-selected request properties. At any point during the request, any service can write a tag to the Census context. From the preceding example, API A and API B can write tags of "API A" or "API B" respectively. Those tags then get forwarded with the request, inside the Census context, to any child services that get called.

As well as tags, any service along the way can record a metric. In our example, the backend database might emit a simple count of API calls, and perhaps also the latency of each call. Whenever a component emits a metric, Census will inspect the request's tags in the Census context, then increment counters on a *per-tag* basis. Counters are maintained locally (in our example, at the database) and only aggregated metrics get reported, periodically, to the Census backends.

Census doesn't capture individual traces at all, because metrics get immediately aggregated within the application (e.g., by the backend database in our example). In the preceding example, the database would record separate counters for APIs A and B. In general, these counters get grouped arbitrarily based on whatever tags are present in the Census context. If you implemented a third frontend API, you could simply start propagating the tag "API C," and the database would automatically group counters for API C.

Doing local aggregation avoids all overheads of generating and reporting individual traces. As a result, Census can propagate tags and record metrics for *every* request. Census is particularly useful for diagnosing uncommon and outlier requests, which might be missed by low sampling rates. On the other hand, Census's main limitation is that it cannot drill down and inspect individual requests.

A second concern about Census is the overhead of propagating tags: the bigger and more complex the system, the more tags you might want to propagate. Census simply limits the number of tags a request can have to 1,000 bytes. This is a new source of overheads that distributed tracing doesn't really have (if we exclude baggage for now). In the next chapter, we talk about context overheads in more detail.

Comparison to Distributed Tracing

Figure 13-3 illustrates the distributed tracing approach compared to the Census approach. There are a few key differences:

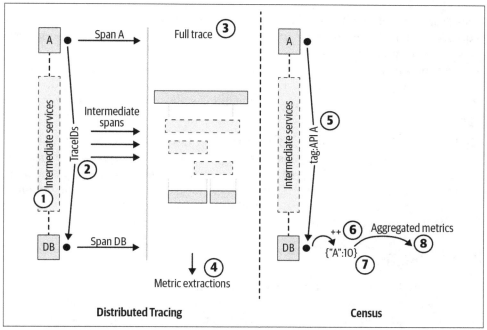

Figure 13-3. A comparison of distributed tracing versus Census.

❶ Distributed tracing emits span data at every component visited by a request, for every request.

❷ Distributed tracing propagates TraceIDs with requests, so that backends can combine spans from the same request.

❸ Distributed tracing emits span data at every component, potentially leading to large traces.

❹ Distributed tracing backends are responsible for extracting metrics from traces, if we want metrics.

❺ Census propagates tags with requests instead of TraceIDs.

❻ Census only emits metric data.

❼ Census locally aggregates metrics.

❽ Census only emits metric aggregates to the Census backend, rather than per-request measurements.

Census is very similar to distributed tracing, in that it propagates contexts with requests so that it can combine data across component and machine boundaries. However, it is not as open-ended as distributed tracing. Census is narrower in scope: it focuses on aggregating metrics, grouped by cross-component tags. Aggregated metrics are an important use case, especially for understanding outliers like 99th-percentile tail latency. Census has directly influenced the inclusion of metrics in OpenTelemetry today.

While Census is not as open-ended as distributed tracing, it does achieve complete visibility of all requests where tracing typically does not. Local aggregation means it can cheaply record metrics for every request. Census doesn't have to sample requests—it records metrics of every request; by contrast, distributed tracing needs sampling to reduce overheads. Like distributed tracing, when you're instrumenting your system, it's up to you to choose which tags to use and which metrics to capture.

Pivot Tracing

Pivot Tracing is a research project from Brown University published in 2015.[3] Pivot Tracing is a lot like Census, in that its core goal is to extract aggregated metrics from distributed applications. Pivot Tracing is designed to help diagnose *unanticipated* problems in distributed applications on the fly, by using a technique called *dynamic instrumentation*. Like Census, Pivot Tracing aggregates data directly at the source rather than generating individual traces of requests. It correlates data across components by propagating contexts, but goes a step beyond the tags used by Census.

Dynamic Instrumentation

When you use distributed tracing, you hardcode instrumentation into our applications, in much the same way that traditional logs and metrics are hardcoded in standalone applications. Dynamic instrumentation is an alternative approach to hardcoding the instrumentation. In a standalone setting, the best-known examples are DTrace, SystemTap, and eBPF. Rather than hardcoding instrumentation at development time, dynamic instrumentation frameworks let you inject code into running programs, without having to recompile or redeploy the program.

---

3 [Mac15]

Recurring Problems

By default, Pivot Tracing records nothing at all. It only injects instrumentation code into your running application when you ask for it to be installed. It thereby targets *active* debugging, where there is a persistent problem in the system, and you are actively investigating the problem by turning instrumentation on and off.

How Does It Work?

Let's go back to our earlier example depicted in Figure 13-1.

In this example, we did two things. First, at the database, we counted database queries and recorded query latency. Second, at the frontends, we were using the API name (A or B) as a tag. Census would then aggregate the query latency, grouped by API name.

You can do the same thing in Pivot Tracing, in roughly the same way. Pivot Tracing provides a more generalized query language for expressing these aggregates. Concretely, to record just the database query latency, you would use the following query:

```
FROM q in DB.ExecuteQuery
SELECT q.duration, COUNT
```

This query refers to DB.ExecuteQuery, which is the source code database method that executes queries. ExecuteQuery is an example of a *tracepoint*—a location in the application source code where Pivot Tracing can run instrumentation. The query causes the database to aggregate the ExecuteQuery method duration every time the method is invoked, as well as a counter. Like Census, these aggregations happen locally at the database, rather than reporting data for every request.

This query accounts for measuring database metrics, but our goal was to also group those metrics by the frontend API type. To do this, we would expand our earlier query to refer to tracepoints for API A and API B, which we will collectively refer to as FrontEnd.HandleRequest.

```
FROM q in DB.ExecuteQuery
JOIN r in FrontEnd.HandleRequest ON r -> q
GROUPBY r.apiName
SELECT r.apiName, q.duration, COUNT
```

The -> symbol indicates a *happened-before join*, a special query operator introduced by Pivot Tracing. This query operator simply means that FrontEnd.HandleRequest has to happen first, then later in the request DB.ExecuteQuery happens. Pivot Tracing will record apiName when the request passes through the HandleRequest method, add it to the Pivot Tracing context, and propagate it along the execution. Then when the request reaches ExecuteQuery at the database, Pivot Tracing will emit the duration of ExecuteQuery, grouped by apiName in the Pivot Tracing context.

The happened-before join is Pivot Tracing's way of formalizing causality and context propagation. In essence, a happened-before join between two tracepoints indicates that information from the first tracepoint should be propagated to the second. In our earlier example, all we're doing is propagating a tag from `HandleRequest` in the frontends, to `ExecuteQuery` at the database.

Pivot Tracing extends beyond just simple single relations. Queries can refer to multiple tracepoints, with multiple different happened-before joins. Pivot Tracing also supports a range of standard query operators such as `unions`, `selection`, `projection`, `aggregation`, and `groupby`. Multiple queries can run side by side without interference, and queries can be nested.

Dynamic Context

For any query that uses a happened-before join, Pivot Tracing needs to propagate data from an initial tracepoint to a later tracepoint. Depending on the query, the exact data that gets propagated varies. In the preceding example, the data was simply a string tag containing the `apiName`—concretely, it would be either *API A* or *API B*. More generally the data could be a set of tuples, partially aggregated data, grouped data, and more. To support this, Pivot Tracing makes use of a general-purpose, dynamic context that the authors termed *baggage*. You've already heard the term used earlier in this book; Pivot Tracing introduced it for arbitrary metadata propagated with requests. Today, *baggage* has been adopted by distributed tracing frameworks to refer to arbitrary key-value pairs.

Like Census, Pivot Tracing avoids substantial overheads by aggregating as much data locally as possible. When a user writes a query, that query is optimized to perform things like filters and aggregations at the earliest possible tracepoint. Nonetheless, baggage size is a concern for Pivot Tracing, and in general, if a tool propagates arbitrary metadata with a request, then it needs to be careful not to propagate too much! We go into this in more detail in the next chapter.

Comparison to Distributed Tracing

Pivot Tracing is much more similar to Census than to distributed tracing, but all three share a few commonalities. All three tools propagate contexts with requests, so that they can combine data across component and machine boundaries. Both Census and Pivot Tracing aggregate data as close to the source as possible, so they can be complete where distributed tracing is not. Unlike Census and Distributed Tracing, Pivot Tracing is the first tool suitable for *unanticipated* problems, as dynamic instrumentation lets developers interactively insert and remove new instrumentation to manually get to the root cause of problems. Pivot Tracing is more open-ended than Census, because it supports a broader set of operations than just tags and aggregations. However, it doesn't provide as rich data as distributed tracing does.

Pivot Tracing is a research project, with an open-source implementation, but there are a few unresolved challenges. First and foremost is managing the overheads and security of using dynamic instrumentation. However, with the growing use of eBPF in production systems, we may see more Pivot Tracing style proliferate in the future.

One alternative way to think about Pivot Tracing is to compare it with distributed tracing backends. In Chapter 10, we described a tracing use case where we aggregate high-level metrics across many traces. Facebook's Canopy is centered around this use case. Whereas a distributed tracing system performs these aggregation queries in the tracing backends, Pivot Tracing "optimizes" these queries by pushing their execution all the way to the original data source.

Pythia

Pythia is a research project from Boston University published in 2019.[4] It is more closely related to distributed tracing than to Census or Pivot Tracing. Like Pivot Tracing, Pythia is intended to help diagnose *unanticipated* problems, by dynamically changing the instrumentation in running systems. The overall output from Pythia is, in fact, distributed traces; however, the data contained in the traces is the set of data most able to explain a performance problem.

Performance Regressions

Pythia's use case is to automatically find explanations for differences in request performance. That is, for a collection of similar requests that have different performance, it will try to find instrumentation that best helps distinguish these two classes.

Consider the example illustrated in Figure 13-4. Suppose a storage service has an in-memory cache to maintain a subset of the hot data in memory. Requests to this system can follow one of two paths:

---

4 [Ate19]

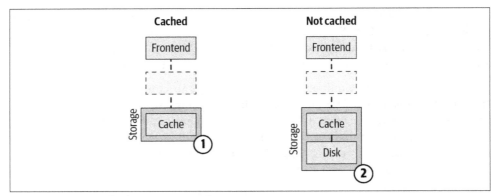

Figure 13-4. A cache hit versus a cache miss.

❶ The fast path—the request looks up data that exists in the in-memory cache, and can immediately return a result.

❷ The slow path—the request looks up data that doesn't exist in the in-memory cache, and has to go to disk to fetch the data.

By default, if you only instrument your RPC framework, then your instrumentation will only capture API calls to the storage service. If you were to plot the latency distribution of the storage service, you'd see a bimodal distribution (see Figure 13-5).

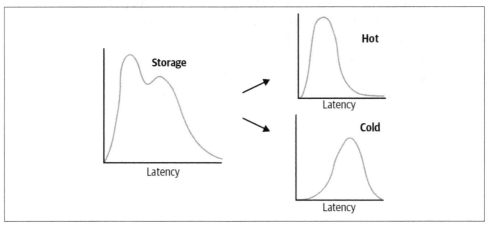

Figure 13-5. The storage service has a bimodal latency distribution.

The goal of Pythia is to automatically identify some internal tracepoints that are present in one mode, but not in the other. For example, slow requests might invoke a fetchFromDisk method that is not present in the fast, cached requests. Pythia would identify and automatically instrument this method. The new output from the system would contain this instrumentation, making it clear to Pythia users why the two request classes are different.

Design

Pythia primarily operates as a distributed tracing backend. It runs as a constant loop, with each iteration performing the following steps:

1. Resolve group requests that are expected to perform similarly.

2. Identify groups that exhibit high coefficient of variation in their response time or other important metric.

3. Search the space of possible instrumentation and identify new instrumentation to enable.

4. Dynamically update the system's instrumentation.

In addition to enabling new instrumentation, Pythia also performs a *garbage collection* step of disabling instrumentation that isn't useful.

Overheads

Pythia introduces a new dimension for managing and evaluating distributed tracing overheads. Concretely, Pythia can automatically determine when instrumentation is *not* useful for explaining performance variations, and disable it. Given some desired computational overhead, Pythia can either increase trace detail and reduce the sampling rate, or decrease trace detail and increase the sampling rate. Both of these are useful for Pythia. Receiving lots of samples quickly is useful for rapidly testing new instrumentation hypotheses, while having high trace detail makes it easier to rapidly localize instrumentation.

Comparison to Distributed Tracing

Pythia is built on top of distributed tracing. However, its use case is more narrow, with a sole focus on explaining performance variations. Unlike distributed tracing, Census, and Pivot Tracing, Pythia does *not* rely on end users to manually explore data and identify problems. Instead, it automates some of this process. For example, while Pivot Tracing is also suitable for explaining performance variations, each successive query must be chosen by the user—a time-consuming manual process. By contrast, Pythia automatically navigates the space of possible instrumentation, leading to much faster problem resolution. Of the tools we've discussed in this chapter, Pythia is the most recent, and is an ongoing project of the Massachusetts Open Cloud initiative.

Summary

When we use distributed tracing, we have to make trade-offs about what to record, and how often to record it. Distributed tracing is very much "all or nothing"—if a request is traced, you get a lot of trace detail. However, none of the trade-offs made by distributed tracing are truly fundamental to profiling, debugging, or monitoring distributed architectures. Census, Pivot Tracing, and Pythia present several different approaches to distributed tracing that are also very effective. Each tool has a different use case, which enables different design choices. Overall, we can observe the following:

- It's useful to be able to turn instrumentation on and off dynamically at runtime. Sometimes instrumentation is useful for human-driven "deep dive" analysis, but not needed the rest of the time.

- Not all instrumentation is created equal. Some instrumentation, like request latency, will always be important; the value of other instrumentation might be difficult to gauge.

- Detailed traces are useful for historical analysis, but for recurring problems, we can insert new instrumentation and "try again," rather than go digging through old traces.

- Tracing doesn't need to be "all or nothing." For example, it can be useful to record a small number of detailed traces and a larger number of simple traces.

- If you're using data to do aggregate analysis, some of those aggregations can be performed directly at the data source, rather than by tracing backends. Early aggregations are far more cost-effective.

- Context propagation adds a new source of overheads.

All of these tools have one thing in common: capturing cross-component causality. In distributed architectures, getting causality between events is very challenging. All of these tools use context propagation in one form or another, as the mechanism for observing and recording cross-component relationships. In the next chapter, we will dive more deeply into context propagation.

CHAPTER 14

The Future of Context Propagation

In this chapter, we're going to home in on context propagation, a powerful mechanism for *many* different use cases beyond just profiling, debugging, and monitoring. We'll refer to this wider class of tools as *cross-cutting tools*—tools designed for distributed architectures. Distributed tracing, Census, Pivot Tracing, and Pythia are all examples of cross-cutting tools. But, cross-cutting tools don't need to be about tracing specifically, nor about recording trace data.

We'll wrap up by taking a look at the Tracing Plane, a 2018 research project from Brown University.[1]

The goal of the Tracing Plane is to abstract and generalize the context propagation used by cross-cutting tools. In Chapters 4 and 5, we talked about the importance of abstract instrumentation and interoperability for distributed tracing. Many of these concerns also apply directly to context propagation too. The Tracing Plane project identifies some of the design considerations for context propagation, and proposes a general solution called *BaggageContexts*. In the future, some of these concepts may materialize as components of our distributed tracing tools.

Cross-Cutting Tools

The goal of distributed tracing is to correlate and integrate data across different components and machines. Distributed traces are used for *offline* analysis—to analyze trace data long after it's been recorded. Distributed tracing has a distinct division between the application-side components of the tool, for instrumentation and generating traces, and the ex post facto aggregation and trace analysis components.

---

1 [Mac18a]

Recently, several academic research projects and industrial prototypes have developed a wider variety of cross-component tools, many of them for *online* tasks. Some of these tools still focus on profiling, debugging, and monitoring, but a distinct set of them go a step further and consider *enforcement*, such as resource management. Instead of just offline analysis, these tools observe and analyze events while requests execute, and potentially make immediate decisions about what actions to take.

The Tracing Plane refers to this broader class of tools as *cross-cutting tools*. Generally speaking, these are tools that deal with end-to-end requests in distributed architectures. Distributed tracing is certainly one in this class of tools, but cross-cutting tools as a whole encompass a broader range of use cases than just recording traces.

Context propagation is a core component of cross-cutting tools. It's the mechanism that lets tools combine information across components and machines. Different tools propagate different contexts—for example, distributed tracing tools propagate Trace-IDs, but metrics tools like Census propagate tags, and Retro, a tool that we have yet to discuss, propagates tenant identifiers. Not all cross-cutting tools use concepts like spans, which are specific to distributed tracing in particular. Likewise, many cross-cutting tools don't collect and store data in backend databases, but instead have control loops that interact directly with the system in real time.

Use Cases

Let's take a look at some example use cases for cross-cutting tools. Some of these are real tools that exist today in production systems; some are research or industry prototypes; others are proposed use cases that have yet to see the light of day. For each tool, we'll touch on three pieces:

- What kind of context propagation the tool uses
- How you go about using the tool in your application
- The background or backend components of the tool

Distributed Tracing

Distributed tracing is the core focus of this book, and the most obvious example of a cross-cutting tool. While there are different implementations out there in the wild, they all follow roughly the same design: they use context propagation to pass around TraceIDs; you have to instrument your systems to record and annotate spans, which under the covers also updates the TraceIDs; and background components buffer and send recorded data over the network to backend tracing servers, for indexing and storage.

In Chapter 13, we introduced Pythia, which we can view as an extension of distributed tracing. Pythia differs in that as a user, you no longer have to exhaustively decide the instrumentation of your system. In the background, Pythia will automatically analyze traces, predict new instrumentation that might be useful, and send instrumentation commands back to the application.

Cross-Component Metrics

The two main example cross-cutting tools for metrics are Census and Pivot Tracing, both of which we described in Chapter 13. To summarize:

Census

Propagates tags with requests. To use Census, your instrumentation will either add tags to the Census context or record a metric. When you record metrics, they are automatically grouped by tags present in the Census context. Census aggregates metrics locally in the background; it only periodically reports its aggregates to the backend servers.

Pivot Tracing

Propagates partial query results with requests, which are typically sets of tuples. To use Pivot Tracing you enable a dynamic instrumentation agent in your application. In response to user-supplied queries, the Pivot Tracing agent dynamically inserts the necessary instrumentation, which will add, remove, and transform tuples from Pivot Tracing's context. In the background, Pivot Tracing agents receive queries from users, and report query results back to users.

Cross-Component Resource Management

Resource management is a difficult problem in distributed architectures, especially ones where you might have multiple users or multiple tenants. An aggressive tenant might send too many requests, potentially overloading services, to the detriment of all other users. This is also sometimes called "resource isolation" or "performance isolation." In large distributed applications, it's useful to coordinate the resource management decisions across services.

In a 2015 project, researchers from Brown University described Retro, a prototype system for end-to-end resource management.[2] Retro uses context propagation to help attribute resource consumption to requests and tenants. To do this, Retro propagates a tenant ID with every request, to identify the user or task that owns each request. To use Retro, you add a Retro agent to your applications. Retro's agent automatically hooks into system calls to measure CPU cycles, disk accesses, network bytes, and a

---

2 [Mac15]

few other generic resources. Any time the application tries to use one of these resources, Retro will consult the active tenant ID, and attribute the measurement to the active tenant.

A second step is to identify places in your application where tenants can be rate-limited. Normally these are places like RPC request queues, where you can impose fair queuing or rate-limiting logic.

Retro has a backend server that makes resource management decisions. It periodically receives resource consumption measurements from all parts of your application, then decides whether any of the tenants should be rate-limited. Retro sends those decisions back to the schedulers in the system.

Managing Data Quality Trade-offs

Many modern applications can make *data quality trade-offs*. A data quality trade-off is when you decide to reduce the accuracy or quality of a result, in exchange for a faster response.

A simple example is a distributed search query that fans out to one hundred machines. Here, you would have a data quality trade-off, with three options:

- Your application could wait for all one hundred machines to return a result, inheriting the latency of the slowest machine.

- You could choose to use only the results from the first 50 machines to reply.

- You might simply use whichever results you have after some period of time has elapsed, such as 80 ms.

In large architectures, there might be many services that can make data quality trade-offs. Each request might hit multiple of these services too. If your goal is to achieve a desired end-to-end request latency, you'd have to decide how to apportion your request latency into latency goals for each service. It's neither easy nor obvious how to do this.

A 2016 project from Facebook described DQBarge, a prototype system for end-to-end data quality trade-offs.[3] DQBarge is designed to make these data quality trade-off decisions automatically.

The authors of DQBarge found certain request-level data to be useful for making data quality trade-offs. DQBarge propagates this information in its context:

---

3 [Cho16]

- At request ingress, DQBarge predicts which child services will be called and in which order. DQBarge estimates how much slack time is available at each service. DQBarge puts this prediction into its context.

- As the request runs, each component measures time *actually* spent in the component and whatever data quality trade-off was made by the component.

- Each component adds CPU and memory load metrics to the DQBarge context.

- The preceding three are done automatically by DQBarge; in addition, developers can instrument their services manually to insert key-value tags into the DQBarge context.

Using this information, DQBarge has machine learning models that run in every service. When a request shows up, data from the DQBarge context is fed into the model to predict an appropriate data quality trade-off (such as an appropriate timeout). These models are created during an offline step using prerecorded distributed traces.

Failure Testing of Microservices

LinkedOut is a 2018 project from LinkedIn that focuses on failure-testing of microservices.[4] LinkedOut systematically injects faults into services at the level of requests. Due to the complexity of microservice architectures, LinkedOut needs to be able to target specific points during request flows to inject faults.

- LinkedOut injects dummy requests alongside production workloads.

- LinkedOut propagates fault instructions with each dummy request. A fault instruction is either an error, a delay, or a timeout. Fault instructions can also include filters specifying where and when faults should occur.

- At each service, LinkedOut inspects the request's metadata, checks the filters on the fault instructions, and possibly executes a fault instruction. LinkedOut only performs a fault injection action if the filters match.

- The LinkedOut backend runs fault injection experiments by propagating various fault instructions with dummy requests, and asserting that the system behaves in the correct way when the actions are triggered.

---

4 [Ros18]

Enforcing Cross-System Consistency

Independent evolution is one of the key benefits of microservice architectures: you develop, deploy, and scale each service independently. As your system grows in scale, you need to start thinking about things like *replication* and *consistency*. Fortunately, these are well-studied topics and a fundamental part of distributed systems. Microservices usually make use of *eventual consistency*, where updates made on one replica will eventually make their way to all other replicas (but not usually immediately). Cross-system consistency becomes a problem when we wire up *multiple* microservices that use eventual consistency.

Consider the following: when a user composes a social media post, the post content is stored in a posts database, then a notification is generated for the user's followers, and stored in a notifications database. Clearly, followers shouldn't actually receive the notification until the post is available to be read from the posts database. However, the posts and notifications databases are separate services that can be replicated at different speeds. It's entirely possible for the follower to be notified of a post that doesn't exist yet in the local replica.

Cross-system consistency problems happen because microservice architectures rapidly grow and evolve in features. Microservices aren't usually designed at the beginning with replication and consistency in mind; instead, they come about later on when the service needs to scale.

Researchers at INESC TEC in Portugal proposed a tool to address this problem.[5] In the preceding example, the tool would prevent a notification from being delivered to a follower until the post had been replicated. To do this, each time a request writes to an eventually consistent service, the tool generates and propagates a causal timestamp with the request. Using causal timestamps, components can infer any preconditions that must be met before the request may proceed. In the background, components maintain and increment causal timestamps as they execute operations.

Request Duplication

One popular technique to reduce tail latency is request duplication—that is, sending multiple copies of a request to different worker nodes. It's difficult to do this in large distributed architectures without blowing up your system with extra requests, because each child service could potentially add further duplication. Researchers at Tufts University have proposed propagating metadata about request duplication choices alongside requests, and having a global external control loop that tweaks when and where duplication decisions should happen.[6]

---

5 [Lof17]

6 [Bas19]

Record Lineage in Stream Processing Systems

In stream processing systems like Spark Streaming or Kafka Streams, the concept of a request is less well defined than in RPC architectures. We might, for example, be interested in the end-to-end flow of a record through the system; however, intermediate processing stages might combine multiple input records into a single output record. Distributed tracing would be capable of capturing this by simply combining the input traces with the output traces; however, when sampling comes into play, it would require every input record to have been sampled. Researchers from the Hungarian Academy of Sciences proposed a hybrid approach, whereby instead of sending trace data to the tracing backends, the trace data is instead written directly to the trace context and propagated with the request (or in this case, record).[7] This leads very quickly to large contexts as the execution progresses; future work will need to address this.

Auditing Security Policies

Security challenges are exacerbated in microservice architectures because of the increased decentralization. Even the original Dapper paper mentions distributed tracing's useful applications to computer security. The authors used Dapper to verify that services were adhering to authentication and encryption policies, by augmenting traces with security protocol parameters. More generally, distributed tracing is an appealing way to audit security policies. Incorrect authentication repeatedly makes the Open Web Application Security Project's top 10 most critical security risks; in microservice architectures it occurs because policies aren't asserted at the time that privileged actions are executed. Distributed tracing would be a mechanism for auditing security policy enforcement; taken a step further, context propagation would be a good way to enforce security policies at runtime.

Testing in Production

Integration testing is a big challenge for distributed architectures, because it's so difficult to replicate production environments and workloads in an offline setting. Testing in production is one way to get around this, but has the added danger of colocating test traffic with real traffic. Context propagation is a simple way of propagating additional metadata with requests, to communicate testing objectives to downstream services. In general, the baggage mechanism of distributed tracing is already an effective way of tagging requests for the benefit of downstream services.

---

7 [Zva19]

Common Themes

Cross-cutting tools all use context propagation, and there are a few common themes:

Contexts are dynamic
>   The cross-cutting tools often read and update the context as requests progress.

Response propagation
>   Sometimes, information from downstream services is propagated *back* to the caller, requiring contexts to be passed back to callers in RPC responses.

Variable context size
>   Distributed tracing usually has fixed-size contexts, since only TraceIDs and flags need to be propagated (excluding baggage). Most cross-cutting tools have variable sized contexts.

Small context size
>   Although contexts are variable in size, most cross-cutting tools factor context size into their design. In particular they aim to minimize context size, since the larger the context, the bigger the runtime cost to propagate it. If the context gets too large, it will introduce unacceptable overheads. For example, Census has hardcoded limits on the size of the tags it's willing to propagate, and drops tags above that limit.

Need for instrumentation
>   No matter which cross-cutting tool you wish to deploy, you have to go and instrument your entire architecture with context propagation. Chapter 2 outlined how enormous this effort can be.

Should You Care?

For some of the use cases we've described, the tools haven't yet made it beyond alpha-stage prototypes, so you might wonder why this information is relevant. Beyond giving a glimpse of the tools we might have in the future, a more concrete goal is to emphasize reusability of the distributed tracing components we have today.

Reusable, interoperable instrumentation is one of the biggest challenges for distributed tracing, and this challenge also extends to cross-cutting tools. Cross-cutting tools all propagate contexts, and they all need instrumentation for propagating contexts. They all follow requests, and the instrumentation needed for propagating contexts always happens *in the same places* for every tool. Do you really want to re-instrument your applications again in the future if you want to deploy any of these tools?

In the past couple of years, this observation led to the inclusion of general-purpose baggage in the OpenTracing spec, and most distributed tracing frameworks today let you propagate arbitrary key-value pairs with requests. This is suitable for several of the use cases mentioned earlier, including metrics, testing in production, and simple resource management. However, baggage is currently underspecified, primarily because it's hard for us to anticipate future use cases.

The final research project we'll talk about is an effort to do just this. Called the Tracing Plane, the project focuses specifically on factoring out context propagation as a general-purpose, reusable component for cross-cutting tools. The project shines a light on some of the subtle challenges to getting this right, and proposes one possible implementation.

The Tracing Plane

The Tracing Plane is a 2018 research project from Brown University, follow-up on work from their earlier Pivot Tracing project.[8]

The idea behind the Tracing Plane is that context propagation is so useful that it should be factored out as a separate component, one that can be reused simultaneously by different cross-cutting tools. The authors proposed an abstraction layering for context propagation, much like OpenTracing is an abstraction layer for distributed tracing.

Figure 14-1 illustrates how distributed tracing would interact with the Tracing Plane. Rather than context propagation being an internal component of distributed tracing, tightly integrated with the concept of TraceIDs and spans, it would instead be a general-purpose component to which distributed tracing is but one client.

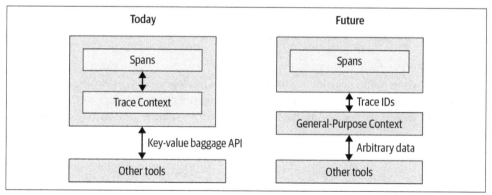

Figure 14-1. The Tracing Plane proposes factoring context propagation as a standalone component.

---

8 [Mac18a]

It's important that context propagation can be shared by multiple tools, because the effort required to add context propagation instrumentation is so high. All cross-cutting tools need instrumentation to propagate contexts alongside requests. This instrumentation is *the same*, regardless of the cross-cutting tool being deployed. If instrumentation can be reused, you only have to instrument your systems once, rather than every time you want to deploy one of these new tools.

Is Baggage Enough?

Distributed tracing already has a notion of baggage, described in Chapter 2 as an array of key-value pairs. Any component can add new key-value pairs to a request's baggage; later components can query values from baggage too. This has already enabled a few interesting use cases. For example, discussions on the Jaeger message board have included proposals for security auditing, traffic labeling, and testing use cases similar to those described earlier.

Unfortunately, this simple definition falls flat whenever we have *multiparent causality*. Multiparent causality occurs in two main ways (see Figures 15-2 and 15-3).

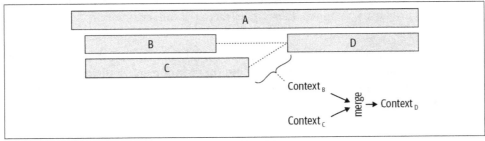

Figure 14-2. Multiparent causality needs to be able to merge contexts.

Multiple parent spans
> This is when some span of execution is causally dependent on multiple parent or sibling spans completing. When this happens, the contexts from both parents or siblings need to be passed to the new span, and somehow combined together.

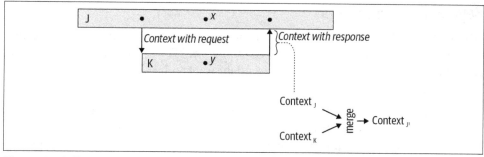

Figure 14-3. Response propagation needs to be able to merge contexts.

Response propagation

Not all distributed tracing implementations need or use response propagation, but many do. In general, it's reasonable that a cross-cutting tool might modify its context, and pass the modified context *back* to the parent. When this happens, the parent needs to merge the response context back with its original context. Remember, the parent might have also continued to do work in the meantime, so the parent might also have modified its own context.

Put simply, you need to be able to *merge* two contexts into one. Merging happens anywhere two concurrent branches of a request join. Merging is fundamental to concurrent programs, and distributed architectures are fundamentally concurrent.

Let's return for a moment to the key-value baggage used in distributed tracing. Suppose service B inserted `priority:low` into the baggage, and service C inserted `prior ity:high`. What should you do? The two baggages now have two different values for the same key. Since keys can only have one value, you'll need to pick one. Today this happens in a crude way: usually one is selected randomly. Alternatively you could go to your code and add more instrumentation to resolve this conflict manually. Neither choice is appealing, and distributed tracing users have bumped into this problem already. The typical message board response is that distributed tracing won't help; you must make the decision yourself.

In simple systems, it might be acceptable for you to manually add instrumentation to resolve these merge conflicts. But in large architectures, this might be too much effort —there might be too many places where merge conflicts can happen, and you might not even be aware of them all. It's difficult to even know ahead of time all of the services that might have your application as a dependency.

Beyond Key-Value Pairs

We saw how different cross-cutting tools propagate different kinds of data, and that data might also have different *merge semantics*. For example, when merging `priority:low` with `priority:high`, you might want to just keep the highest priority level, in this case keep `priority:high`.

Other kinds of data have other merge semantics. For example, Census treats its tags like a `set`. If this was implemented as keys and values, the ideal result of merging `tags:A` with `tags:B` might be the set union `tags:A,B`. A more elaborate example is a counter. A simple tool that counts RPC invocations might want to add values: merging `count:5` with `count:2` should produce `count:7`.

Unfortunately, there is no one correct way of merging contexts. It's up to the cross-cutting tool to decide how this should happen. Fortunately, it's usually quite easy to write concisely what data gets propagated and how it should get merged.

The Tracing Plane introduced a language for this called BDL, or, Baggage Definition Language. For the preceding priority example, we would write:

```
bag PriorityExampleTool {
        int32 Priority = 0;
}
```

This definition is stating that the `PriorityExampleTool` wants to propagate a field called "Priority" of type `int32`. By default in BDL, merging two `int32` fields will keep the larger one.

At this stage, our goal by showing you BDL is to be illustrative rather than exhaustive; for now, it suffices to know that definitions in BDL look and behave a lot like Google's Protocol Buffers (a popular interchange format for structured data).

Let's look at another example:

```
bag Census {
        set<string> Tags = 0;
}
```

This definition defines Census as propagating a field called `Tags` that is a set of strings. By default in BDL, merging two sets will perform a set union.

As we have mentioned, BDL looks and behaves a lot like Google's Protocol Buffers. It has the typical built-in primitive types that you would expect, along with some special built-in types: sets, maps, flags, and counters. All types in BDL have explicit merge semantics (such as set union for sets). BDL supports nested definitions and has many of the useful properties offered by other interchange formats, such as support for unknown fields when mixing multiple different versions of a bag definition.

Compiling BDL

BDL is all well and good for *declaring* data used by cross-cutting tools, but we haven't said yet what it actually compiles to, or how it's used. The Tracing Plane project also defines an underlying serialization format for BDL called *BaggageContext*. This is similar to how Protocol Buffers has a well-defined underlying serialization format.

From a BDL definition, a command-line compiler will generate source files that you can include in your projects. For example in Java, compiling the Census declaration would produce a source file Census.java, as shown in Example 14-1.

Example 14-1. Command-line compiler

```
public interface Census { ❶

        public Set<String> getTags(); ❷
        public void setTags(Set<String> tags);

        public byte[] writeTo(byte[] baggageContext); ❸
        public static Census readFrom(byte[] baggageContext); ❹

}
```

The compiled code defines an interface ❶ and an implementation (not shown) representing the Census bag. The code includes methods to get and set values for Tags ❷ and methods to serialize ❸ and deserialize ❹ the data. Notice that baggageContext is simply a byte array. To use the compiled code is straightforward (see Example 14-2).

Example 14-2. Using the compiled code

```
public class Example {

        public static void main(String[] args) {
                byte[] emptyBaggageContext = new byte[0]; ❶

                Census census = Census.readFrom(emptyBaggageContext); ❷

                Set<String> tags = new HashSet<String>();
                tags.add("API-A");
                census.setTags(tags); ❸

                byte[] baggageContextWithTag = census.writeTo(emptyBaggageContext); ❹
        }
}
```

❶ Initially our baggageContext contains nothing; this is equivalent to an empty array.

❷ Using `readFrom` we can extract a Census bag from the empty `baggageContext`. Since the `baggageContext` is empty, the Census bag will contain no tags.

❸ We create a tag "API-A" and add it to the Census bag.

❹ We use `writeTo` to inject the Census bag into `baggageContext`. We receive back a nonempty `baggageContext` that contains the serialized Census bag.

All of these operations are designed to be quite computationally efficient.

BaggageContext

In the preceding example, `baggageContext` represented the generic, serialized form of a bag. You can think of BaggageContext as being like our opaque trace contexts in distributed tracing. BaggageContext needs to be passed around with requests, included in RPC headers, and so on. As in the preceding example, distributed tracing would use BaggageContext to store its TraceIDs; then anywhere you create spans, you would read and write tracing data directly to and from the BaggageContext.

Merging

BaggageContext provides one additional extremely useful property: it can be merged. The BaggageContext format is carefully designed such that two *serialized* instances can be merged together easily and efficiently, without needing to either deserialize the objects or even understand the datatypes contained within. The BaggageContext library has the core interface shown in the following example:

```
public class BaggageContext {

        public byte[] merge(byte[] baggageContextA, byte[] baggageContextB);

        public byte[] trim(byte[] baggageContext, int size);

}
```

We won't get into the details of the implementation here, but at the heart of the BaggageContext is a simple byte-wise comparison scheme. The `merge` API combines two BaggageContext instances at the byte level, without actually interpreting the values. Duplicating an instance is easy—it can simply be copied.

Overheads

In addition to merging, the BaggageContext library provides a `trim` API call. This is used for managing overheads. The idea behind trim is to limit the size of the BaggageContext being propagated. For example, a service might only be willing to propagate 1000 bytes; using `trim`, the service can enforce this limit. This is a lot like how Census operates today, by discarding tags above a given size threshold.

Like `merge`, `trim` correctly discards data at the byte level, without interpreting the values in the BaggageContext. Trimming has two nice properties. First, when data is discarded, the `trim` operation adds a small (1-byte) marker to the BaggageContext to indicate that a trim occurred. This can be used by cross-cutting tools later, as a hint that some data was being propagated but at some point had to be thrown away. Second, `trim` discards data based on an implicit priority ordering that is baked into the serialization format.

Summary

BaggageContext and BDL may come across as a heavyweight way of doing context propagation—after all, simple key-value pairs seem so much nicer! However, BDL used many of the lessons offered by existing approaches to data serialization, specifically Protocol Buffers. As a result, the serialized overhead of BaggageContext is minimal, but we get all sorts of nice properties that are difficult or impossible to achieve with key-value pairs:

- All BaggageContext data has explicit merge semantics, making it clear how to resolve merge conflicts.
- Merge conflicts are resolved automatically, correctly, and without the need for custom instrumentation.
- Services can propagate BaggageContext instances without needing to be able to interpret them, as BaggageContexts are just bytes.
- Services only interpret BaggageContext instances when they actually use or manipulate the data contained within.
- BaggageContext instances can be resized without needing to interpret them.
- Cross-cutting tools can update their bag definitions, and use multiple versions concurrently, with correct conflict resolution.
- When you instrument your system, all you need to do is propagate BaggageContexts. The only API you need to use is the `merge` and `trim` API. You don't need to know anything about the tools that might later use the BaggageContext.
- You don't need to revisit your instrumentation to deploy new cross-cutting tools.

In the future, a more principled approach to context propagation is quite likely. Whether the approach we described here is the one that gets used is anybody's guess. Certainly, future context propagation needs to solve the problem of key-conflicts, and BaggageContext provides an elegant solution to this.

As we said back in Chapter 10, distributed tracing is young, and it's still evolving. The tools we use in the future might not be the same as the tools we use today. The lessons we've learned with projects like OpenTracing and OpenTelemetry are ones we can apply to other areas that are less mature, such as context propagation. For now, knowing this might not change the way you choose to use distributed tracing. But we hope we've helped to broaden your perspective on what future tracing tools might do.

The State of Distributed Tracing Circa 2020

One of the biggest challenges in writing this book has been figuring out what merits inclusion. We've attempted to provide a broad, and somewhat timeless, overview of the fundamental concepts and techniques underpinning the technology as it exists today. For everything we touched on, however, there's more that we left out. This appendix will attempt to give you a snapshot of popular tools for distributed tracing, both open source and commercial, that you might find useful.

Open Source Tracers and Trace Analysis

These are some popular open source tracers and trace analyzers:

Zipkin (https://zipkin.io)
> One of the most mature open source tracing tools available today. We discuss it in more depth in "Zipkin" on page 54. It provides, in addition to a trace analyzer, a number of instrumentation libraries for popular frameworks such as ASP.NET Core, a variety of Java frameworks (such as Jersey, JAXRS2, Apache HttpClient, and Spring Cloud), and more.

Jaeger (https://www.jaegertracing.io)
> A newer open source tracing tool and a Cloud Native Computing Foundation (CNCF) project. The more lightweight nature of Jaeger has made it extremely popular for cloud-native developers, and it is the default trace analyzer for the popular service mesh Istio. Jaeger also fully supports the OpenTracing API, making it compatible with hundreds of integrations into existing frameworks and libraries.

SkyWalking (https://skywalking.apache.org)
> An Apache Foundation project that has found a great deal of popularity in China. Its goal is to be an all-in-one application performance management tool. It

supports not just distributed traces but also metrics, and can ingest data from a variety of tracing formats.

Haystack (https://expediadotcom.github.io/haystack)
A distributed tracing analysis system built by Expedia. It supports OpenTracing, allowing you to make use of hundreds of existing integrations. It supports trace analysis and allows you to create custom alerts based on performance data.

Pinpoint (https://naver.github.io/pinpoint)
An APM tool that supports monitoring of Java- and PHP-based distributed systems. One unique characteristic of Pinpoint is that it exclusively instruments your code through agents and plug-ins, which means you can't do explicit instrumentation of your source code and are required to run the agent.

Appdash (https://github.com/sourcegraph/appdash)
An application tracing system for Go that is based on Google's Dapper. It's primarily intended for instrumenting Go-based applications, but offers support for the OpenTracing API and has clients in Python and Ruby as well.

In general, Jaeger and Zipkin are the two most popular and mature open source tracing tools. They have large user and contributor communities, and offer a fairly straightforward setup and installation process.

At the time of this writing, OpenTelemetry is still in alpha, but by the time this book is printed it's anticipated to be in beta or moving toward a 1.0 release. One of the design goals of OpenTelemetry, in addition to providing a standard API and SDK for instrumentation, is to provide high-quality automatic instrumentation for popular frameworks and libraries both through wrappers around that code and also through agents. We anticipate that this movement toward instrumentation as a focus of the open source world will lead to distributed tracing being a built-in feature of RPC frameworks, libraries, and other software products.

Commercial Tracers and Trace Analyzers

There's a huge variety of commercial performance monitoring and distributed tracing vendors. In an effort to be impartial, we'll simply list the most notable ones here. In general, these are all SaaS products that do the heavy lifting in terms of storing, analyzing, indexing, and alerting based on your trace data. Some of them offer proprietary agents and other tools to ease instrumentation. Many, if not most, support open source instrumentation standards such as OpenTracing, OpenCensus, and OpenTelemetry:

- AppDynamics (*https://www.appdynamics.com*)
- Datadog (*https://www.datadog.com*)

- Dynatrace (*https://www.dynatrace.com*)
- Elastic (*https://www.elastic.co*)
- Epsagon (*https://www.epsagon.com*)
- Honeycomb (*https://www.honeycomb.io*)
- Instana (*https://www.instana.com*)
- Lightstep (*https://www.lightstep.com*)
- New Relic (*https://www.newrelic.com*)
- Splunk (*https://www.splunk.com*)
- Wavefront (*https://www.wavefront.com*)

Language-Specific Tracing Features

Not every language is created equal when it comes to distributed tracing. Some languages offer tools, features, and projects that you may wish to employ in instrumenting your code. We'll look at a few of them here.

Java and C#

As two of the most common languages in use around the world, it's no surprise that Java and C# have wide support for distributed tracing. A variety of proprietary and open source agents and automatic instrumentation plug-ins exist for most popular service and RPC frameworks, including:

- Spring
- Akka
- JAX-RS
- JDBI
- JDBC
- Apache HttpClient
- Netty
- OkHTTP
- Java Flight Recorder (JFR)
- Web Servlet Filter
- gRPC

C# also supports a wide variety of instrumentation plug-ins, such as:

- ASP.NET MVC
- ASP.NET WebAPI
- ASP.NET Core MVC
- Entity Framework Core
- gRPC

In addition, both of these languages feature a variety of automatic instrumentation tools that operate on the bytecode of compiled software, such as the Java Special Agent or C#'s Fody plug-in. It's also possible to use a variety of aspect-oriented programming frameworks (such as C#'s PostSharp) to write tracing plug-ins that allow you to easily decorate method declarations in order to trace them.

Go, Rust, and C++

Go, Rust, C++, and C are somewhat more challenging to instrument because they lack some of the niceties available to us in managed runtimes like the JVM or CLR. However, their popularity as microservice languages means that there are a great many instrumentation tools available for them.

Go supports automatic instrumentation primarily by wrapping existing libraries with tracing code. Generally, you use these by modifying your import path to point to a traced version of the library, but there are other implementations that provide function wrappers—such as the ones used earlier in this text, in the MicroCalc example code.

Rust supports tracing as a first-class citizen through its `tracing` crate (package, in Rust parlance), which was formerly known as `tokio-trace`. This crate provides an interface to popular OSS tracing APIs such as OpenTracing and OpenTelemetry. This package is becoming widely supported throughout the Rust ecosystem, and provides helpful methods for tracing at the local function level in addition to distributed requests.

C++ is supported by the OpenTracing API, as well as OpenTelemetry. There's little in the way of automatic instrumentation or tracing agents for C++, but tracers exist for most commercial and OSS tracing systems that support C++ as it is part of service mesh tracing (through its integration into tools like Envoy and Nginx).

Python, JavaScript, and Other Dynamic Languages

Dynamic languages tend to have excellent support for distributed tracing instrumentation, through either plug-ins or agents. We'll focus just on JavaScript and Python, but much of this is generally applicable to other similar languages (for example, most of what we write about JavaScript applies to TypeScript and other languages that run on V8 or other JS runtimes).

JavaScript instrumentation can be thought of in two major groups—browser- and Node.JS-based. Browser instrumentation is primarily interested in instrumenting HTTP libraries, such as the XMLHttpRequest or fetch libraries. These plug-ins tend to be fairly straightforward, just importing the libraries and going from there. Since JavaScript makes it easy to add hooks to existing functions, quite a bit of browser instrumentation falls into this category. There are also packages, like OpenCensus Web, which hook into the underlying browser API to trace page load timings and user interactions in the browser.

For Node.JS, instrumentation plug-ins and middleware exist for many popular and widely used libraries and frameworks, such as the following:

- Express
- Connect
- gRPC
- Restify
- Native modules (dns, http, net, etc.)
- MySQL and MySQL2
- pg (Postgres)
- Redis
- MongoDB

This isn't an exhaustive list, but it's representative of the breadth of integrations available.

Python, similarly, allows for dynamic instrumentation by simply importing a tracing library into your application code, as method signatures can be intercepted and rewritten by imported code. Some of the frameworks and libraries that are instrumented for Python are:

- Django
- Flask
- Tornado
- Cassandra
- Memcached
- MongoDB
- MySQL

- Postgres
- Redis
- gRPC
- Requests
- gevent

The best way to discover these and other integrations for your language is to browse the various tracing registries available at OpenTracing (*https://opentracing.io/registry*) and OpenTelemetry (*https://opentelemetry.io/registry*), as they tend to be somewhat exhaustive.

Context Propagation in OpenTelemetry

In Chapter 14 we discussed context propagation as it applies not only to distributed tracing, but also to other applications in microservice architectures. As of this writing, OpenTelemetry has adopted a proposal to separate its context mechanism and model from the distributed tracing and metric models to support a wider variety of use cases. As the exact translation of this proposal into specification has not occurred at this point, we'll describe the overarching goals of this context propagation model, how it factors into the overall OpenTelemetry project, and its intended use.

Why a Separate Context Model?

Earlier in the book we discussed the advantages of context propagation as a mechanism that applies to use cases beyond simply profiling and monitoring microservice architectures, also known as *cross-cutting tools*. Today, the practical realities of how developers build software has meant that these cross-cutting tools are often tightly coupled to some other particular component or dependency in their software. An example of this is in OpenTracing—the ability to propagate key-value pairs through trace context baggage is quite useful for passing messages around an application for telemetry purposes (for example, using data carried in the baggage from an upstream service to isolate a particular event or metric later in the request), but we have also seen usages of it where developers use it as an out-of-band message channel to send commands or control flow indicators to later services in a request. Another example, outside of an existing telemetry tool, would be gRPC's context class, which is commonly used as a way to propagate security principles and credentials across API boundaries.

OpenTelemetry's context model primarily seeks to address two main concerns—extensibility of the context propagation mechanism, and a cleaner separation of concerns between observability and context propagation. Extensibility is fairly straightforward as a design goal. A clean separation between the context propagation mechanism and the observability components allows for end users to consume and utilize just the context propagation mechanism if they wish, without requiring them to depend on the observability tool for nonobservability concerns. This makes it easier for developers to build new applications built on context propagation, such as A/B testing, lower-level request routing, and authentication/authorization schemes. In addition to these extensibility goals, separation of concerns in OpenTelemetry itself is a critical goal. By moving context propagation into its own, self-contained component, it becomes easier to understand and reason about without having to understand all of the observability APIs. Furthermore, it allows for the context propagation mechanism to have multiple self-contained types of propagation—for example, you may want to sample your trace context and throw away certain traces, but if you're passing security data through the propagation mechanism, you'd never want that to be discarded.

The OpenTelemetry Context Model

OpenTelemetry's context propagation model defines a "top level" set of cross-cutting concerns which integrate with the business and application logic of a service, and a "bottom level" context propagation layer that can store and manage state across the life span of a request in a distributed system, as illustrated in Figure B-1.

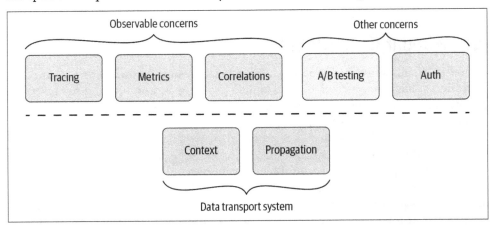

Figure B-1. Overview of the context propagation system.

The top level includes functions such as distributed tracing, metrics, and correlations along with other nonobservability functions. These observability APIs are discussed more generally in "OpenTelemetry" on page 34, however, the correlations function is not. Correlations are a feature of OpenTelemetry that allows you to propagate index values throughout a request to assist in correlating observability events that occur in one service with some piece of data provided by an upstream service in order to

---

establish a causal link between them. As a simple example, you could link the version of some upstream component or dependency (like an OS or browser version) with a particular failure in a downstream component or service. The API for correlations is based on the W3C CorrelationContext specification (*https://oreil.ly/9Ycf3*), which we'll take a look at in more detail now.

W3C CorrelationContext and the Correlations API

Much like the W3C Trace-Context specification's goal of ensuring a standard format for the propagation of trace context, correlation context ensures a standard format for passing user-defined correlation data through a request. The `CorrelationContext` header(s) in a request are limited to 180 key-value pairs, with a maximum size of 4,096 bytes for a single pair, and a total length of 8,192 bytes for all pairs in a single header.

Here, we show example headers, and keys and values are URL-encoded:

```
// A single correlation context header
Correlation-Context: userID=janeDoe,isTrialUser=false,token=entropy9

// Multiple headers are allowed
Correlation-Context: userID=janeDoe
Correlation-Context: isTrialUser=false,token=entropy9
```

At the time of this writing, the W3C standard is a public working draft, and is not finalized, so these details may change in the future.

OpenTelemetry seeks to adopt an API that allows for observability components (tracing, metrics, etc.) to interact with the correlation context through a simple set of setters and getters. The proposed methods are as follows:

`GetCorrelation(context, key) -> value`
Returns a value from a given key in the correlation context

`SetCorrelation(context, key, value) -> context`
Returns a context with the given key-value pair

`RemoveCorrelation(context, key) -> context`
Returns a context with the given key removed

`ClearCorrelations(context) -> context`
Returns a context with correlations removed (used if crossing a trust boundary)

`GetCorrelationPropagator() -> (HTTP_Extractor, HTTP_Injector)`
Returns an implementation of the injector and extractor methods needed to deserialize a correlation context from an upstream process or serialize them for propagation to a downstream process.

Distributed and Local Context

Outside the general scope of correlation context, OpenTelemetry itself needs to interact with the underlying context API. Broadly, these interactions can be thought of as interacting with a distributed, or a local, context. Distributed context we've already discussed; it's how you propagate data across API boundaries. Local context interacts with this in two ways. The first is to allow in-process access to the distributed context, and either access or modify it as required by the service. The other is to hold values that are intended to scope a single request inside of a single process, shared by its threads or subprocesses. The intention of the local context API is not only to encapsulate the correlation context, but also to act as a wrapper for local resources (such as process-wide attributes) that would be applied to telemetry sources within the context's scope. This local context should be managed either by passing an explicit context object from function to function, or automatically by registering it in thread-local storage (or language equivalent).

Examples and Potential Applications

The specifics of the context propagation mechanism in OpenTelemetry have yet to be fully implemented (but should be by the time you read this), but we would be remiss to not at least demonstrate some of the functionality that it should enable in pseudocode.

Our example posits a simple routing scenario, where two versions of a client service exist. In this scenario, you might wish to have different backend services handle requests differently from each client version, and capture some performance data on the response times of each request. To put it in more concrete terms, consider a messaging application where you are adding new features, but wish to ensure that users of all client versions can continue to communicate. You would need to either force client updates for your end users so that they are all using the same version of the back-end service or create logic in your back-end service that could handle multiple different client versions at the same time. Both of these have drawbacks—end users may not wish to update, and the complexity of adding handlers for each client version in a single backend may balloon the complexity and maintainability cost of the code. Using context, however, you could easily route requests to the appropriate service based on some value in the correlation-context header. An example of this in pseudo-code can be seen in the following example:

```
func init() {
    baggageExtractor, baggageInjector = Correlations.HTTPPropagator() ❶
    traceExtractor, traceInjector = Tracer.W3CPropagator()

    Propagation.SetExtractors(baggageExtractor, traceExtractor) ❷
    Propagation.SetInjectors(baggageInjector, traceInjector)
}
```

```
func main() {
    init()
    // Define handlers, process context, etc.
    router.Handle("/api/chat", handleRequest(context, this.request))
}

func handleRequest(context, request) -> (context) {
    extractors = Propagation.GetExtractors()
    context = Propagation.Extract(context, extractors, request.Headers) ❸

    context = Tracer.StartSpan(context, ...) ❹

    clientVersion = Correlations.GetCorrelation(context, "clientVersion")

    switch (clientVersion) { ❺
        case "1.0":
            result, context = fetchDataFromServiceB(context)
        case "2.0":
            result, context = fetchDataFromServiceC(context)
    }

    context = request.Response(context, result)
    Tracer.EndSpan(context)
    return context
}

func fetchDataFromServiceB(context) -> (context, data) {
    req = MakeRequest(...) ❻

    injectors = Propagation.GetInjectors() ❼
    req.Headers = Propagation.Inject(context, injectors, req.Headers)

    data = req.Do()
    return data
}
```

❶ Note that baggage and Trace Context are propagated separately to avoid correlations being sampled out.

❷ Extractors and injectors are set globally, so that we're able to properly inject and extract all headers from our outgoing and incoming requests.

❸ The extract function will run all registered extractors, so both our trace context and our correlation context are present in the local context.

❹ This span will be the child of whatever span was extracted from our incoming request, and the new span will be in the resulting context.

❺ Keys need to be known by the receiving service in order to inspect them; there's no way to enumerate all of the keys in a correlation context.

❻ Create a new outgoing HTTP request to our new service. We don't describe `fetchDataFromServiceC` here, but it would be similar.

❼ This injects both the correlation context and the trace context into the outgoing request.

Notice that the inject and extract functions in the preceding example don't specifically reference a tracer or any other OpenTelemetry component at all; this is a by-product of the separation of concerns between observability and context. You should also notice that many of the functions are returning a context object rather than manipulating the state of an existing one. Context objects are intended to be immutable, so you'll need to be sure that you're passing the correct context into function calls or assigning it to thread-local storage, as appropriate.

Keep in mind that the preceding example is intended not to be exhaustive; it's more of an idea of how you could use these distributed and local contexts for purposes other than simply propagating trace context. The majority of this work should be handled for you, behind the scenes, by the OpenTelemetry SDK and various helper libraries. We have included it in this text to ensure that you're aware of it, though, and to get you thinking about the possibilities of the correlation context as a more general way to pass data across API boundaries in a standards-compliant way. It's possible that in the future, this context layer may migrate to a completely separate project, independent of OpenTelemetry as a way for multiple open source projects to benefit from it and standardize on a single distributed context layer.

You can read more about the OpenTelemetry context layer at OpenTelemetry's GitHub repository (*https://oreil.ly/GqfRV*).

Bibliography

[Abr13] Abraham, Lior, John Allen, Oleksandr Barykin, Vinayak Borkar, Bhuwan Chopra, Ciprian Gerea, Daniel Merl, Josh Metzler, David Reiss, Subbu Subramanian, Janet L. Wiener, and Okay Zed. 2013. "Scuba: Diving into Data at Facebook." Facebook paper. *https://research.fb.com/wp-content/uploads/2016/11/scuba-diving-into-data-at-facebook.pdf.*

[Agu03] Aguilera, Marcos K., Jeffrey C. Mogul, Janet L. Wiener, Patrick Reynolds, and Athicha Muthitacharoen. 2003. "Performance Debugging for Distributed Systems of Black Boxes." *ACM SIGOPS Operating Systems Review* 37(5): 74-89. *https://pdos.csail.mit.edu/~athicha/papers/blackboxes:sosp03.pdf.*

[Aka17] Akamai. 2017. "Akamai Online Retail Performance Report: Milliseconds Are Critical." Press release. April 19, 2017. *https://www.akamai.com/uk/en/about/news/press/2017-press/akamai-releases-spring-2017-state-of-online-retail-performance-report.jsp.*

[Ate19] Ates, Emre, Lily Sturmann, Mert Toslali, Orran Krieger, Richard Megginson, Ayse K. Coskun, and Raja R. Sambasivan. 2019. "An Automated, Cross-Layer Instrumentation Framework for Diagnosing Performance Problems in Distributed Applications." *SoCC '19: Proceedings of the ACM Symposium on Cloud Computing* (November 2019): 165–70. *https://doi.org/10.1145/3357223.3362704.*

[Bar04] Barham, Paul, Austin Donnelly, Rebecca Isaacs, and Richard Mortier. 2004. "Using Magpie for Request Extraction and Workload Modelling." *Proceedings of the 1st ACM SIGOPS European Workshop*, Leuven, Belgium, September 19-22, 2004.

[Bas19] Bashir, Hafiz Mohsin, Abdullah Bin Faisal, Muhammad Asim Jamshed, Peter Vondras, Ali Musa Iftikhar, Ihsan Ayyub Qazi, and Fahad R. Dogar. 2019. "Reducing Tail Latency via Safe and Simple Duplication." Presented at CoNext 2019: 15th International Conference on Emerging Networking Experiments and Technologies, Orlando, FL, December 9-12. *https://arxiv.org/pdf/1905.13352.pdf.*

[Bey16] Beyer, Betsy, Chris Jones, Jennifer Petoff, and Niall Richard Murphy, eds. 2016. *Site Reliability Engineering: How Google Runs Production Systems*. Sebastopol, CA: O'Reilly.

[Che02] Chen, Mike Y., Emre Kıcıman, Eugene Fratkin, Armando Fox, and Eric Brewer. 2002. "Pinpoint: Problem Determination in Large, Dynamic Internet Services." *Proceedings of the 2002 International Conference on Dependable Systems and Networks*: 595-604. *http://roc.cs.berkeley.edu/papers/roc-pinpoint-ipds.pdf*.

[Cho14] Chow, Michael, David Meisner, Jason Flinn, Daniel Peek, and Thomas F. Wenisch. 2014. "The Mystery Machine: End-to-End Performance Analysis of Large-Scale Internet Services." Presented at 11th USENIX Symposium on Operating Systems Design and Implementation, Broomfield, CO, October 2014. *https://www.usenix.org/system/files/conference/osdi14/osdi14-paper-chow.pdf*.

[Cho16] Chow, Michael, Kaushik Veeraraghavan, Michael J. Cafarella, and Jason Flinn. 2016. "DQBarge: Improving Data-quality Trade-offs in Large-Scale Internet Services." Presented at 12th USENIX Symposium on Operating Systems Design and Implementation, Savannah, GA, November 2016. *https://www.usenix.org/system/files/conference/osdi16/osdi16-chow.pdf*.

[Dan15] Dang, Huynh Tu, Daniele Sciascia, Marco Canini, Fernando Pedone, Robert Soulé. 2015. "NetPaxos: Consensus at Network Speed." *SOSR '15: Proceedings of the 1st ACM SIGCOMM Symposium on Software Defined Networking Research* (June 2015) 5: 1-7. *https://doi.org/10.1145/2774993.2774999*.

[Erl11] Erlingsson, Úlfar, Marcus Peinado, Simon Peter, and Mihai Budiu. "Fay: Extensible Distributed Tracing from Kernels to Clusters." *SOSP '11: Proceedings of the Twenty-Third ACM Symposium on Operating Systems Principles* (October 2011): 311-26. *https://doi.org/10.1145/2043556.2043585*.

[Fon07] Fonseca, Rodrigo, George Porter, Randy H. Katz, Scott Shenker, and Ion Stoica. 2007. "X-Trace: A Pervasive Network Tracing Framework." *Proceedings of the 4th USENIX Symposium on Networked Systems Design & Implementation*. *https://people.eecs.berkeley.edu/~istoica/papers/2007/xtr-nsdi07.pdf*.

[Fow14] Fowler, Martin. 2014. "Microservice Prerequisites." MartinFowler.com. August 28, 2014. *https://martinfowler.com/bliki/MicroservicePrerequisites.html*.

[Kal17] Kaldor, Jonathan, Jonathan Mace, Michał Bejda, Edison Gao, Wiktor Kuropatwa, Joe O'Neill, Kian Win Ong, Bill Schaller, Pingjia Shan, Brendan Viscomi, Vinod Venkataraman, Kaushik Veeraraghavan, and Yee Jiun Song. 2017. "Canopy: An End-to-End Performance Tracing and Analysis System." *SOSP '17: Proceedings of the 26th Symposium on Operating Systems Principles*, October 2017. *https://doi.org/10.1145/3132747.3132749*.

[Lin06] Linden, Greg. "Marissa Mayer at Web 2.0." *Geeking with Greg*, November 9, 2006. *http://glinden.blogspot.com/2006/11/marissa-mayer-at-web-20.html*.

[Lof17] Loff, João, Daniel Porto, Carlos Baquero, João Garcia, Nuno Preguiça, and Rodrigo Rodrigues. 2017. "Transparent Cross-System Consistency." *PaPoC '17:*

Proceedings of the 3rd International Workshop on Principles and Practice of Consistency for Distributed Data, April, 2017. *https://doi.org/10.1145/3064889.3064898.*

[Mac15] Mace, Jonathan, Peter Bodik, Rodrigo Fonseca, and Madanlal Musuvathi. 2015. "Retro: Targeted Resource Management in Multi-Tenant Distributed Systems." Presented at USENIX Symposium on Networked Systems Design and Implementation, Oakland, CA, May 2015. *https://www.usenix.org/system/files/conference/nsdi15/nsdi15-paper-mace.pdf*

[Mac18a] Mace, Jonathan, and Rodrigo Fonseca. 2018. "Universal Context Propagation for Distributed System Instrumentation." *EuroSys '18: Proceedings of the Thirteenth EuroSys Conference* (April 2018): 1–18. *https://doi.org/10.1145/3190508.3190526.*

[Mac18b] Mace, Jonathan, Ryan Roelke, and Rodrigo Fonseca. 2018. "Pivot Tracing: Dynamic Causal Monitoring for Distributed Systems." *ACM Transactions on Computer Systems* 35(4): 1-28, October 2015. *https://www2.cs.uic.edu/~brents/cs494-cdcs/papers/pivot-tracing.pdf.*

[May10] Mayer, Marissa. 2010. "Google Speed Research." Filmed at Web 2.0, San Francisco, CA, April 2010. *https://www.youtube.com/watch?v=BQwAKsFmK_8.*

[Med17] Meder, Sam, Vadim Antonov, and Jeff Chang. 2017. "Driving User Growth with Performance Improvements." *Medium.* March 3, 2017. *https://medium.com/pinterest-engineering/driving-user-growth-with-performance-improvements-cfc50dafadd7.*

[Mic13] Mickens, James. 2013. "The Night Watch." *Login: Logout.* November 2013. *https://www.usenix.org/system/files/1311_05-08_mickens.pdf.*

[Mil17] Mills, David L. 2017. *Computer Network Time Synchronization: The Network Time Protocol on Earth and in Space*, 2nd ed. Boca Raton, FL: CRC Press.

[Ros18] Rosen, Logan. 2018 "LinkedOut: A Request-Level Failure Injection Framework." *LinkedIn Engineering Blog*, May, 2018. *https://engineering.linkedin.com/blog/2018/05/linkedout--a-request-level-failure-injection-framework.*

[Sam16] Sambasivan, Raja R., Ilari Shafer, Jonathan Mace, Benjamin H. Sigelman, Rodrigo Fonseca, and Gregory R. Ganger. 2016. "Principled Workflow-Centric Tracing of Distributed Systems." *SoCC '16: Proceedings of the Seventh ACM Symposium on Cloud Computing, October 2016.* *http://dx.doi.org/10.1145/2987550.2987568.*

[Sig16] Sigelman, Ben. 2016. "Towards Turnkey Distributed Tracing." *Medium.* June 15, 2016. *https://medium.com/opentracing/towards-turnkey-distributed-tracing-5f4297d1736.*

[Sig19] Sigelman, Ben. 2019. "How 'Deep Systems' Broke Observability…And What We Can Do About It." Filmed October 16, 2019, Systems @Scale 2019, San Jose, CA. *https://atscaleconference.com/videos/systems-scale-2019-how-deep-systems-broke-observability-and-what-we-can-do-about-it.*

[Sig10] Sigelman, Benjamin H., Luiz André Barroso, Mike Burrows, Pat Stephenson, Manoj Plakal, Donald Beaver, Saul Jaspan, and Chandan Shanbhag. 2010. "Dapper, a Large-Scale Distributed Systems Tracing Infrastructure." Google paper. *https://research.google/pubs/pub36356.*

[Sou09] Souders, Steve. 2009. "Velocity and the Bottom Line." O'Reilly Radar, July 1, 2009. *http://radar.oreilly.com/2009/07/velocity-making-your-site-fast.html.*

[Sta19] Stack Overflow. 2019. "Developer Survey Results 2019." *https://insights.stackoverflow.com/survey/2019.*

[Wu19] Wu, Yang, Ang Chen, and Linh Thi Xuan Phan. 2019. "Zeno: Diagnosing Performance Problems with Temporal Provenance." Facebook paper presented at 16th USENIX Symposium on Networked Systems Design and Implementation, Boston, February 2019. *https://www.cs.rice.edu/~angchen/papers/nsdi-2019.pdf.*

[Zva19] Zvara, Zoltán, Péter G.N. Szabó, Barnabás Balázs, and András Benczúr. 2019. "Optimizing Distributed Data Stream Processing by Tracing." *Future Generation Computer Systems* 90: 578-91. *https://www.sciencedirect.com/science/article/abs/pii/S0167739X17325141.*

Index

A

abstract instrumentation, 32
active span, 21
agent-based instrumentation
    about, 15
    deployment of tracing, 106
    library-based versus, 15
    monolithic server tracing, 26
    portability of open source, 59
    tracer architecture, 104
aggregate analysis
    about, 195
    automated root cause analysis, 198
    Canopy, 219
    critical path aggregate analysis, 171
    errors seen via traces, 171
    Kolmogorov-Smirnov statistic, 194
    performance changes, 197
    sampling and, 214
    traces, 171, 209
        (see also trace aggregations)
    traces organized, 212
aggregate traces (see trace aggregations)
aggregation of data (see data aggregation)
agnostic nature of distributed tracing, 6
    abstract instrumentation, 33
    importance of, 201
    service mesh transport layers, 75
    spans agnostic, 224
AllReduce communication in ML, 231
Amazon Web Services (AWS)
    tracing header, 32, 53
    X-Ray distributed tracing, 53
analyzing data (see data analysis)

anomalous metrics via trace aggregations, 210
API services
    API gateway tracing, 101
    best practices custom instrumentation, 70
    best practices example framework, 65
    distributed tracing challenge, 242, 247
    endpoint and trace aggregations, 211
    HTTP API idioms used in book, 19
    Jaeger sampling API for OpenTracing, 47
    OpenCensus, 48
    OpenTelemetry, 35, 39, 41
    OpenTracing, 44, 47
    RESTful API, 19
    Web APIs for frontend tracing, 28
AppDash, 270
application performance management (APM)
    tools, 140
application programming interface (see API
    services)
application versus system instrumentation, 13
attributes of spans (see tags)
attribution for code from book, xxii
automated alerts, data presented, 185
automated data analysis
    deviation from normal, 193
    fully automated, 176

B

B3 context headers, 45, 54
backend services
    client app tracing challenges, 227
    clock skew, 110
    data outside your control, 110
    malicious users, 112

tags into, 233
unique position in software stack, 224
Rust tracing features, 272

S

safety valves, 84
sampling, 96
    aggregate analysis and, 214
    aggregate critical path analysis, 171
    application throughput, 121
    bias, accounting for, 131
    biased sampling, 165, 187
    Canopy, 220
    centralized sampling decisions, 128
    coherent sampling, 240
    collectors for, 108
    costs of tracing, 124, 143, 240
    Dapper latency and throughput metrics, 121, 143
    Dapper network and storage costs, 123
    Dapper percentage of transactions, 143
    data volume reduction, 132
    frequency of, 131
    minimum requirements, 124
    observability tool volume limits, 150
    response-based, 127
    sampling rates, 126, 143
    selecting traces, 130
    strategies, 126
    time period, 172
    TraceID on spans, 129
    up-front sampling, 126
saturation, 155, 180
scalability of distributed software, xv
scope manager for span contexts, 23
Scuba (Facebook), 145
searches
    extremely large datasets, 143
    logs, 143, 190
    trace search queries, 168
    traces, 167, 189
security audits via traces, 259
    gRPC context class for security, 275
segments (spans) in X-Ray, 53
serverless technologies
    challenges of, 5
    tracing-friendly architectures, 23
service graph, 76
service level agreement (SLA), 181

service level indicators (SLIs)
    automated alert data presented, 185
    defining baseline performance, 180
    improving baseline performance, 156
    metric labels, 136
    traces for gathering, 90
service level objectives (SLOs)
    business metric–based, 181
    defining baseline performance, 180, 185
    failing to meet, 181
    SLIs compared with, 136
    traces for gathering, 90
service meshes
    abstract instrumentation, 33
    beginning instrumentation at edges, 71
    definition, 75
    deployment leveraging, 102
    instrumentation best practices, 75
    instrumentation challenges, 76
    migration strategy via, 57
    open source instrumentation benefits, 60
services (see microservices)
sidecar proxies of service meshes
    definition, 75
    deployment of tracing, 106
    tracer architecture, 104
    tracing, 75
    tracing challenges, 76
site reliability engineering (SRE), 135, 136, 184
SkyWalking (Apache Foundation), 269
SLIs (see service level indicators)
SLOs (see service level objectives)
spans
    about, 38, 223
    active span, 21
    all microservices producing, 25
    benefits, 223
    benefits not enough, 225
    best practices, 79
    best practices example tracing, 70
    beyond spans (see beyond spans)
    context propagation, 16, 37
    cost of tracing and span selection, 117
        (see also cost of tracing)
    created under OpenCensus, 49
    created under OpenTelemetry, 38
    created under OpenTracing, 45
    creation safety valve, 84
    critical path, 160

open source tracers and trace analyzers, 269
OpenCensus, 48
OpenTelemetry context layer, 280
OpenTelemetry integrations and plug-ins,
    58
OpenTracing integrations and plug-ins, 58
O'Reilly Media online, xxii
Web APIs for frontend tracing, 28
X-Ray, 53
Zipkin, 54, 269
user impact of performance
    aggregate user behavior, 192
    automated alerts on symptoms, 186
    chaos engineering, 189
    critical path, 160
    measuring performance, 154
    observability, 146
    portion of user requests that fail, 155
    which users, 154, 166

V
vendor URLs, 270
    vendor lock-in, 33, 33, 58
verbosity of traces, 87
version attributes, 37, 94, 188
virtualization, xiv
visibility of OpenCensus, 246
visualization tools
    cumulative distribution function, 194
    dashboards of operations centers, 147
    flame graph, 140, 144
    histograms (see histograms)
    historical data, 191, 193

Kibana, 139
    TensorFlow TensorBoard, 230

W
W3C
    best practices example tracing headers, 69
    TraceContext, 45, 54, 277
WAN connectivity loss, 29
Web APIs, URL for frontend tracing, 28
web clients
    abstract instrumentation necessity, 32
    best practices example microservice, 62
    browser tracing, 120, 273
    client app tracing challenges, 227
    data outside your control, 110
    distributed tracing, 27
    JavaScript instrumentation, 273
    request-response systems, 202
    response latency in history, 202
white box instrumentation, 12
    tracing-friendly architectures, 23

X
X-Ray (Amazon), 53
X-Trace, 206, 207

Z
Zeno temporal provenance, 235
Zipkin (Twitter), 54
    OpenZipkin, 140, 233, 269
    trace searches, 189
    URL, 54

About the Authors

Austin Parker is principal developer advocate at Lightstep, where he works as a core contributor and maintainer to the OpenTracing project. Prior to Lightstep, he was a software architect at Apprenda, building enterprise platforms using Kubernetes.

Daniel Spoonhower is a cofounder of Lightstep, where he's building performance management tools for modern software systems. Previously, Spoons spent almost six years at Google, where he worked on developer tools as part of Google's internal infrastructure and Cloud Platform teams. He has published papers on the performance of parallel programs, garbage collection, and real-time programming. He has a PhD in programming languages from Carnegie Mellon University but still hasn't found one he loves.

Jonathan Mace is a tenure-track faculty member at the Max Planck Institute for Software Systems, where he leads the Cloud Software Systems research group. His research centers on ways to understand, monitor, and debug large distributed systems. His notable work includes Pivot Tracing, which introduced the concept of baggage used by distributed tracing today; Canopy, Facebook's internal performance tracing system; and his PhD work on abstractions for tracing, which received Honorable Mention for the 2018 Dennis M. Ritchie Doctoral Dissertation Award.

Rebecca Isaacs is a software engineer currently focused on the performance tuning and debugging of large-scale datacenter services. She was previously a research scientist, most recently at Google. She first started thinking about tracing for distributed systems over 15 years ago while at Microsoft Research, which she joined after obtaining a PhD from Cambridge University and a BSc from the University of Glasgow.

Colophon

The animal sniffing the subtitle on the cover of *Distributed Tracing in Practice* is a long-nosed bandicoot (*Perameles nasuta*), a marsupial found in a narrow range along the coast of eastern Australian rainforest and woodlands.

Long-nosed bandicoots have brownish gray fur and a short tail, weigh about two pounds, and stretch about one foot long. The lifespan is typically five to six years. These bandicoots dig distinctive conical holes when they forage with their clawed toes and characteristic snout. They forage for insects, fungi, and plants at night and nest in shallow dirt holes during the day. The long-nosed bandicoot's pouch faces backward to protect its young from dug-up soil.

When the conservation status of the long-nosed bandicoot was last assessed in 2015, authorities listed the species as of Least Concern, but Australia's Department of Agriculture, Water, and the Environment found it at risk of extinction after the bushfires of 2019–20. Many of the animals on O'Reilly's covers are endangered; all of them are important to the world.

The cover illustration is by Karen Montgomery, based on a black and white engraving from *Meyers Kleines Lexicon*. The cover fonts are Gilroy Semibold and Guardian Sans. The text font is Adobe Minion Pro; the heading font is Adobe Myriad Condensed; and the code font is Dalton Maag's Ubuntu Mono.

O'REILLY®

There's much more where this came from.

Experience books, videos, live online training courses, and more from O'Reilly and our 200+ partners—all in one place.

Learn more at oreilly.com/online-learning

CPSIA information can be obtained
at www.ICGtesting.com
Printed in the USA
JSHW042200110321
12425JS00005B/168